MENDED BY THE MUSE

Mended by the Muse: Creative Transformations of Trauma is an in-depth exploration of the relationship between trauma and creativity. It is about art in the service of healing, mourning, and memorialization. This book addresses the questions of how artistic expression facilitates the healing process, what the therapeutic action of art is, and if there is a relationship between mental instability and creativity. It also asks how self-analysis through art-making can be integrated with psychoanalytic work in order to enrich and facilitate emotional growth.

Drawing on four decades of clinical practice and a critical reading of creativity literature, Sophia Richman presents a new theory of the creative process whose core components are relational conceptualizations of dissociation and witnessing. This is an interdisciplinary book that draws inspiration from life histories, clinical case material, neuroscience, and interviews with creators, as well as from various art forms such as film, literature, paintings, and music. Some areas of discussion include: art born of genocide, confrontation with mortality in illness and aging, and the clinical implications of memoirs written by psychoanalysts. Visual images are interspersed throughout the text that illustrate the reverberations of trauma and its creative transformation in the work of featured artists.

Mended by the Muse powerfully articulates how creative action is one of the most effective ways of coping with trauma and its aftershocks—it is in art, in all its forms, that sorrow is given shape and meaning. Here, Sophia Richman shows how art helps to master the chaos that follows in the wake of tragedy, how it restores continuity, connection, and the will for a more fully lived life. This book is written for psychoanalysts as well as for other mental health professionals who practice and teach. It will also be of interest to graduate and post-graduate students and will be relevant for artists who seek a better understanding of the creative process.

Sophia Richman is a psychoanalyst and psychologist who has been in private practice for over forty years. She is affiliated with the New York University Postdoctoral Program in Psychotherapy and Psychoanalysis, where she is on the supervising faculty. She is the author of the award-winning memoir, *A Wolf in the Attic: The Legacy of a Hidden Child of the Holocaust* (Routledge, 2002) and she is a painter.

PSYCHOANALYSIS IN A NEW KEY BOOK SERIES

DONNEL STERN
Series Editor

When music is played in a new key, the melody does not change, but the notes that make up the composition do: change in the context of continuity, continuity that perseveres through change. Psychoanalysis in a New Key publishes books that share the aims psychoanalysts have always had, but that approach them differently. The books in the series are not expected to advance any particular theoretical agenda, although to this date most have been written by analysts from the Interpersonal and Relational orientations.

The most important contribution of a psychoanalytic book is the communication of something that nudges the reader's grasp of clinical theory and practice in an unexpected direction. Psychoanalysis in a New Key creates a deliberate focus on innovative and unsettling clinical thinking. Because that kind of thinking is encouraged by exploration of the sometimes surprising contributions to psychoanalysis of ideas and findings from other fields, Psychoanalysis in a New Key particularly encourages interdisciplinary studies. Books in the series have married psychoanalysis with dissociation, trauma theory, sociology, and criminology. The series is open to the consideration of studies examining the relationship between psychoanalysis and any other field—for instance, biology, literary and art criticism, philosophy, systems theory, anthropology, and political theory.

But innovation also takes place within the boundaries of psychoanalysis, and Psychoanalysis in a New Key therefore also presents work that reformulates thought and practice without leaving the precincts of the field. Books in the series focus, for example, on the significance of personal values in psychoanalytic practice, on the complex interrelationship between the analyst's clinical work and personal life, on the consequences for the clinical situation when patient and analyst are from different cultures, and on the need for psychoanalysts to accept the degree to which they knowingly satisfy their own wishes during treatment hours, often to the patient's detriment.

MENDED BY THE MUSE

Creative Transformations of Trauma

Sophia Richman

Routledge
Taylor & Francis Group

NEW YORK AND LONDON

First published 2014
by Routledge
711 Third Avenue, New York, NY 10017

and by Routledge
27 Church Road, Hove, East Sussex BN3 2FA

Routledge is an imprint of the Taylor & Francis Group, an informa business

Library of Congress Cataloging-in-Publication Data

Richman, Sophia, 1941–
    Mended by the muse : creative transformations of trauma / Sophia Richman.
        pages cm
    Includes bibliographical references and index.
    1. Arts—Therapeutic use.   2. Psychic trauma—Treatment.
3. Creative ability—Psychological aspects.   I. Title.
    RC489.A72.R53   2014
    616.89'1656—dc23
    2013041332

ISBN: 978-0-415-88363-4 (hbk)
ISBN: 978-0-415-88364-1 (pbk)
ISBN: 978-0-203-84358-1 (ebk)

Typeset in Times New Roman
by Apex CoVantage, LLC

FOR SPYROS AND LINA

MY LOVING AND SPIRITED MUSES

CONTENTS

ILLUSTRATIONS

ACKNOWLEDGMENTS

Without Donnel Stern's suggestion that I write a book for his series, on a subject of my interest, it is not likely that this book would have been written. His encouragement, wise guidance, and thoughtful editing have been invaluable to the process.

My husband, Spyros Orfanos, my partner in life and companion in the world of the intellect, has provided the spark that ignited me and inspired me to write; he is my Muse and my witness. Additionally his careful reading and rereading of the manuscript, in all its stages, and the emotional support that he so generously provides are gifts that I am forever grateful for. I am also appreciative of the eloquent and passionate chapter that he has contributed to this book.

Special thanks to Helen Epstein and Marilyn Papayanis, my dear friends who devoted hours to reading and editing the manuscript and whose thoughtful comments and wise suggestions have enriched it. Other friends and colleagues who have read sections of this manuscript and contributed helpful comments include Darlene Ehrenberg, Laura Geringer, Stefanie Solow Glennon, Marcia Greenleaf, Sandra Hershberg, Joan Lipton, Clemens Loew, Helen Neswald, and my dear friend Elaine Kulp Shabad, whose unwavering support deserves special mention.

My friend and fellow traveler in the child survivor world, Nelly Toll, gave me my first opportunity to publish an oil painting of mine in her book *When Memory Speaks: The Holocaust in Art* in 1998. Several years earlier, I had discovered Nelly's memoir, *Behind the Secret Window*, where she had revealed how, as a child of 8, she had used writing and painting to help her cope with the experience of hiding in a confined space for over a year. The influence on my creative life of hidden children like Nelly Toll needs to be acknowledged.

I am grateful for the opportunity to have interviewed Ofra Bloch, the filmmaker; Susan Erony, the visual artist; and Clarice Adler, the nonagenarian; I thank them for their open and giving participation. I also want to acknowledge my appreciation to the patients who granted me permission to discuss our work together in order to illustrate my ideas about trauma and creativity.

Some of the contemporary artists who have generously contributed their artistic work include Catherine Angel, Marilyn Charles, Susan Erony, and David Newman. I have been touched by their enthusiasm about my project. I also wish to thank Mark Baron, the son of the artist Hannelore Baron, who has generously made available his mother's artwork and biographic information.

With gratitude, I acknowledge those who made it possible for me to include the fascinating artwork of Marian Kołodziej—Sue Shapiro, who alerted me to his art; Father Ron Schmidt, S.J., who facilitated my acquiring permission to use it; Andrzej Krajewski, who put me in touch with Halina Slojewska-Kołodziej, who granted her permission for me to reproduce her late husband's work; and my cousin Tadeusz Wielecki, who helped me with details of the transaction overseas.

My parents, Leon and Dorothy Richman, and my daughter, Lina Orfanos, have inspired me to record their stories of tragedy and of triumph; I am thankful that I can share their personal material with readers. My late parents, both Holocaust survivors, gave testimony during their lifetime because of a strong conviction that their story of survival needed to be told. Lina, always courageous and generous, gave me permission to write about her life—without a moment of hesitation.

This publication has been supported by a grant from the Psychoanalytic Society of the Postdoctoral Program, Inc. This organization is the graduate society of the New York University Postdoctoral Program in Psychotherapy and Psychoanalysis.

A final thank you to the members of the Routledge staff whom I have had the pleasure to work with closely. In particular, I wish to acknowledge Kate Hawes and Kirsten Buchanan of Taylor & Francis and Sheri Sipka and her team at Apex CoVantage. Always pleasant, competent, and responsive these women helped to smooth the way for what often seemed like a mysterious and wondrous process.

INTRODUCTION

Painting was my first passion. When I received a set of oil paints in adolescence, I fell in love with the smell, the rich texture, the brilliant and varied colors, and the freedom—compared with watercolors, which require a commitment that cannot be undone, oils are most forgiving. Unlike many of the artists I write about in this book, I rarely use painting to express my inner world; I prefer the aesthetic challenge and the control of recreating the image before my eyes as skillfully as I can. Yet what is internal and uniquely *me* somehow always gets expressed—in the strokes, in the nuances of color, in the choices made with every dip of the brush. I have always found it fascinating to note how unique each painting is when a group of individuals are at their easels looking at the same still life or model. Each finished product has the indelible stamp of the individual artist, regardless of the subject matter, the technique, or the particular painting that she happens to be working on. Like a signature is unique to the signer, so a work of art is unique to its creator. Even if we've not seen a particular van Gogh work before, we usually recognize it as a van Gogh when we see the brush strokes, the vibrant colors, and the composition. The self has a way of emerging without conscious intention; it is inevitably expressed in whatever we create.

Although I sometimes wish that I could be as free to express spontaneous feelings and imaginative associations in my artwork as I can in my writing, nevertheless, I find the activity of making art immensely gratifying. I love the sensation of surrendering to the process. No matter what is going on in my life, when I am in the studio at my easel, I am fully engaged and totally focused. Only what is on the canvas matters at that moment—getting the effect I want, a pleasing sense of harmony, just the right shade of purple, the perfect line, the rhythm of recurrent shapes, the movement of dark and light flowing through the painting. I lose my sense of time; if there are sounds, I don't hear them; I have no awareness of my body's needs. I am in an altered state of consciousness; I am one with my canvas, which is coming alive before my eyes.

This is the state that Mihaly Csikszentmihalyi (1990, 1996), known for his research on creativity, has called "flow" and has written about extensively since the mid 1970s. In a recent video conference presentation, Csikszentmihalyi (2004) spoke about the genesis of his interest in creativity. He attributes its beginning to

1

his childhood experiences in war-torn Europe, when he observed that while most of the adults around him were devastated by the war, some were able to somehow transcend the tragedy and keep a positive attitude. Gradually he began to understand that engagement in creative endeavors provided people with meaning that helped them cope with the difficulties and tragedies of life.

Like Csikszentmihalyi, I have been drawn to the subject of creativity in its relation to traumatic circumstances for as long as I can remember. My own mother was one of those adults he refers to who managed to keep a positive attitude in the aftermath of war despite her momentous losses. Although she would not have referred to herself as creative, I believe that it is largely thanks to her talents that we survived in hiding. In the midst of war, she took on a false Catholic identity, created a convincing narrative as a cover story, and gave a flawless performance for more than three years—all this while protecting the life of her toddler and hiding her husband out of sight in the attic. Among her personal gifts were an unusual capacity to dissemble, a sharp social intelligence—she could pick up on the subtlest nuances in communication—and an ability to improvise and problem-solve under great pressure. These characteristics, along with the capability to be flexible and to adapt to quickly changing and terrifying circumstances, are in my view testaments to her creativity.

There are no universally accepted definitions of creativity. There may be as many definitions as there are people who attempt to define this elusive phenomenon. My mother's type of creativity was a version of what has been known as "everyday creativity" born of necessity. Extreme times are often times of heightened creativity and innovation. Attempts to master traumatic circumstances and to cope with their aftermath can be ingenious and inspired. Creativity under those circumstances is part of a survival capability (Richards, 2007), and it is associated with flexible adaptation: the ability to shift one's perspective and to improvise. Under normal circumstances, the criteria for creativity include novelty, usefulness, and authenticity; the qualities associated with creativity are openness to the world, curiosity, tolerance of ambiguity, and unpredictability.

When I refer to *creativity* in this book, I am not limiting it to the expression of artistic talents and skills or to the creation of a unique product of lasting value for society. Unlike many writers on the subject including Freud (1910/1999) and more current contributors such as Csikszentmihalyi (1996), Kandel (2012), Knafo (2009), Simonton (1999), and Storr (1993), who discuss creativity in relation to eminent artists who have made significant creative contributions, I am not addressing the talented and famous, although some of the people I write about are in fact very talented and well-known. I use the term *artist* loosely, referring to the individual engaged in the process of making art, without judgment regarding the quality of the product. My emphasis here is on creativity as a potential that exists in all of us to some degree—the ability to find unique ways to express ourselves and to solve the problems that we face by shifting our perspective. In that sense, creativity can be an attitude, an act, an idea, or a product that changes or influences an existing situation, thereby allowing individuals to work through

2

and master some of the significant issues with which they struggle, including traumatic circumstances.

The word *trauma* like the word *creativity* is another much-used term; according to some, it is so overused as to have become almost meaningless (Boulanger, 2007). For my purposes, however, I choose to use the term in its broadest sense, conceptualizing it as a subjective phenomenon falling on a continuum ranging from the inevitable losses that we experience in our daily lives due to the human condition, to exposure to extremely violent and catastrophic events outside of common human experience. Trauma, regardless of its specific nature, is defined by the experience of the survivor, whether it is consciously registered or not; it involves a highly stressful situation that leaves the person emotionally, cognitively, and physically overwhelmed and feeling helpless and vulnerable.

My central thesis in this book is that creative action is one of the most effective ways of coping with trauma and its aftereffects. Art in all its forms provides us with opportunities to repair what has been torn asunder by events that have overwhelmed us and rendered us helpless. It is in art, in its various forms and symbolic disguises, that our sorrow is given shape and meaning. By expressing the internal pain, the artist externalizes it, fashions a container for it, and invites others to become witnesses to his suffering. Art facilitates mourning; it restores continuity and connection and helps to master the chaos that follows in the aftermath of tragedy.

A few words about my choice of title for this book: *Mended by the Muse.* Although in the text I use the word *healing,* I am aware that this term has its limitations. Can one ever fully heal from emotional wounds, particularly of the magnitude endured by survivors of catastrophic trauma? It is questionable that psychic pain can ultimately be "healed." In my view, healing is more of a goal to be approximated than a result reached. Intense suffering can be lessened with time, with therapy, or with artistic expression—but scars do remain even after wounds have healed, and the pain of past losses can be triggered by current events. So, for the title of this book, I have chosen the concept of *mending* rather than healing. Mending, to me, suggests that a tear has been repaired, but the damage can still be observed if one looks closely.

The Muse, as conceptualized in the title of the book, is a relational presence in what would otherwise be a solitary activity of making art; it is an embodied image of an imaginary other who serves a mirroring, inspiring, and witnessing function for the artist. Like an imaginary friend, the Muse exists in the intermediate area of experience—the potential space between psychic reality and the outside world (Winnicott, 1967).

What draws a writer to her subject is usually what is personally compelling; this idea has been wittily expressed as "research is me-search." In the field of psychoanalysis, there is a growing recognition that our understanding of human behavior begins with our self-understanding (Barron, 1993) and that the subjective world of the theorist is inevitably translated into her view of human nature (Stolorow & Atwood, 1979). In my case, the connection between creativity and

3

trauma has been personal for many years, in my own life and the life of my family. It is my personal experience, and the experience of my father and daughter, that has inspired this book, as will become evident to the reader.

My own life experience is an example of the fact that engagement in the creative process can be immensely reparative. I was drawn to the arts from a very early age—drawing, painting, writing, and dancing. As a hidden child during the Second World War, I had to be extremely cautious about what I said out loud; speaking became associated with danger, but other forms of expression were safer. Although I didn't make the connection between my personal history of trauma and my longing for self-expression until many years later, it exerted a powerful pull and led me to seek opportunities for release and repair.

At one point in my adolescence, I thought that I might have a career in fine arts. When I was in my last year of high school, I signed up for an art history class, and it was there that I was first introduced to the "art of the insane"—as it was referred to at the time. The field of art therapy had not yet become a discipline, although some pioneers like Margaret Naumburg (1950) were introducing their students to the concept of healing through art. Today, Naumburg is considered to be the primary founder of American art therapy (Malchiodi, 2005). She was psychoanalytic in her formulations and viewed her clients' art expressions as symbolic communications of unconscious material. Kris (1953) pointed out that Naumburg's "creative therapy" has significant advantages over traditional ways of working with schizophrenics because the regressive behavior can be meaningfully channeled and the ego can recapture control through the shaping of the artistic material: "'Creative therapy' supplies to the relationship a form of anchorage from which it may swing to more archaic patterns and to which it can safely return" (p. 99).

Impressed with Naumburg's work, I contacted her and we met one afternoon. I was then in my freshmen year of college. She encouraged me to major in psychology and eventually to attend her graduate classes in what she called "dynamically orientated art therapy." I followed her advice, but after a brief flirtation with art therapy, I fell in love with psychoanalysis. So the ideas that are explored in this book had their beginning as far back as 1958—more than 55 years ago, when I first began to contemplate the relationship between trauma and creativity. At the time, I had neither an awareness of its relevance to my life, nor an understanding of the theoretical underpinnings of these ideas. My study of psychoanalysis led to a better understanding of both.

Through the years of my practice, I have continued to be fascinated with this theme, and I have written a number of articles on the subject. Most of these articles were an outgrowth of my experience authoring a memoir titled *A Wolf in the Attic: The Legacy of a Hidden Child of the Holocaust* (2002). In this memoir, I explored the long-term impact of my childhood in hiding on my adult life and choices. While the memoir was written for a general readership, the articles that followed were meant for a professional audience. They focused on the experience of writing (Richman, 2006b), compared it with the development of narrative in psychoanalysis (Richman, 2009), and explored the effects of self-disclosure on my work with patients (Richman, 2006a). A couple of these articles are reprinted here as separate chapters.

The current work can be seen as an instance of process reflecting content. In other words, the process of writing this book represents the implementation of the very theme it seeks to demonstrate—namely, the working through and transformation of traumatic experience into a creative product. For me, it is the actualization of mending through artistic action; it represents an integration of my personal and professional experience of the role of the arts in healing, informed by theoretical and conceptual contributions of psychoanalysts and others in the mental health field grappling with the concepts of creativity and trauma.

This book focuses on the healing potential of creativity and offers a new theory about the creative process using relational concepts and extending them to the artistic realm. It highlights the role of dissociation and witnessing and identifies these functions as integral to the creative process. These ideas are illustrated by various clinical examples and interviews with artists, as well as by examples from applied psychoanalysis, literature, film, visual arts, and music.

The first chapter introduces the basic theme of the book and gets the reader immediately acquainted with what is meant by creative transformation of trauma. Traumatic experiences have a ripple effect that continues throughout life and functions as a powerful inner force that draws the survivor like a magnet to situations and events that allow her to work through pain: to give it shape, to release it, to express it to others, to make sense of it, and to find some meaning in it. Art takes place in the transitional space, partly internal, partly external; self-expression through the creative arts can be one of the most effective means to healing. This will be illustrated by an analysis of three generations of trauma survivors in my own family who spontaneously turned to the arts as a means of self healing.

Chapter 2 is essentially a selective literature review that examines the contributions of psychoanalytic thinkers on the subject of creativity from various theoretical perspectives, beginning with Freud and the drive theory model of sublimation and gradually moving into more contemporary thinking on the subject. Not much has been written on creativity from a relational perspective, and this work attempts to formulate a new theory on the subject. Thus, the theoretical overview in this chapter provides the context for a relational theory of the creative process to be formulated in subsequent chapters.

Chapter 3 moves in the direction of a relationally informed theory of the creative process. The chapter begins with an exploration of the widespread belief that there is a relationship between creativity and psychopathology. Shared mental processes, such as regression and dissociation, are identified as the connecting link between them. In the second part of this chapter, the concept of dissociation is discussed and elaborated. Dissociation is here understood as an altered state of consciousness that is essentially neutral and paradoxical in nature. On the one hand it functions as a defense mechanism that, under traumatic circumstances, is subject to involuntary states of cognitive and affective alterations of consciousness; on the other hand, it can be enlisted temporarily in the service of the creative process. Thus, the same dissociative process that is responsible for moments of inspiration when the artist is deeply immersed in creative work is also responsible for fragmentation of the self when the individual is beset by trauma. The central role of dissociation in the creative process is consistent with data emerging in neuroscience. Researchers have found that in altered states of consciousness, like flow or meditation, there is temporary deactivation of prefrontal areas of the brain. As a result of a temporary hold on the workings of the frontal lobes, thinking becomes more meandering, less directed, and available for making creative connections. This state, which corresponds to the inspirational phase of the creative process, is then followed by the elaboration phase, in which the frontal lobes take over in order to evaluate and develop previously generated ideas.

Chapter 4 begins with an examination of the essential role of witnessing in the creative process. Although making art seems to be a solitary activity, the presence of another is implied; the artist is alone in the presence of an imaginary other designated as a potential reader, viewer, audience, or Muse. For the trauma survivor, whose experience has been chaotic and fragmenting, the witness can serve a holding function as well as a validating and integrating one. I conceptualize the imagined witness as a dissociated self-state that serves the crucial function of mirroring, affirming, and validating. When traumatic experience is transformed into a work of art, a poem, a collage, or a photograph, the survivor is able to bear witness to her own experience; the final product is an external presence and a memorial to what has been lost. The remainder of the chapter provides a series of examples that illustrate how artistic expression can be enlisted in the service of preserving memory, mourning, and working through of traumatic loss. In a section on the healing alliance of creativity and trauma, additional case examples from the literature illustrate how artistic activities allow unformulated experiences of pain and loss to be given form, thereby providing a means of repair. A section on the therapeutic action of art is followed by a clinical case vignette of a patient who spontaneously brought expressive written material into sessions. The vignette illustrates how the integration of such material into the analysis can deepen the dialogue and enrich the work.

Chapter 5 continues the theme of survivor art but makes it specific to the survival of massive psychic trauma. Widespread theoretical assumptions held by some Holocaust scholars are critically examined, and it is concluded that these ideas tend to perpetuate misconceptions about survivors. For instance, the notion that there is a "generic" survivor experience that results in the destruction of cognitive functions, such as the capacity to symbolize, narrate, or self-reflect (Laub & Auerhahn, 1989), fails to take into consideration the complexity and diversity of emotional responses to massive psychic trauma and the multiplicity of self-states in which the survivor exists in the aftermath of trauma. Even when art is recognized as the one area where symbolization can be expressed (Laub & Podell, 1995), the art of trauma is so narrowly defined that it excludes the creative work of many survivors. The ability to use one's imagination to represent and symbolize traumatic experience and to create a coherent narrative is what allowed many survivors to hold on to their sanity and to begin the long road toward recovery in the aftermath of genocide. The remainder of the chapter focuses on the experiences and the art of several survivors whose work is a testament to the powerful healing effect of artistic self-expression.

Two interviews are featured in chapter 6, one with a filmmaker/psychoanalyst and the other with a visual artist. Both women happen to be dealing with intergenerational reverberations of war trauma in their personal histories; in childhood they each were faced with the unacknowledged trauma of a significant other that presumably influenced the nature of their art in later years.[1] The filmmaker is especially interested in transgenerational Holocaust trauma; she is exploring it in a documentary film about an adult child survivor and her artist daughter whose paintings and collages reflect both the trauma and its effect on the mother–daughter relationship. The visual artist is interested in the manifestations of genocide, including the Holocaust and its long-term reverberations in our culture. Through her artwork she gives voice to what is silenced and memorializes what is in danger of being forgotten. These interviews highlight the themes identified in earlier chapters, such as the role of dissociation and witnessing in the creative process, as well as the potential of art to impart meaning, to organize chaos, and to provide a sense of mastery and control.

Chapter 7, written by Spyros D. Orfanos, is titled "Music and the Great Wound." As an expert on the work of the great composer and activist Mikis Theodorakis, whom he has interviewed over many years, Orfanos was invited to contribute this chapter. This essay on music and trauma begins with an ancient Greek myth about Eros and Thanatos and ends in modern-day Greece. A short and selective history of music and psychoanalysis is presented, and creativity is discussed as both a relational and a memorializing aesthetic. Central to the theme is "Song of Songs," the first aria from Theodorakis' *Mauthausen Cantata*. Its performance illustrates the immense complexity of grasping what relations exist among musical creativity, meaning, and trauma. Further, the aim is to discuss the song in relationship to its total historical surrounds and the various subjectivities involved.

Chapter 8 examines the effects of biographic self-disclosure on the part of the analyst on the analytic dyad and on the treatment process. Currently, there is a great deal of information on the internet about the personal life of the analyst, but little data on the impact of such disclosures on the analytic work. Several clinical vignettes illustrate the complex reactions of patients as they came up in the treatment. Various issues explored in this chapter include the impact of personal disclosures on the transference/countertransference matrix and the development of potential problems as well as potential benefits. Some of the concerns relate to intrusion of the analyst's subjectivity into the analytic space and analyst vulnerability. Positive outcomes include the creation of an atmosphere of heightened emotional intensity and intimacy, and the facilitation of a collaborative spirit that ultimately enriches the analytic work.

Chapter 9 focuses on Carl Gustav Jung's autobiographical works—*The Red Book* and *Memories, Dreams, Reflections*. His life and his works are wonderful illustrations of the themes explored in this book. Much of the material to be found in Jung's memoirs, which ultimately became the basis of his metapsychology, was arrived at through a process that he called "active imagination." This technique, which he developed in order to reach deep into his psyche, was a type of meditation or visualization. Jung's work has had great influence in areas outside of psychoanalysis. Artists, particularly those who identified themselves as Surrealists or Abstract Expressionists, were most appreciative of his emphasis on mythology and unconscious symbolism. Through his own personal explorations and his work with patients, Jung concluded that artistic expression as well as dream interpretation can help restore emotional health and aid in recovery from trauma. While Jung's influence has reached far beyond the confines of psychoanalysis, for many years his contributions to psychoanalysis were not truly recognized. It is striking how many of Jung's ideas are similar to, or compatible with, contemporary relational psychoanalysis. Jung's model of personality is a dissociative one in which the psyche is viewed as a multiplicity of part-selves. A number of Jung's ideas seem ahead of their time and have anticipated some of our current thinking in psychoanalysis, such as the mutual field created by analyst and analysand, the necessity of deep involvement on the analyst's part, the recognition of mutual influence in analysis, and the desirability of transformation for both the analyst and the patient. Despite some ambivalence about self-exposure, Jung's willingness to self-disclose at a time when most analysts were preoccupied with neutrality and anonymity was not only courageous, but also in keeping with his belief that we learn about psychoanalysis not only from patients, but also from the observation of our own unconscious.

The notion of a last chance to fulfill what has been set aside before it is too late is a powerful theme in the life of those who are confronting their mortality, either as a result of life-threatening illness or of aging or both. In illness or in old age, existential concerns such as death, isolation, and meaninglessness take center stage, as I indicate in chapter 10, the last chapter of the book. Both physical illness and the gradual deterioration of the body associated with aging can be seen as potentially traumatic events—with an attendant sense of irreparable loss, helplessness, and disturbance of self-image and identity. The first part of this chapter focuses on the trauma of physical illness. Two case examples illustrate how art-making can facilitate the process of working through major losses and help to restore a sense of control and connection with others. Both of the artists use mixed-media productions—a technique that seems particularly well-suited to the expression of emotional fragmentation and a desire for wholeness in the aftermath of trauma. The second part of this chapter addresses issues of aging. It's a time of decline and a time of endings. The body shows signs of deterioration, losses accrue, contemporaries die, and memories begin to fade. With retirement, there is more time to contemplate one's life and the inevitability of death. Simonton (1989) has noted that creativity tends to undergo resurgence in the later years of life, a pattern that he believes is related to the contemplation of death. Stage theorists Jung and Erikson wrote about this stage of life as presenting specific challenges, as well as opportunities for growth and renewal. Knowing that one will cease to be stirs a desire to leave a mark on the world—some sort of generativity, a sign of one's existence. The tasks at this stage of life include life review and retrospective evaluation, the maintenance of a sense of continuity over the life span, an acceptance of limitations, and a creative adaptation that holds some possibility of transcendence, as well as the potential for fulfillment of interrupted or submerged aspects of self. These ideas are illustrated with two case examples, one from the life and work of a contemporary writer, the other from my clinical practice. Also included in this chapter is a brief section on data from neuroscience about the effects of aging on the brain. We know that diseases such as Alzheimer's selectively affect different parts of the brain and that the parts involved in creativity can remain relatively intact for a long time. The aging brain is actually similar to the creative brain with respect to a broader focus of attention and distractibility.

The art of trauma is vast and rich. We see evidence of it all around, inside and outside of the consulting room. Picasso's *Guernica,* Anne Sexton's anguished poetry, and Eric Clapton's haunting ballad "Tears in Heaven," written after the death of his young son, are but a few poignant examples. This book will argue for a complex understanding of the therapeutic action of art, and of how creativity and trauma interact and mutually influence one another. The coming chapters invite the reader to explore variations on this theme and, in the process, to identify personal, public, and collective examples of the Muse in action.

Note

1. This commonality of experience was discovered during the interviews.

1

OUT OF DARKNESS

*Il fallait . . . faire sortir de la pénombre ce que j'avais senti,
de le reconvertir en un équivalent spirituel. Or ce moyen qui me
paraissait le seul qu'était-ce autre chose que de créer une oevre
d'art?*

*(I needed to retrieve from the shadows that which I had felt, and
transform it into some spiritual equivalent. But the way to do it,
the only one I could see, what else could it be but to create a work
of art?)*[1]

—M. Proust (1908–1912, in Segal, 1991, pp. 86–87)

The year was 1944; I was a toddler living in Nazi-occupied Poland with my
mother—two Jews out in the open passing as good Catholics. Hidden in our attic
was my father, who had escaped from a concentration camp a year earlier. As a
3-year-old I had the responsibility of keeping his existence a secret from the rest
of the dangerous world. An excerpt from my memoir *A Wolf in the Attic* (Richman,
2002) describes an experience that is forever imprinted on my mind, one of the
few memories from those early years in hiding:

> The sun is streaming through the window. I sit at a large table. *Tatush*
> [Daddy] sits across from me. We hear steps outside of the door. *Tatush* is
> very scared. He motions to me—he puts his hand on his lips. I know he
> wants me to keep the secret. The woman outside asks me if I'm alone. I
> lie; I say yes. She goes away. (p. 52)

This traumatic memory has always been available to me. When my father wrote
his own memoir he described the same experience in this way:

> "One day when my wife went to the village for shopping . . . I was sitting
> in the room with our little daughter. Somebody knocked at the door. It
> was the landlady with her dog. She asked my daughter, a 2-and-a-half

year old kid, '*Zosia,* who is there with you?' I shook my head giving a sign to my daughter that nobody is with her." (quoted in Richman, 2002, p. 52)

The impact of this event is recorded in my memoir in the following paragraph:

Apparently, at barely 3 years of age, I understood the importance of keeping the secret of my father's existence. On that day, the wrong answer could have cost all three of us our lives. Those years in hiding have left their legacy. From time to time, in certain circumstances, I experience an inhibition in speaking that I believe has its roots in a time when words uttered out loud had the power to save or destroy. (Richman, 2002, p. 53)

And that is how my young voice, a voice just beginning to speak, was lost! It would take many years for me to find it again.

Decades later, at a symposium "Trauma and Autobiography," I spoke about this incident. Anna Ornstein (2006b), the discussant of my paper (Richman, 2006b) pointed out that in traumatic memory, the emotional core of a traumatic experience is remembered, even if there are distortions in the details as evidenced by this memory. Both my father and I vividly remembered the essence of the event—that a woman was trying to enter the room and that this situation presented a grave danger because of the potential discovery of my father's presence.

For me, this event told from two different perspectives (the child's and the adult's) highlights developmental variations in the nature of traumatic memory. When those two memories are juxtaposed we note how differently the same event is processed by a young child versus an adult, both in a state of terror. My father's recall of the event is a narrative of the facts; he described the meaning of the situation, while my own memory is closer to the sensory experience. For me, it is the image and kinesthetic sensation that constitutes the memory. Thus I remember the large table (probably large because I was so small); I remember the light shining through the window, the seating arrangement—my father sitting across from me. I also have a body memory of the experience, an awareness that the voice I heard at the door was coming from behind me, slightly above, and to the right of my body (Richman, 2006c).

Daniel Schacter (1996) wrote about emotional memories and their persistence, intensity, and flashback quality. As an example, he told the story of Melinda Stickney-Gibson, an artist who survived a horrific fire by jumping out of a third-floor window; he described the impact that this traumatic experience had on her life and art. Her paintings clearly reflected her ordeal. She began painting darkly introspective works on lead, steel, and concrete—a contrast to her former bold expressive canvases, alive with colors of mauves and blues. After the fire, she used only orange, black, and okra—the colors of fire. "Her new artwork became a vehicle for repetitively and exhaustively exploring her traumatic memory" (p. 193). Notably, the exploration was almost entirely involuntary; the images seemed to appear unbidden, and it was only after they were painted that Melinda made a connection to the fire.

Like Melinda, my father and I eventually found a way to articulate our traumatic memories through artistic means. We both independently, and at different points in our lives, wrote autobiographical narratives that bore witness to what had happened to us that day, during the war years, and beyond.

Creativity Born of Trauma

This chapter will focus on the interface between trauma and creativity. I am interested in how human beings are able to use creative approaches to express and work through their pain or their preoccupations. When I refer to creativity in this context, I am not limiting it to the expression of artistic talents and skills or to the creation of a unique product of lasting value for society, but rather in its broadest sense as a unique capacity for self-expression. The term *trauma*, like the word *creativity*, is used here in a broad context—as a subjective phenomenon falling on a continuum ranging from inevitable losses due to the human condition to exposure to catastrophic events that are experienced as a threat to psychic and/or physical survival.

It is my contention that sustaining losses and suffering function as a powerful inner force that draws us like a magnet to situations and events that allow us to work through our pain: to give it a tangible form, to release it, to communicate it, to make sense of it, and to extract some meaning from it. This is all part of a healing process that goes on in myriad conscious and unconscious ways until, if we are fortunate, we come to terms with our despair and reach a state of mind that could be called "acceptance."

When trauma is experienced in childhood, it shapes us and becomes a dominant theme in our life, influencing our identity and our choices; but even when trauma strikes in adulthood, it cries out for expression, selectively influencing our perception and determining our preoccupations. We are driven to find release and express our psychic pain. We develop symptoms that plague us, but that can also be seen as creative solutions to our internal conflicts. Through them, we memorialize our suffering (Shabad, 2001). In the long run, symptoms are not an effective solution; they often create new problems for us; they become a source of shame and ultimately don't protect us from anxiety.

There are, however, more effective means toward healing. Major life choices, such as marriage or career, offer opportunities for psychological repair through the creation of relationships and situations that allow for the fulfillment of thwarted needs. For instance, it has been observed that many trauma survivors are drawn to the helping professions. Through identification with their patients, survivors can work through their own experiences from a distance and feel a sense of power in the process—a situation that counters the helplessness previously felt in the face of traumatic events in their own lives.

One of the most powerful and effective routes toward emotional healing is through creative expression—literary, visual, music, and the performing arts. Engagement in the process of creativity can be immensely reparative (Bose, 2005; Knafo, 2003; Kogan, 2012; Laub & Podell, 1995; Orfanos, 2010; Ornstein, 2010; Pollock, 1989a, b; Richman, 2006b; Rose, 1996). Through the symbolic or direct expression of the trauma experience, the survivor can bring some order into emotional chaos. Creative self-expression provides an opportunity to mourn, to find meaning, and to regain some sense of continuity and connection. When the artist has a special talent and the world recognizes it, the public recognition becomes a source of self-esteem as well—a quality usually in short supply in the life of the survivor. However, even when the artist is not especially talented or is unaware of the connections between the trauma experience and its expression, the engagement in the process of making art can be gratifying and reparative. By expressing the internal pain, the artist externalizes it, fashions a container for it, and invites others to become witnesses to his suffering. Those witnesses allow the survivor to be known and to feel less alone.

For the many survivors who have written memoirs, painted their memories, or expressed their sorrow in music or through dance, art serves the witnessing function on multiple levels, including becoming a witness to oneself and one's own suffering. The need for witness is universal and ubiquitous; we come to know ourselves through the recognition of others (Stern, 2010a). But for the trauma survivor, whose experience has been chaotic and fragmenting, the witnessing function is especially vital; it provides opportunities for repair through connection and integration. The ability to step outside of oneself and see the product that one has created through the eyes of another (i.e., the witness) allows a person to shift perspective and achieve some distance—a state that is helpful to gain mastery over the chaotic feelings that follow in the wake of trauma.[2]

How does art help master trauma? What is the therapeutic action in the creation of art? These are the basic questions that I want to address briefly and that will be further developed in chapter 4. Rose (1987), who has written extensively on the subject of art and trauma, proposed that "both creative and clinical processes follow the fundamental psychic principle of attempting to master passively experienced trauma by active repetition" (p. 44). Creative work externalizes inner processes and connects the person more intimately to the outside world. What begins for the creative artist as the task of mastering one's personal past becomes a process of externalizing and transcending it.

This conceptualization is consistent with my thinking on the subject. In the aftermath of trauma, artistic work helps the survivor to come to terms with the internal chaos generated by the experience. I see the process of creation as a purposeful (although not always conscious) symbolic reenactment of traumatic experiences that facilitates the working through of overpowering affects. By externalizing what is experienced internally as overwhelming and fragmenting, and by fashioning it into a creative product, the artist brings the traumatic experience into the light of day for a new viewing. In that sense, the artist becomes witness to her own trauma as she transforms it into a work of art. This enables the artist to reflect on the trauma, something initially terrifying with no boundaries or definition, and to define and integrate it into a coherent meaningful narrative.

A similar idea is well expressed by Bose (2005) when he wrote,

> The function of the work of art, in a reciprocal process between the art object and its maker, in the making and in the performing of it, can then be seen as being able to reassert the ability to find meaning and symbolic form and therewith again to communicate to an other, to have a witness and to also communicate with oneself and with dissociated aspects of self-experience. (p. 69)

What exists inside as *unformulated* (to borrow a term from Stern, 1997) chaos can be formulated, that is, given shape and meaning and witnessed by self and other. Through the creative process, painful disorganizing and overwhelming affects are shaped into images or ideas that have a substance and a reality. This process counteracts the tendency toward dissociation, the common legacy of trauma. The creative product exists as evidence of one's experience at a moment in time and, as such, it endures the vicissitudes of shifting self-states. Thus, it facilitates the integration of disparate self-states into a coherent and continuous sense of self. Although Bromberg (1998) does not conceptualize this process as one of integration, he basically expressed a similar idea—that the capacity to feel whole while recognizing that one is made up of many selves is the essence of self-acceptance and creativity.

At this point, I would like to illustrate the transformation of trauma into creative self-expression by discussing three generations of trauma survivors in my family—my father before me and my daughter after me—who have turned to the arts as a means of self-healing.

"WHY?" Making Sense Through Memoir

My father, Leon Richman, was a concentration camp survivor who found in writing and in painting his royal road to healing. Even with his limited talent in both art forms, he experienced immense satisfaction in the process; his impulse to create became a driving force, giving meaning and purpose to his life. Leon Richman was born in 1901 to a Jewish family living in a *shtetl* in southeast Poland. He, the youngest of four, had great aspirations. He was the most educated of his siblings, actually spoke many of the 13 languages he had learned, and enjoyed painting, writing, and learning. In his youth, he had aspired to be a physician, but the options for a poor Jew were quite limited at the time. He ended up in banking, a profession that satisfied his preoccupation with money, which was legendary, but not his creative or intellectual interests.

After the Second World War broke out, Leon ended up in a concentration camp, where he desperately clung to life for over a year. He managed to get himself assigned to a factory, which provided him access to some materials that he could write on. There he made the decision that, should he be fortunate enough to

14

survive, he would tell the world about the horrors that transpired in the camp. For that purpose, he kept scraps of paper with notes including names of perpetrators and victims, and details of murderous incidents. When he saw an opportunity to escape, Leon made sure that those precious notes were in his possession.

Following his daring escape, his good fortune continued. Through the help of some gentile friends, he located my mother and me. We were hiding out in a village some miles away from the city of Lwów, passing as a Catholic widow and her child. There he found shelter in the small, cramped attic space attached to our apartment, where he remained hidden for several years until liberation. Confined to that tiny space, he spent his days putting those notes into manuscript form. At night, when the unsuspecting landlords were asleep, he slipped out of the attic and came into the apartment where my mother waited to hear the next installment of his writing. In this way, Leon was able to share what he had endured alone during the most terrifying year of his life. In my mother, he found the caring and interested witness that he must have imagined when he made the commitment to the project.

After liberation, Leon's motivation to tell the world what had happened in the concentration camp seemed to wane. His focus was on creating a new life for himself and his family, and the energy required for that precluded a focus on artistic activities. The writing experience in hiding seemed to have served its purposes, namely, it had provided him with a sense of control and mastery over the humiliating experiences he had endured in the camp, and it had enabled him to reconnect with my mother. As to his commitment to tell the world—it would have to wait for another 30 years. By that time, he had retired, and fortuitously the world had become interested in the stories of survivors. He had the manuscript translated from Polish into English and had it published through a vanity press (Richman, 1975). He gave the book the title *WHY?*, presumably revealing his continual struggle to make sense of the incomprehensible tragedy of what had happened to him and to his people.

By then, Leon had also returned to another interest of his youth—painting. In striking contrast to the rageful and bitter tone of the book, his paintings depicted peaceful, bucolic scenes and lovely landscapes painted from life when he was on vacation. These scenes, done in a child-like primitive style with bright colors, were meant to memorialize places that he had enjoyed. I presume that the beauty of nature that he tried to capture in these landscapes was meant to counterbalance the ugliness of human nature that his wartime experiences had imprinted on him. Only one painting stood in stark contrast to these pretty pictures—it was a self-portrait that revealed his tormented face; an expression of horror in his eyes captured a self-state that must have felt like his essence (see Figure 1.1). That painting was not displayed as were the others. It was never framed and was tucked away for me to find after his death.

Although generally the paintings and the writing seemed so different in terms of the mood that they conveyed, they had one thing in common—they revealed

Figure 1.1 Leon Richman, *Self-Portrait* (1975). Tempera on paper 9 × 12 inches. The original is in color. Photo: Steve Hockstein/Harvard Studio. Private collection.

Leon's commitment to record what he had seen and experienced as accurately and as objectively as possible. In so doing, he placed himself in the position of witness; his intention was to show the reader/viewer facts rather than emotions, believing that he could remain objective and keep his feelings out of the picture. Leon was not a social man; he had few friends and had difficulty communicating with people. Yet, like most of us, he had a need to be known, and it is through his art that he was able to meet that need. The illusion that he was keeping himself out of the picture provided the safety that allowed him to reveal his thoughts and perceptions.

The idea of going into psychotherapy to address his post-traumatic symptoms was alien to my father, as it was for most of his contemporaries. Leon, whose attitude toward religion was one of disdain, would often announce that he didn't "believe" in therapy—as if he was referring to a new religion deserving of his contempt. My choice of psychology as a profession always baffled him, and he was quite critical of it.

After the war, most adult survivors did not turn to psychotherapy for help. Their mistrust of authority, their terror of retraumatization, and their need to deal with the realities of everyday life in a new world made delving into the past a threatening endeavor. The fact is that most probably would not have found the real help they needed anyway because the mental health professionals of the 1950s and 1960s were not especially knowledgeable about or attuned to the aftereffects of massive psychic trauma.

For those survivors who could not turn to a stranger for help—and in point of fact, the analyst is always a stranger at the beginning of an analysis—there were other roads to healing. The "other" who witnesses can be an affirming empathic person in the life of the survivor or even an internalized presence, such as an imagined audience, a lost parent, or the concept of God—the ultimate all-knowing presence.

Once art is created, there is the potential for a real witnessing presence. This shift from internal vision to external witness represents a significant achievement, for it encourages the restoration of connection with others, a connection that the trauma experience threatened or ruptured. Furthermore, it is the exercise of these capacities that fosters self-healing. Art allows people to express symbolically what they may not be able to express directly or verbally. Survivors of trauma often struggle with conflicting needs around the issue of self-expression—whether to reveal or to conceal what has happened to them (Herman, 1992). They have a deep-seated conviction that no one could possibly understand what they have lived through. Yet, at the same time, they have the human desire to be known and recognized, and for their experience to be validated.

Art provides a compromise between the need to be known and the impulse to hide for self-protection; it allows the trauma survivor to let people into his private world and connect with them on his own terms and from a safe position. "Depicting anything in the external world, whether by painting it, drawing it sculpting it, or describing it in words, requires that a certain distance be interposed between the artist and the object which he is attempting to portray" (Storr, 1993, p. 197). In the process of creating an artistic product, the trauma survivor achieves the necessary distance to be able to bear the pain of revisiting the traumatic experience.

While all forms of artistic expression can be instrumental in self-healing, writing is particularly well suited for the integration of cognitive and emotional aspects of self (Lepore & Smyth, 2002), especially when it is autobiographical. By autobiographical writing, I mean any writing that expresses the author's individuality, whether it is a poem, a story, a memoir—anything that reveals who we are. In my experience, memoir writing especially lends itself to the restoration of a sense of continuity that was disrupted by trauma. In the last 40 years, a new genre of nonfiction literature has emerged: first-person narratives about bearing witness and giving testimony to tragic events (Nachmani, 2005). In that process, an author transforms the unspeakable into something that can be communicated and used to educate and to memorialize. Nachmani refers to narration or the telling of one's story as "proof of life."

The creation of narrative is an important aspect of the therapeutic experience, whether it is the product of an ongoing psychotherapy or it occurs in the privacy of one's studio. The narrative that emerges through artistic self-expression helps to organize experience and give it a context and a meaning. It can put one in touch with deep inner knowledge that is not readily available in the conscious waking state. Self-discovery is an exhilarating experience; it is affirming, organizing, and empowering.

The uncertainty of what will emerge when putting pen to paper or brush to canvas can be exciting, but it can also be threatening or destabilizing. Under such circumstances, creativity cannot flourish and the artist may turn to psychotherapy, a holding environment in which it is possible to delve into the depths of one's soul under the watchful eye of an empathic therapist. But for trauma survivors who have experienced massive betrayal at the hands of others, trusting others with one's life story is not always an option. Survivors seem to know intuitively what the relational position in psychoanalysis has highlighted, namely, that narrative developed in the analytic setting is a joint construction, the result of mutual influence between patient and analyst (Aron, 1991; Epstein, 2009b; Hoffman, 1998; Stern, 2010a). Entrusting oneself to the influence of a powerful other (the analyst) is a dangerous endeavor for those who fear being in someone's power and control. For those individuals, like my father, their creative activity becomes their sole form of therapy.

Finding My Voice

During his lifetime, I never could acknowledge that my father and I actually shared a number of interests and that he had influenced me in some of my choices. Love of learning, a passion for painting, and a desire to put personal experiences into writing are all important themes in my own life, as they were in his, but I did not recognize them as shared interests or as something that could potentially bring us closer. It was only after I wrote my memoir (Richman, 2002), about 20 years after my father's death, that I could let myself see how much we had in common and what an influence he had on my life.

When I think about the turning point when I first allowed myself to face my childhood trauma and its impact, I place it around the time that my father first published his memoir in the mid 1970s. Up until that point, the Holocaust had been a shadowy presence in our home, kept at bay by silence or whispers between my parents and their survivor friends. When my father told the world about his concentration camp experience through his memoir, he emerged into the open and gave me permission to do the same. His self-disclosure paved the way for my own. The process of writing changed my relationship with my father. It allowed me to see him as a separate person with strengths and weaknesses, a product of his culture and a victim of traumatic life circumstances. I came to admire the difficult choices that he had made throughout his life and gained new respect for his courage.

Writing a memoir was a life-changing experience for me, as I imagine it had been for my father as well. I embarked on it shortly after termination from my analysis. It came to be a way to continue the process of analysis on my own. My analyst was most encouraging of the process. Whenever I ran into him in the analytic community, he would pointedly ask if I was writing. But in truth, I didn't need his encouragement. The process was so gratifying and preoccupying that nothing could hold it back.

Although I had read many memoirs written by others, I had written little autobiographical material in my adult life. Once I made the decision to write, I was surprised at how effortless, exciting, and gratifying the project was. My words and thoughts flowed with amazing facility. I had always enjoyed the process of writing, but didn't realize how fulfilling telling the story of my life would be. As I wrote, I began to discover new things about myself and make sense of events and choices that I had not understood before, despite years of analysis. By examining the totality of my life, I began to see the intricate patterns in its fabric. Events that had existed in my mind as separate entities became part of the larger picture, and reenactments that had puzzled me suddenly began to make sense in their context.

When I was engaged in writing, it often felt as if I entered into a trance-like state with an altered sense of time and a suspension of critical judgment. One of the most interesting things for me was the absence of an internal critical censor. The censor who inhibits me whenever I'm about to speak seemed totally absent during the writing process. The internalized other (the projected reader) was an amorphous presence without distinguishing characteristics, but seemed to be an interested observer, a witness, someone who wanted to know more about me and my life. Perhaps the amorphous presence represented my mother, my first reader-listener, who loved to hear my school papers and received my writing with unwavering admiration. Over the years I have found other affirming listeners, like my analyst and my husband.

When I first began writing, the events of my early life seemed fragmented and lacking in coherence—I didn't even have a mental time line of the historical events that had shaped my life. Writing fostered continuity by bringing structure and meaning to what had transpired and helped me to make sense of emotional experiences that had felt disconnected and confusing. It also connected me with family both known and unknown to me—the latter sensed as shadows whose existence had been cut short as they vanished into the maelstrom. Seeing my life in context not only allowed me to understand myself better, but it encouraged me to function as a witness to historical events both on a global and personal level. I accepted the identity of being one of the last living witnesses to the Shoah (Kestenberg & Brenner, 1996; Richman, 2007) and found it to be both a source of pride and a responsibility. I was empowered by the notion that I could give voice to those who had been silenced and provide them with an opportunity to be remembered. As Elie Wiesel wrote in his blurb to my memoir, "Thanks to her scholarly effort, more names and tales will be remembered" (Richman, 2002).

My narrative did not stop with the story of the war years, as so many Holocaust memoirs do; instead, the narrative continued into my adult life. I decided that what needed to be told was the long-term psychological impact of war trauma on character, personality, and life choices. Additionally, I suspect that part of my motivation was to address and challenge my parents' assertion that I was unaffected by what had transpired when I was so young. While my parents were no longer alive to give me the recognition I sought, at least I could set the record straight—a common motivation of memoir writers.

The writing of my memoir also gave me the opportunity to work through other traumatic experiences that had occurred in my adulthood. The narrative that readers of the memoir often find most compelling is the story of my daughter, Lina, and her journey out of darkness.

"What the Eye Cannot See"

Lina was born when I was in my 40th year and was welcomed into the world by both sets of grandparents, for whom she was the first and long-awaited grandchild. For my parents, she represented new life on a family tree whose branches had been broken during the Second World War. From early on, Lina was exposed to the trauma of the Second World War through the stories that both sets of grandparents told. Although her paternal grandparents were Greek Orthodox and not subjected to the persecution that was directed against Jews, they had also suffered under German occupation. Their children heard many stories about hunger and fear and how the entire community on the small island of Ereikousa in Greece had conspired to successfully hide Greek Jews from the Nazis.

Lina's sense of herself was not directly impacted by her history. She never thought of herself as a second-generation survivor. She has always been partial to the Greek side of her family, the side with many cousins who meet for celebrations and dance with abandon. The thriving Greek American community in the United States has a strong sense of identity, in contrast to the few remaining relatives on my side whose ethnic and religious identity was deeply affected by circumstances of displacement and the need for safety. The few relatives who survived on my mother's side had converted to Catholicism before the war and had hidden their

Jewish roots from the generations that followed, while those who survived on my father's side had migrated to the United States before the war and held on to the Jewish traditions of their ancestors. So Lina, who like her parents identifies herself as an atheist, grew up in a diverse community surrounded by cousins of varied religious orientation: Catholics, Jews, and Greek Orthodox.

Lina's early years seemed charmed. She was cherished by immediate family just because of her existence, but she also had special gifts. From very early on, she showed an aptitude for music, and by the age of 7 she was appearing on the Metropolitan Opera stage in New York City in the Children's Chorus. She had inherited her hauntingly beautiful voice from my aunt Jadzia, my mother's sister, who was murdered with her 5-year-old daughter in 1942 when they were discovered in their hiding place. It is a triumph to know that Jadzia's beautiful voice, silenced by the Nazis during the war, has lived on in her niece's daughter.

At the age of 14, Lina's childhood came to a sudden end when she was diagnosed with a brain tumor. According to her neurologist, the huge tumor (the size of an orange) had been growing inside her head for many years and had been surreptitiously creating damage, which had manifested as strange symptoms and perplexing behavior. The child who could read at the age of 2 and whose IQ score was 160+ on the Stanford-Binet at the age of 3 was dyslexic by the time she reached early adolescence. She developed a strange gait, and her toes began to curl downward. Her fingers gripped the pencil so tightly that writing hurt and the words were barely legible. Her headaches were becoming more common, and all of the psychological explanations that we manufactured did not fit the picture we watched unfold before our eyes. The physicians and psychologists who were consulted were as baffled as we were about what was happening to her.

In the meantime, Lina was drawn to poetry. She wrote it constantly, ignoring the pain in her fingers as they gripped and twisted around the pencil in claw-like fashion. Only poetry and music seemed to hold her attention. Her love of music and her beautiful voice appeared unaffected by what was happening to the rest of her body.

Once diagnosed, she underwent a series of harrowing brain surgeries. As she was being wheeled into her first surgery, clinging to her teddy bear, we heard her humming "America," an upbeat song from *West Side Story*—her favorite musical. Since she was a toddler, she had used music to soothe herself; as she drifted off to sleep, I could hear her humming the Brahms melody she had learned from the mobile over her crib. Music was truly a transitional phenomenon (Winnicott, 1953) for her, an intermediate space where she could find comfort and security when she needed it.

I believe that poetry writing also brought her into this transitional area of experience, providing her with a safe place where she could contemplate her internal world and its relationship to external reality. The poetry that she wrote before she consciously knew of the tumor growing inside of her brain reflects an intuitive knowledge, as the following poem written two months before her diagnosis suggests:

"Darkness"

My heart glistens
in the open
sun.

The beauty that surrounds me
is closing in.

A painter paints my picture
but he does not know what's inside
my soul.

I blink and
darkness surrounds my body.

Everything turns into
dust.

Poetry writing is a common adolescent experience, and dramatic self-expression is not unusual at that age, but for Lina it represented something that went beyond the usual adolescent angst. In this, as in the other poems she was writing at the time, her vulnerability was palpable. She had a sense that something was going wrong inside of her that was not visible to others. The school counselor tried to discourage her from writing such "depressing" poetry, naively thinking that happier poems would make her feel better, but Lina would not be influenced; she knew what she needed and was driven to express what was tormenting her. What's more, it seemed to help.

Loewald (1978/1980c) writes: "In great poetry and creative prose . . . there is an interweaving of primary and secondary process by virtue of which language functions as a transitional mode encompassing both" (p. 204). While I am not suggesting that Lina's writing is great poetry, the merging of primary and secondary process in her poems allowed her to put amorphous primitive experiences into words so that she could make sense of what she was feeling and communicate it to others.

It was only during the recovery period that the tone of her poems changed. The following poem was written six months after surgery, while we were vacationing on Ereikousa, the home of her paternal relatives.

"Untitled Poem"

A young girl
sits outside a home
far away from her problems.

A relaxing breeze
cools her head
and the
music that is played
calms her.

Pussy willow flows in the
wind.

Everything is
calm.

The song may stop
but the music still
continues.

In this poem, Lina uses multiple senses to enter a kind of meditative state in which she experiences an inner calm and a sense of well-being. This is the transitional state that Lina has been able to move into, and derive strength from, since childhood. The last sentence "The song may stop / but the music still / continues"—reaffirms her sense of self-continuity in the wake of the fragmenting potential of trauma. One of Lina's common phrases in describing herself and her relationship to music was always, "Music *is* my life." In that context, she is letting the reader know that her life continues; she has survived and she believes that there will be music in her future. Ultimately, it is an expression of a sense of optimism that some believe is the essence of resilience (Anthony & Cohler, 1987; Tedeschi, Park, & Calhoun, 1998).

Stricken during her adolescence, a time when most young people enjoy a sense of omnipotence and invulnerability, Lina was dealing with life and death issues. For the first year after her surgeries she kept a calendar marking off each passing day, and on January 16—the anniversary date of her surgery—she printed the words "I'M ALIVE!"

Not only was Lina robbed of her adolescence, but even now, 19 years later, she continues to live with the emotional and physical scars of her illness. Shortly after the first surgery, we had been informed by her neurooncologist that a portion of the tumor that was located in her hypothalamus could not be excised, and although it was benign, it was life-threatening and would have to be monitored for the rest of her life. Both the tumor and the surgery had done irreversible damage to her brain, which would affect her functioning in ways that could not be predicted at the time. The hypothalamus is a crucial part of the brain, and one of its many vital functions is the control of hunger. In most survivors of these types of tumors, both appetite and metabolism are permanently affected, resulting in "hypothalamic obesity," an intractable condition unresponsive to any intervention.

For anyone, but for a young woman in particular, this is a difficult life sentence to have to face. Yet Lina demonstrates a remarkable capacity to cope with the traumatic circumstances of her life. Despite countless assaults on her mind and body, her zest for living remains strong and she faces her situation, for the most part, without bitterness or self-pity. But that's only one side of Lina. There is also anger and anxiety and areas of vulnerability so poignantly revealed in the following poem, written 10 months after her surgery.

"What the Eye Cannot See"

A girl with skin soft
as a velvet blanket sat
on the limb of a tree.

The cool wind
brushed against her face.

She stared off into the
sky and noticed its color.

A smooth, silky
grayish blue that any moment
would change color.

It looked as though
it would rain.

The leaves slumped over
hunchbacked.

The girl looked
far beyond the scene
and saw a world
filled with
hatred and
anger.

In this poem, Lina reveals her precarious position in the world. While she looks "normal" to others, they cannot see her vulnerability; she's out on a limb, and her soft skin cannot protect her from the harsh elements. The weather could turn destructive at any moment, and like the leaves on her metaphoric tree, she could be overcome (slumped over) and deformed like a hunchback. As she looks ahead, she sees a world filled with hatred and anger—perhaps a reference to the rejecting attitudes of others towards her disability and her own projected anger at her fate.

This is the other side of her resilience, the hidden side that people tend to forget when they encounter Lina. According to Valent (1998), there is an internal dialectic in the term *resilience*. We can focus on the side that expresses the triumph of having overcome a tragedy, or we can look at the devastation caused by it. Resilience is not a dichotomous trait but exists on a continuum. Like other survivors of trauma, Lina is both resilient and vulnerable at different times and in different situations or self-states. Her life is a testimonial to the indomitable human spirit, but it is also an example of trauma's debilitating long-term effects.

As used by most people, the concept of resilience often conceals the fact that while a person may function well in the world, there is a considerable price that must be extracted for this seemingly good health and adjustment. For instance, we know that dissociation enables the survivor of trauma to cope—but at what sacrifice? What aspects of self have to be denied in order to function well? Furthermore, high levels of anxiety and depression may not always be observable, and vulnerabilities may come to light only under certain specific circumstances.

Poetry served Lina well during the period of her life when she was traumatized, first as her body and mind were assaulted by the effects of the brain tumor, and later as she struggled to regain her equilibrium in its aftermath. Coming to terms with a disability requires a long working through process (Thomas & Siller, 1999). The grief and depression following the realization that life would never again be the same found expression in her poetry. Somehow, she had to mourn and still go on with life as a high school student, and it was through her poetry writing that she found a way. Serendipitously, the school had been offering workshops taught by professional writers, so Lina eagerly signed up. The experience was immensely therapeutic; in addition to helping her express her feelings in writing, it also allowed her to develop relationships with talented adults empathic to her situation.

Poetry facilitated mourning, but it was in music that Lina consistently found solace. Her musical ability was evident from the start of life. She had a heightened sensitivity to sound and a special responsiveness to music. As she developed, we could see her talent unfold. According to Nass (1989), creative individuals have a different sensorimotor system than others; they have greater access to body processes and body rhythms.

As a largely primary process, nonverbal, somatic, and kinesthetic mode of communication, music taps the earliest developmental roots; it is the language of emotion. Of all of the arts, music is the most direct means of self-expression; it is the form of symbolism that is the closest to the representation of pure feeling (Hagman, 2005). Because of its relationship to affect and its connection with body rhythms, music is particularly well-suited to the expression of varied and intense emotions, moods, and states of mind, and it has the power to help regulate potentially disorganizing affects.

Stein (2004a, 2004b), a professional pianist turned psychoanalyst, has written about the role of music in mourning and trauma. He finds that there are important connections between temporal aspects of music and traumatic experience: "The use of slow rhythmic counting, cradlelike rocking, or other lulling associated with early life are thus a not uncommon means of self-soothing during traumatic events" (2004a, p. 759).

Music, according to Stein, possesses unique properties among the arts in its potential to evoke and convey a range of affects connected with grief, and consequently plays a special role in mourning, serving the mourning process for composer, performer, and listener. He wrote, "Music can be composed or listened to (1) for grieving, (2) for solace and comfort, (3) to provide a sense of belonging, (4) to provide a sense of hope that life can go on, and (5) to provide a sense of triumph over adversity" (Stein, 2004b, p. 792).

In my view, of all of the instruments, it is the human voice that is most suited to express grief and mourning. Another psychoanalyst from a musical background, Glennon (2003), a gifted singer, wrote about her personal experience of mourning the death of her husband with the help of vocal music. She found that putting the pain of loss into the aesthetic container of a song aided her mourning process, and that the creation of something beautiful from the chaos of pain led to a sense of inner calm. She recorded a series of songs that had special meaning for her, with lyrics that captured her feelings, then found that her listeners were also helped in accessing the pain over losses in their own lives. She concluded that the act of expressing authentic emotion gives the sufferer a sense of mastery over their pain. Authentic artistic expression facilitates not only the process of mourning, but also the emergence of other emotions, which counters the tendency towards dissociation or defensive numbness.

With her command of her vocal instrument and her natural expressiveness, Lina found in music the ideal medium to work through her trauma. Fortuitously the tumor was located on the left side of the brain, which meant that while language was adversely affected, non-verbal areas sustained less damage. Her musicality remained intact; it was the medium for the expression of her deepest emotions; a source of immense gratification and self-esteem.

The recognition of her musical talent by others was always a source of positive self-regard, which became particularly significant during a time of heightened vulnerability and shame associated with a sense of being damaged. When performing, Lina seemed able to put such negative feelings aside and bask in the affirmation and admiration of her audience. In striking contrast to her physical awkwardness in daily life, when Lina performs she seems to take great pleasure in her body and communicates an unusual sensuality and self-confidence.

Writing about performers in general, Hagman (2005) pointed out that "in performance, the musician creates something beautiful and perfect, the externalization of an ideal level of self-experience through the most authentic interpretation of the musical text. The musician experiences himself or herself as transcendent, perfect, powerful and whole" (p. 108). In Lina's case, the transformation is even more striking because of her physical limitations. When Lina performs, the narcissistic injury of having sustained irrevocable physical and mental damage is replaced by a healthy narcissism (Kohut, 1957) derived from exercising a special skill and talent and being recognized for it.

In addition to serving important intrapsychic functions, music serves relational needs. Through empathic resonance, inner mental states that cannot be put into words can be communicated to others and shared. Since early childhood, Lina has been a highly social person, and despite the isolating potential of trauma, she has managed to maintain intimate connections. In the face of trauma, communication becomes difficult, if not impossible; language, which is our usual means of organizing and narrating experience, is often inadequate to the task. Words do not always effectively convey the experience of grief and suffering; the sense of isolation may endure and sometimes prevail. Music allows for a different kind of expressivity and fosters a different kind of connectedness to others.

As a performer, Lina and her audience are often one. In those who watch and listen to her, she finds witnesses and participants to share her experiences. Through empathic resonance and affective communication, Lina's emotional rendering of a song evokes similar emotions in her listeners. Besides her relationship to her audience, Lina also dialogues with other musicians as they create sounds together. Musical group activity can be a gratifying social experience, providing the artist with a sense of belonging to a special group (Kohut, 1957). For many years, Lina sang in choruses, but in the last decade she has been a solo performer. Whether she sings in a chorus, backed by an orchestra, or accompanied by an ensemble, she enjoys being a part of a special, talented group who resonate and share a life-affirming creative process.

Since her graduation from college 11 years ago, Lina has been concentrating on singing the music of the renowned Greek songwriter and composer Mikis Theodorakis—a choice encouraged and nurtured by her father, Spyros D. Orfanos, a psychoanalyst and amateur ethnomusicologist, who is a great admirer of this man and his work.[3] Theodorakis, a musical genius and an activist, is also a trauma survivor. During the Second World War and the Greek Civil War, he was imprisoned and tortured but managed to continue to compose powerful melodies and symphonies, which were smuggled out and eventually turned into popular song cycles, oratorio, operas, and symphonies. Through music, he was able to symbolize and memorialize trauma; for him and his fellow countrymen, music has been the mechanism of salvation and testimony (Orfanos, 1997, 1999, 2010).

Certain composers, more than others, are able to capture or communicate a sense of grief (Stein, 2004b), and Theodorakis is the leading contemporary composer of mourning music in Greece, a country that values the ongoing nature of mourning. His compositions integrate powerful words and sorrowful sounds that evoke passion, longing, and loss. The aesthetic structure allows the listener to enter a safe holding environment where these powerful emotions can be experienced and shared.

Concerts featuring the music of Theodorakis have certain similarities to the commemorative events and rituals described by Bassin (2011) and Slochower (2011). Both types of events create a transitional space for remembering and mourning in a protected setting in the presence of others for a limited period. Audiences and parishioners find themselves in a facilitating environment in which to access and memorialize their losses, both individual and collective.

Lina's affinity for this music goes beyond her connection with her father. These songs of loss and suffering resonate with her and provide her with an opportunity for the creative working through of her own trauma. Music is a powerful communicator of affect, and Lina's personal tragedy has given great emotional texture to her voice, the vehicle through which she expresses her emotions about the tragedies that have happened to her and to her people.

In the fall of 2007, when Lina was in her late 20s, she was asked by Theodorakis to sing one of his best-known and loved pieces of music—"Song of Songs" from the *Mauthausen Cantata*, a cycle of songs dealing with the trauma of the Holocaust—at a concert in Athens dedicated to the victims of the fires that had raged in Greece that summer. The televised event took place at the ancient amphitheater at the foot of the Acropolis and was attended by over 5,000 people. Lina found herself among the brightest stars and luminaries of Greece, the only guest star from America. She sang this sorrowful song of mourning, based on the poetry of the concentration camp survivor poet Iakovos Kambanellis, both in Greek and in Hebrew. As she sang with the full orchestra, images of the Holocaust were projected on a huge screen behind the stage.

For Lina, that magical moment in time represented a masterful integration of the different strands of her life; it brought together her father's Greek heritage, her mother's Holocaust history, and her own legacy of loss and resilience, all expressed in her hauntingly beautiful soprano voice. Over these past few years, Lina has come to consider this to be her signature song. Ironically, never having identified herself as a second-generation Holocaust survivor, with this piece of her heritage, she has somehow found her way to represent it in the world. In the most recent concert in Greece featuring the work of the composer, she was introduced as "a child of the Holocaust."

For those present in the amphitheater that night, Lina became a symbol of triumph over trauma. Few in the audience were aware that she had survived her own tragedy and that the song she sang, which tells the story of a beautiful young girl lost in the Holocaust, could just as well refer to the part of Lina herself who was lost when illness overtook her. As the lover narrator mourns the loss of his beloved, Lina mourns her lost adolescence, her damaged body, and her lost potential.

Each song holds the possibility of serving as a moment of mourning when the singer and members of her audience can safely enter that transitional space, acknowledge what has been lost, experience the grief in the presence of witnesses, and then be free to move into another self-state—one invoked by the next song, be it a playful or romantic one. Music remains central in Lina's life, a source of great pleasure for her and for her audiences. Whether she sings music of mourning or lighter fare, like sensual love songs or joyful and playful ones, her passion is expressed and communicated with every note. For her, singing is an affirmation of life. Like her mother and her grandfather, Lina has turned to creative self-expression as a way to mourn, to work through trauma, and ultimately to transcend it.

While each of the three generations has found its own unique voice, all three have shared the intoxicating experience of mastering and transforming loss and misfortune into something of meaning and value. Concomitantly, the self has undergone a transformation as well—from victim, to survivor, to creator or artist, and in that process, the sense of agency and vitality has been restored.

Notes

Sections of this chapter previously appeared in *Contemporary Psychoanalysis, 42* (2006), 639–650, and *Psychoanalytic Dialogues, 23* (2013), 362–376.

1. My translation from the French.
2. In chapter 4 I will elaborate further on the significance of the witnessing function.
3. Chapter 7 will provide a more detailed account of some of this material.

2

UNDERSTANDING CREATIVITY
The Theoretical Landscape

In 1818, during the early German Romantic period, the artist Caspar David Friedrich created his now familiar oil painting, *The Wanderer above the Sea of Fog*. This work depicts a young man in a black coat in the foreground standing on a rocky precipice, his back turned toward us. He is bracing himself with a walking stick against the wind that blows his hatless hair in tangles. Stretched before the wanderer lies a fog-shrouded landscape composed of rocks and shapes of trees in lowland plains, faded mountains in the far horizon of clouds, and perhaps very far away—one can't be sure, maybe it's just more fog—an ocean. About this painting, the historian John Lewis Gaddis (2002) wrote,

> The impression it leaves is contradictory, suggesting at once mastery over a landscape and the insignificance of an individual within it. We see no face, so it's impossible to know whether the prospect confronting the young man is exhilarating, or terrifying, or both. (p. 1)

This image is a good starting point for understanding the theoretical landscape on creativity. Conceptual mastery of the subject is elusive. How one understands creativity is a matter of one's point of view. For the ancient Greeks, theory (*theoria*) was defined as an active process of looking at, viewing, and contemplation, and it was acknowledged to be speculative. It was dynamic and constructive, not necessarily a system of ideas or statements held as an explanation of a group of facts. Theorizing about creativity often feels like an effort to reconcile oil and water; yet there are some points of view that feel more compelling than others. If the aim of a theory is to assume a higher view, at least for a time, then it should also elaborate and enrich, even if such actions only partially lift the fog.[1]

In theories that strive to explain creativity, process and content are inevitably intertwined. In a sense, every theory is a creative construction, a framework that allows us to view things in new ways and from a different perspective. Theories of creativity are thus examples of the very same phenomenon they seek to explain: formulations about the creative process that reflect on the imaginative and intellectual capacities of their creators. Furthermore, theories are the creation of those with a particular interest in the subject, and so their constructions tend to mirror the experiences and the psychodynamics of their creators. Issues that are personally significant will find their way into formulations, revealing as much about the theoretician as about his/her ideas. The subjective world of the theorist is inevitably translated into his view of human nature (Stolorow & Atwood, 1979).

Understanding creativity is a particularly challenging task, and each new theory builder attempts to bring his/her own particular spark to it. Some theorists, like McDougall (1995), find that there is an enigmatic dimension to creative expression that evades our comprehension; nevertheless, many have attempted to shed some light on this mysterious process. Despite the fact that theories of creativity are subjective offerings, they are often presented as indisputable, objective truths that belie their hypothetical nature.

After surveying the extensive literature, I have found myself quite disappointed with the elaborate and somewhat sterile theoretical formulations about the nature of the creative process and the motivational hypotheses attributed to the artist, particularly those deriving from the drive theory model that reigned supreme in the early days of psychoanalysis and that persists in some forms to this day. I have a personal aversion to jargon, and terms like *libidinal energy cathexis* and art as *archaic residue* do not resonate with me. In my opinion, the elaborate, often abstract conceptualizations of most theoreticians fail to truly capture the essence of art; they are neither experience-near nor do they convey the excitement or the transformational capacity of the creative experience. I agree with Greenberg and Mitchell (1983) that when the creation of art is reduced to constructs, such as sublimation or reconciliation of the pleasure and reality principles, it strains our intuitive understanding of art: "Where does the theory account for the experience of being elevated by an encounter with a work of great beauty, of being awed by the creative potential of our fellow men?" they ask (p. 269).

In my own analytic training in the early 1970s, theory and metapsychology were viewed with skepticism if not outright suspicion. A number of the interpersonal psychoanalysts, whom I studied with, were less interested in abstract theoretical ideas and more focused on clinical and experiential material. They seemed to be going through a period in which intellectual activities were not as appreciated as they currently are (Stern, 2010b). The phenomenological orientation, while not atheoretical, minimized the power of explanatory interpretation and historical reconstruction in favor of an approach that emphasized the uniqueness of experience and the nature of interpersonal engagement in the present. My supervisors and some of the teachers whom I respected maintained that presuppositions often interfere with the phenomenological goal of entering the patient's experiential world and seeing it from her perspective; it is only through mutual exploration with the patient that one is able to arrive at an understanding of the meaning of an event for that individual. Perhaps that is why I am wary of theoretical speculations and have never really been comfortable with metapsychology. I appreciate the Sufi proverb quoted by Edgar Levenson, one of the most creative writers of the Interpersonal School: "No problem is too difficult to be solved by a theoretician!" (Levenson, 2005).

That said, however, I will attempt to do a brief and selective review of the theoretical literature on creativity in order to anchor my own understanding of the creative process in the ways that it is similar to and different from what has been offered before. It is not my intention here to survey the vast literature on creativity; there is no dearth of theories on this subject. The topic inspires countless generative ideas, but because of the constraints of time and space, I will choose to limit my exposition to the ideas that have had a lasting influence in the field, stimulating the work of well-respected theoreticians and clinicians. I will focus on ideas that interest me and are most relevant to the theme of the present work—creativity and trauma. Some of these concepts will be elaborated in later chapters as they become relevant to the discussion of the material at hand. In my attempt to be selective, inevitably and regretfully I will leave out some who may have made important contributions.

Since the early days of psychoanalysis, art and artists have captured the imagination of theoreticians in our field. Psychoanalytic theorists writing about creativity have been preoccupied with some of the following questions: What are the motivating factors involved in the creative process? What is the basic function of a work of art? What is the role of the unconscious and the primary process in the creation of art? Does the creative process involve regression? Is there a relationship between creativity and psychopathology? What is the therapeutic action of art? These are a few of the themes that will be explored in this chapter and the next two.

Sublimation Rules: Drive Theory Models

Sigmund Freud, himself one of the most creative individuals of the 20th century, was deeply invested in understanding creativity, but by his own admission he did not feel confident in grasping its essence, as evidenced in his often-quoted statement that, when it comes to creativity, "psychoanalysis must lay down its arms" (1929/1961, p. 177). In "The Autobiographical Study," written toward the end of his life, he concluded that "[psychoanalysis] can do nothing towards elucidating the nature of the artistic gift, nor can it explain the means by which the artist works—artistic technique" (1935/1952 p. 73). Although he felt that the essence of creativity eluded psychoanalysis, he did focus on the role of unconscious motivation in creativity (Arieti, 1976).

According to Freud, the primary motive for creative endeavors is the gratification of unconscious libidinal wishes that have been inhibited in their aim and transformed through the power of imagination. He coined the term *sublimation* to denote this diversion of sexual energy into socially acceptable forms, such as cultural and artistic activities. Freud saw parallels between dreams and artist's creations in terms of defensive processes involved. He wrote, "the unconscious mechanisms familiar to us in the 'dream-work' are thus also operative in the processes of imaginative writing" (1935/1952, p. 74). While artist's creations are the imaginary gratifications of unconscious wishes that, much like dreams, are subject to compromise between the forces of repression and gratification, unlike dreams they are meant to arouse interest in other people, in whom they evoke and gratify similar unconscious wishes. Freud (1935/1952) also drew parallels between the neurotic and the artist in that both withdraw into a world of imagination in order to cope with the painful transition from the pleasure principle to the reality principle. Both struggle for self-expression and conflict solution, but only the creative person can do this in a socially valued way because, as Freud points out, the neurotic is incapable of sublimation. In the following chapters, a more detailed and nuanced account of the relationship between neurosis and psychopathology and creativity will be offered.

Although the word *creativity* rarely appears in his writing, Freud was preoccupied with imagination and fantasy and the subject was very important to him (Eigen, 1983). Nevertheless, in contrast to the voluminous contributions he made in other areas, Freud has left us with relatively few writings on the subject: a paper, "The Relation of the Poet to Day-Dreaming" (1908/1958) and a few works of applied psychoanalysis in the form of pathographies of artists like da Vinci (1910/1957) and Dostoyevsky (1929/1961), among others. By analyzing the artwork and the writings of these creators, Freud attempted to reconstruct their past and to understand their psychological motivations, their inner conflicts, and their psychodynamics. He looked at the artist and his work as if he were conducting an analysis.

With the advent of ego psychology in the 1920s, there was a fresh look at creativity as originally conceptualized by Freud, but most psychoanalysts of that period continued to operate within the theoretical framework of the Freudian school. While still maintaining roots in the drive theory model, ego psychologists focused their attention on adaptive and conflict-free areas of functioning. The ability to create was considered to be one of the cognitive functions of the ego, an enduring trait of the personality rather than the result of a state of conflict (Noy, 1972). Noy (1979) regarded the creative act as an attempt to resolve fragmentation and to regain a state of mental health. Most psychoanalytic theorists writing about creativity have grappled with the question of what agencies or levels of mind operate when the artist is engaged in creation. Richard Chessick (1999) reviewed some of the theoretical contributions of those studying the creative process and found that the belief that artistic creation flows from the unconscious is most common. Yet there are widely varying perceptions of the degree to which different levels of awareness are involved. Like Kubie (1958), who believed that all three systems of symbolic function—the conscious, the unconscious, and the preconscious—operate together, Hanly (1986) held that the integrity of form and content in art needs to be understood in the light of what we have learned about all three agencies of the psyche. This integrity cannot, for example, be understood adequately in terms of either ego functions alone or primary process alone. Rather it needs to be viewed from a multifaceted perspective according to which the function of art involves catharsis as well as a quest for maturation, reparation, restoration, and psychic integration (Chessick, 1999, p. 279 referring to Hanly).

Ernst Kris (1952), an art historian turned psychoanalyst, used his familiarity with the lives of numerous artists and his interest in the creative activities of psychotics to refine and modify Freud's ideas about artistic motives, and to add to an understanding of the creative process. Some have referred to Kris as the founder of the modern psychoanalytic theory of art (Noy, 1972). Working within the Freudian energic paradigm, Kris extended and elaborated on the concept of sublimation. According to Kris, sublimation in creative activity has two characteristics: the fusion in the discharge of instinctual energy and the shift in psychic levels. The artist possesses a special capacity to bring about a shift in the psychic level so that the ego can allow controlled regression to primary process function. Rather than positing unconscious motivation as the source of creativity, as his predecessors had done, Kris (1952) saw it as one of the organizational functions of the ego—its capacity for self-regulation of regression and control over the primary process (p. 28). He coined the phrase "regression in the service of the ego," a phrase that was picked up and repeated by generations of theorists writing about creativity. Noy (1972), writing about Kris in the 1970s, observed that Kris's theory of the relationship between primary process and artistic creativity was the first to depart from a psychoanalytic view about the primary process as chaotic and archaic. The artist's regression to primary process is a sign of strength rather than a weakness.

But Kris's contributions go beyond this concept. For instance, he understood the creative process as composed of two separate phases—"inspiration" and "elaboration"—each involving a shift in psychic level and a corresponding shift in ego functions. During the first "inspirational" phase, the artist is in a passive receptive state with the subjective experience of a flow of thoughts and images driving toward expression, while in the second phase, the ego asserts itself and the artist has the experience of purposeful action and is actively engaged in problem-solving, evaluating, and communicating with the outside world.

Lawrence Kubie (1958), like Kris, located the source of creativity in preconscious, rather than in unconscious, activity. He saw the creative person as one who had retained his capacity to use his preconscious functions more freely than others, even those others who may be equally talented. The content of preconscious mentation, according to Kubie, derives from certain universal experiences that originate in infancy and early childhood. These primitive experiences, which are the building blocks of both the creative and the neurotic processes, include events such as transitions through varied states of consciousness, disturbing experiences of body difference, developmental experiences of an inner and outer world, and the need to bridge the gap between them. These developmental experiences are among the child's primary encounter with reality, and much of life is spent struggling to master universals that are expressed in symbolic and disguised forms through symptoms, dreams, myths, or art.

Like other ego psychologists who examined the concept of sublimation, Kubie (1958) found it to be antiquated, clinically inept, and inaccurate. He maintained that it was based on the inaccurate assumption that unconscious conflicts can be resolved if they can be expressed in socially valuable forms like art. In fact, says

Kubie, when unconscious processes predominate, behavior is rigid and unmodifiable, and creativity is stifled. When the artist uses his talent to project his own internal struggles, it can take over his creative thinking, distorting it to serve his unconscious needs, as happens in dreams or symptom formation. The successful artist, according to Kubie, is able "to free preconscious processes from the distortions and obstructions interposed by unconscious processes and from the pedestrian limitations of conscious processes" (p. 143). While the preconscious system is the essential implement of all creative activities, preconscious processes don't operate by themselves; they are under the influence of conscious and unconscious systems of symbolic function. At every moment of life, all three levels are active concurrently. Shifts in consciousness occur during process of falling asleep, in hypnotic states, and under the influence of alcohol and drugs; there is a continuous movement between immature and mature levels of symbolic function, a play of dissociative and reintegrative processes.

Another psychoanalyst who used Kris's concept of regression as a springboard for his own ideas about the creative process was Phillip Weissman. Weissman (1968) considered the notion of controlled regression in the service of the ego as limited theoretically and clinically. Instead, he offered the idea that a dissociative or desynthesizing function, along with an integrative function of the ego, better describes nonregressive ego functioning in creativity. He perceived the dissociative function as essential for the temporary liberation of the established order of the psyche, so that new and creative products could result through restructuring and integration.

Several psychoanalysts had identified dissociation as a phenomenon in creativity. Both Glover (1943) and Beres (1959) had previously shown that the capacity for dissociation is a predominant feature of ego functioning in the creative process. Kris (1952) himself had confirmed this and, in addition, had suggested that the more creative the artist, the greater the dissociation between his personal life and his creation.

Weissman elaborated on the idea of dissociation, which he explained in structural terms; he saw the dissociative or desynthesizing function of the ego as a capacity of the ego to dissociate itself from its established object relationships and demands from the id and the superego:

> Applied to the creative person, the dissociative function re-emerges whenever he is in search of a creative state. The dissociative function liberates him from his customary mode of operation and permits emerging drive-derived cathexis to new treatment by the ego and the superego. It is probable that the dissociative function (rather than ego regression) is receptive to the new id-derived cathexis available to the ego. This constitutes the optimal state of the ego for creative inspirational activity. (Weissman, 1967, p. 43)

Weissman held that the dissociative and synthetic functions are utilized in both the inspiration and elaboration phases, and that these two aspects of creative activity operate together.

35

In the next chapter, I will elaborate on my own understanding of the creative process in relation to the dissociative process. While I share Weissman's recognition of the importance of dissociation in creativity, my own conceptualization of the process is quite different from his, as I do not think in terms of drive theory, but rather view dissociation from a relational perspective.

Phyllis Greenacre (1957) was another ego psychologist who made reference to dissociation in the artist. For instance, she noted a split in the self-presentation and sense of identity of the artist into a "creative self" and a more "conventional self," and felt that regardless of presence of psychopathology, the dissociative function enables the creative person to temporarily detach his creative self from his personal self.

Greenacre (1957, 1959) wrote extensively about the characteristics that distinguish talented individuals from the rest of society. Many of her findings were based on her work with young gifted children who later became artists. In trying to identify the basic characteristics of creative talent, which she believed is innate, she noted that early in life, creative individuals demonstrate greater sensitivity to sensory stimulation and earlier and greater reactivity to form and rhythm. They show an unusual capacity for awareness of relations between various stimuli, suggesting the presence of a heightened sense of subtle similarities and differences. Other characteristics that she identified were a predisposition to empathy, a heightened responsiveness to external objects and to one's own body state, a continual access to primary process thinking, and an enhanced capacity for symbolization.

One of the implications of a greater-than-average sensitivity to sensory stimulation is a widening of experience to include not only the primary object but also more peripheral objects, which in turn allows for less dependence on the primary object. The way that Greenacre (1957) formulated this phenomenon is that the ego of the child who ultimately becomes an artist is capable of dissociating itself from the real objects and develops a "love affair with the world" (p. 58). This capacity makes these children less reliant on having good relationships with their caretakers and protects them from difficult life experiences.

Like other theorists who wrote about the relationship between children's play and adult creativity (Freud, 1908/1958; Oremland, 1998; Rank, 1932/1989; Winnicott, 1971/1990), Greenacre was interested in this subject and wrote a number of elegant and insightful articles on it (1957, 1958, 1959). She elaborated on Freud's (1908/1958 observation that there is a similarity between the fantasy of especially creative individuals and the imaginative play of young children, with both play and fantasy serving the dual functions of trying out new behavior and gratifying a wish that all will turn out well. She argued, "It is clear that much complex play is acted-out fantasy; and that fantasy of special quality is the stuff of which creative productions are made" (1959, p. 73). Greenacre observed that the play of young children is repetitive and imaginative, and often used in order to master difficult situations—a way of practicing and working through anxiety by repetition of a disturbing experience.

Greenacre also took issue with the notion of sublimation as defined by Freud, pointing out that creative activities actually tend to stir passions. She maintained that the energy utilized in creative activity is often not well "neutralized" and does not fit with our idea of sublimation, which actually may be more applicable to less creative individuals. "Growth and development of creative power is undoubtedly sometimes aided by the loosening up of personal conflicts and the liberation of energy that is then available for less restricted productions. But I doubt whether development through sublimation comprises the major growth of creative abilities in all, or even perhaps in most artists" (1959, p. 74).

Another important theorist who had difficulty with the way that Freud used the concept of sublimation was Heinz Hartmann. Writing about the contradictions and inconsistencies in Freud's use of the concept of sublimation, Hartmann (1955) pointed out that in the earlier writings, sublimation referred to culturally or socially valuable achievements only, which implied that very few had this capacity, whereas later conceptualizations referred to sublimation as a more fundamental psychological process. To quote Hartmann, "With Freud's later proposition, we will tend to see in sublimation not a more or less occasional happening but rather a continuous process" (p. 16), which implies that there is an essential relation between creativity and the ego.

Similarly, Eigen (1983) has noted that Freud did not have a unified theory of creativity. The complexity and constant evolution of Freud's thinking made it apparent that his conflicting views about the basic nature of psychic life was reflected in apparent contradictions in his concept of creativity. Eigen proposed that Freud's formal and informal theories of creativity differed with regard to the degree of order or chaos present in psychic life. On the one hand, there was a formal theory of creativity in which order was imposed on chaos through the defensive process of sublimation. In that theory, artists were given privileged status and sublimation was an achievement that very few individuals were capable of. On the other hand, in the informal theory, psychic life was seen as basically orderly, and creativity was perceived as an aspect of healthy development potentially available to all. The essential issue, according to Eigen, hinges on the place of creativity in the life of most people. When "creativity is seen as normative for all people and pathology as creativity gone wrong," then "healthy development and creativity are necessarily linked" (p. 44).

Loewald (1988), who reframed many Freudian concepts, reformulated Freud's theory of sublimation. Taking issue with the energic basis of sublimation, he proposed that rather than viewing sublimation as a conversion or displacement of instinctual energy into aims that are socially more valued, we can conceptualize sublimation as an aspect of the human capacity to allow one object or activity to stand for another (i.e., to symbolize or represent it).

For Loewald, it is not that humans convert one form of energy (i.e., sexual or aggressive) into some other form of energy (i.e., activity of any kind), and it is not that a higher aim (e.g., creativity) is substituted for a lower aim (e.g., procreativity). The principle is that, humans have the capacity to entertain the notion that one object or activity can come to stand for (symbolize, represent) another. (Frank, 1991, p. 477)

A similar point was made by Susan Deri (1990), when she wrote that Freud and some of his followers focused on the pathological manifestations of symbolization and did not do justice to this universal, normal, and biologically essential process. Deri maintained that human beings cannot cope directly with the complexity of inner and outer stimulation without the mediation of symbols. Symbolization is therefore a biological necessity that coincides with ego development. According to Deri, symbols are tools for the synthesizing function of the ego; they transform energy from primary to secondary process for purposes of safeguarding the homeostatic equilibrium of the organism and thereby provide order from unbounded chaos. She emphasized the fact that deviation, as well as their normal prototypes, serve the same dynamic function—to bind energy and transform it. She wrote, "Since symbol formation is essentially a structure or gestalt-forming process, it can produce structures of highly creative value as well as psychologically distorted forms. This complex and affectively colorful inner world of the artist finds expression in the creation of aesthetic symbolic structures" (p. 529).

This concept of symbolic representation had been one used by Freud in his explanation of the dream process. Loewald's reformulation of the concept of sublimation represented a major shift in psychoanalysis from its reliance on theoretical explanations based on the principles of biology and physics, and came closer to Freud's belief that psychoanalysis is part of psychology.

Rather than viewing sublimation as a defense against instinctual life, Loewald saw it as a reconciliation of both instinctual and spiritual experience. In a book review essay on *The Freud/Jung Letters*, Loewald (1977/1980a) wrote, "Psychoanalysis, I believe shares with modern existentialism the tenet that superpersonal and transcendental aspects of human existence and of unconscious and instinctual life can be experienced and integrated convincingly . . . only in the concreteness of one's personal life" (p. 416). In the same passage, he equates sublimation and true ego expansion (in psychoanalytic terminology) with authentic transcendental experiences and insights ("spirituality").

Anton Ehrenzweig (1967), an art and music teacher trained as a psychoanalyst, developed an elaborate theory of creativity emphasizing the organizing role of the unconscious. He believed that in order to take account of artistic experience, a substantial revision of traditional Freudian theory was needed. He took issue with the classical concept of the primary process as lacking in structural potential, pointing to the contradiction presented by the highly organized structure of art. He resolved this contradiction by arguing that most of the aesthetic and structural qualities of art are actually the result of primary process activity. He postulated an unconscious scanning process responsible for organizing pictorial space, use of color, and rhythm. There is—as the title of his book indicates—a hidden order in art. What we associate with undifferentiated primary process fantasy, namely, chaos and destruction, is only the beginning for the artist. Through a process of unconscious scanning, the artist is able to bring about the integration of his work. According to Ehrenzweig, the creative process involves a necessary psychic disintegration. A natural rhythm exists between various psychic layers involving disruption and re-integration; it is a rhythm by which the ego voluntarily seeks it own temporary dissolution in order to make contact with the hidden powers of unconscious perception (Milner, 1967/1987). Ehrenzweig challenged Kris's view of creativity as regression, seeing it instead as a progressive phenomenon.

Ehrenzweig postulated three phases of creativity. In the first stage, which he referred to as *projection*, fragmented parts of the self are projected by the artist into the work. As the ego disintegrates into partial fragmentation, the artist faces chaos and has to manage his heightened anxiety. The second stage, referred to as *dedifferentiation* or *unconscious integration*, involves an unconscious process of scanning that allows for the integration of these fragmented self-states. This stage is associated with a sense of oneness in which there is a suspension of boundaries between self and not-self and between the inside and the outside world. The oceanic experience of fusion, with its lack of differentiation, occurs in deeply unconscious levels. In the last stage, referred to as *introjection* or *re-introjection*, there is an integration of previously split-off parts of the self into the ego, and the artist becomes more detached from his work as the art object assumes an independent existence and otherness. Thus, according to Ehrenzweig, in the creative process, there is a constant oscillation between the surface mind and the depth mind, with the latter undoing the split of subject and object that is the basis of logical thinking (Milner, 1956/1987).

While many analysts have tried to remain within the system laid down by Freud with regard to the primary and secondary process, as well as the levels of the mind (conscious, preconscious, and unconscious), some have found it necessary when writing about creativity to develop a different language and different conceptualizations. Two of these are Silvano Arieti and Michael Balint. Arieti (1976) used the term *tertiary process* to designate the special combination of primary and secondary process mechanisms that operate when the artist is engaged in creation. The tertiary process, with specific mechanisms and forms, blends the two worlds of mind and matter, and, in many cases, the rational with the irrational. "Instead of rejecting the primitive (or whatever is archaic, obsolete, or off the beaten path), the creative mind integrates it with logical processes in what seems a 'magic' synthesis from which the new, the unexpected, and the desirable emerge" (p. 13).

Michael Balint (1968) coined the term *the area of creation* to describe the area of the mind where creativity originates from. It is one of the three areas that extend through the ego—the other two being the area of the Oedipus conflict and the area of the basic fault. The area of creation is where all artistic, philosophical, and scientific innovation begins. Balint understood levels of the mind in the context of relationships and noted that while the oedipal and basic fault levels of mind involve outside objects, this is not the case in the area of creation, where there is no external object present. The subject is alone, and his intent is to produce something out of himself. When a completed work of art is produced, it then becomes an external object. The important point that Balint made is that while there are no objects in the area of creation, for much of the time the subject is not entirely alone either. The other may be present, silently observing. Balint proposed to use the term *pre-object* to refer to this concept. He described the pre-object as primitive and lacking in organization until the work of creation renders it whole. At that point, verbal interaction with external objects can take place.

My own concept of *witnessing presence*, which will be elaborated in chapter 4, is meant to capture this idea of an internalized other as an amorphous, undefined presence providing a witnessing affirming function.

Before leaving this section on the drive theory models of creativity, the work of Melanie Klein needs to be mentioned because of its powerful long-term influence. Klein, as interpreted by Hanna Segal (1964), believed that one of Freud's greatest contributions to psychology was the notion that sublimation is the outcome of a successful renunciation of an instinctual aim. What Klein added was that a successful renunciation requires a process of mourning, and that this process sets off a reparative drive to restore loved internal and external objects that have been destroyed by the infant's fantasized destructiveness. According to Kleinian theory, from the earliest stages of development the infant searches for symbols in order to deal with painful experiences such as aggression, anxiety, and mourning. Art as a symbolic activity is thus the expression of an urge to repair and restore loved objects. Art allows relief from internal pain through an activity that is experienced as reparative and enlivening (Kogan, 2012).

Personally, I found the later work of Hanna Segal (1991) on the subject of art more accessible and more in keeping with my own observations. For instance, she said that the need to create is compelling and that art is not only an internal communication but a communication with others. She emphasized the emotional aspects of art, believing that form, whether it is musical, visual, or verbal, can move us so deeply because it symbolically embodies an unconscious meaning—a certain kind of archaic emotion of a preverbal kind. The artist seeks to locate his conflict and resolve it in his creation by the process of working through.

The Person at the Center:
Existential and Humanistic Models

The concept of sublimation and the models of the mind as presented in the theory-driven ego-psychological perspective were rooted in a one-person psychology. The sources of creativity, its role in human existence, and whether it was viewed as a regressive or progressive phenomenon are pivotal issues handled differently depending on the theoretical model considered. As Freud was developing his libido theory and applying it to the arts, some of his younger colleagues like Jung and Rank were developing their own ideas about the creative process and psychoanalysis. At first they were devotees, and Freud welcomed the opportunity to mentor these young men who admired him greatly. But eventually, as their ideas differed from his own and took a turn that he did not approve of, Freud became intolerant of their theoretical directions and broke with them. For both Jung and Rank, the creative process allows for the release of what is most healing in the psyche.

Carl Jung conceptualized the creative process in a dramatically different way from the man who had been his mentor before their theoretical differences created an irreparable rupture in their relationship. Jung's theories, with their mystical and religious overtones, represented a significant shift in the understanding of motivations for creativity from the Freudian biologically based instinctual drives to spiritual ones. Jung's memoirs open a window into the creative process as it attempts to deal with the traumatized and vulnerable self. We will have a closer look at the relationship between Jung's internal world and his metapsychological theories and will illustrate the healing potential of creative production in chapter 9.

Otto Rank, another student of Freud who was originally a devotee, also came to view creativity in a very different way from his mentor. Although at first Rank was committed to drive theory and used the concept of sublimation of sexuality to explain the creative impulse, he gradually came to understand creativity as primary and deriving from the life impulse, and in fact wrote that the creative impulse "has something positively antisexual in its yearning for independence of organic conditions" (1932/1989, p. xxiii).

Rank defined creativity in its broadest terms and made it the central concept in his understanding of humanity: "Creativeness lies equally at the root of artistic production and of life experience" (1932/1989, p. 38). According to him, there is a universal progressive creative process underlying all of the phenomena of life. The human urge to create finds expression in works of art, as well as religion and mythology; it produces the whole culture. What distinguishes the artist from the rest is that he is the most dramatic example of man's general striving for self-expression and growth. "In any case we can say of all artistic creation that the artist not only creates his art, but also uses art in order to create" (1932/1989, p. 7). The impulse to create originates in an inherent striving toward ever higher and more complex levels of integration (Menaker, 1982).

Rank's is a psychology of the self that greatly differs from Freud's view of personality. In contrast to Freud's emphasis on the oedipal phase of development as the foundational source of art, myth, and religion, Rank emphasized the pre-oedipal period as the basic source of all human culture (Menaker, 1982). He believed that attachment to the mother is the central dynamic in living, and that separation in all its forms is a basic issue for humankind. From the beginning of life until its end, man deals with separation—first from the state of oneness with the mother, later separation of the individual from the collective, the artist from his creative product, and ultimately the separation of the person from life itself. For Rank, separation anxiety and guilt are inevitable concomitants of attachment.

Another idea that is central in Rank's understanding of man is the concept of *will* (or what we would call *agency* today), which he understood to be a prewired force that impels the individual to strive for separateness, uniqueness,

41

and individualization. This thrust, however, inevitably brings man into conflict with his need for connection and merger. Thus, human development is a lifelong process involving a negotiation between a yearning for connection and a desire for individuation; life is an oscillating movement between separation and merger.

Creation is an act of individuation. The first creative act of the artist is his own self-creation, his appointment of himself as "artist." Artists begin the creative process by separating from their fellow human beings and liberating themselves from their influence, but eventually they need the recognition of others for their creations to attain immortality. Rank recognized his own creative personality and strongly identified with artists. Born into a culturally impoverished home, Rank's determination and will to overcome his humble beginnings exemplifies the ideal he wrote about. Ultimately, he became one of the most original and seminal thinkers in the psychoanalytic field, but not without personal struggles for selfhood.

Stolorow and Atwood (1979) identify narcissism as a basic issue in Rank's life and connect his struggle for self-esteem regulation with his theories. According to their thesis, Rank found opportunities for narcissistic reparation and self-esteem in art and in elegant theoretical constructions. He believed that the artist, like the neurotic, is driven by narcissistic conflicts; both have an exaggerated fear of the destruction of the self, but the artist deals with the dread of self-loss in a more effective way. He is able to satisfy his narcissistic needs through creative production. Ultimately, Rank saw neurosis as a failure in creativity. Rank's ideas about the difference between the artist and the neurotic will be further explored in the next chapter, which features selected writings on the subject of creativity and psychopathology and their points of intersection.

Rank's psychology is essentially existential in character. He addresses the basic concerns of human existence—life, death, alienation, and choice—giving them prominence in his theory of creativity and psychotherapy. According to Rank, the fact that all things are ultimately transient and that death is inevitable fills us with intense anxiety and elicits defenses that are more or less effective. We all must come to terms with the finiteness of our existence and live our life as fully as possible. The fundamental human dilemma is how to manage both the Life fear and the Death fear. The artist, like the neurotic, experiences these fears in an intensified way, "but with the difference that in the neurotic the fear of life predominates and so checks all expression in life, while the artist-type *can* overcome this fear in his creation and is driven by the fear of death to immortalize himself" (1932/1989, p. 387).

The artist manages his fear of life and his fear of death by externalizing the conflict into the work of art, where he has some measure of control over psychic chaos. At the same time, the urge to create can be so intense and total that the artist may need to protect himself against the threat of being swallowed up by the creative process. Artists, as Rank sees them, can become so intensely absorbed in their work—sometimes to the point of exhaustion and complete self-surrender—that their ego needs to erect necessary protection. Inhibitions or refusal to complete the work can be seen in that context as protections against the intensity of the creative process.

Rank can be viewed as the forerunner of object relations theory, self psychology, and existential psychoanalysis (Menaker, 1996; Wadlington, 2001). Rollo May, who considered Rank to be the most important precursor of existential therapy, wrote, "I have long considered Otto Rank to be the great unacknowledged genius in Freud's circle" (Krim, 1999, p. 167). "Unacknowledged" is a mild term considering the fact that Rank's voice was actively silenced because his ideas diverged from classical Freudian theory (Krim, 1999; Wadlington, 2001). The way that Rank describes the artist's dilemma is precisely what can be said about him and his relationship to the prevailing psychoanalytic orthodoxy. According to Rank, the artist is forever struggling to separate himself from the community and prevailing ideology, and the most creative artists are those able to reach out beyond themselves and their own ideology and give birth to fresh ways of seeing the world. For Rank, lifelong creativity is related to the continual capacity to separate from "internal mental objects," such as internalized institutions and beliefs, and from the restrictions of culture, social conformity, and the so-called wisdom of others. Rank lived out what he preached and suffered the consequences of "excommunication" from the psychoanalytic community.

Rank's understanding of the role of the unconscious in the creative process was quite different from the prevailing view among his peers. Although he did not deny its existence, he took issue with what he perceived to be an overvaluation of its importance and the tendency to minimize the part played by conscious will in artistic and poetic creation. As an example, he wrote about the artist's use of the Muse metaphor as a way of avoiding responsibility for his actions and the existential guilt associated with the creative process. Thus he wrote, "The invocation of the Muse, the demand by the poet himself for unconscious inspiration, is perhaps not infrequently a pretext—a poetic license even—for a more unrestrained expression of himself. If he is inspired by poetic frenzy, he is less responsible for what he says" (1932/1989, p. 423).

Rank's prolific creativity is evident in his extension of psychoanalytic theory to the study of mythology and art. He is also credited with ideas advanced for his time about the significance of affects in human life, the importance of cultural context, and the recognition that there is no "I" without a "thou," thus anticipating the relational orientation in psychoanalysis. Rank's influence can be recognized in the writings of humanistic, existential, and interpersonal thinkers who followed in the second half of the 20th century.

For most existential and humanist thinkers, the concept of creativity and the concept of the self-actualizing, healthy human being are synonymous. Like Rank before them, Maslow (1962), May (1994), Schachtel (1984), and Winnicott (1971/1990), among others, perceived the creative process to be a prime example of the human capacity for growth rather than a way of compensating for what is lacking. The shifting zeitgeist of the 1960s from seeing man as a natural science–determined organism to seeing him as a conscious being capable of bringing his consciousness to bear on his experience and behavior was reflected in a focus on the self-actualizing aspects of creativity (Basescu, 1967/2010; Orfanos, 2010).

Ernest Schachtel (1984), an interpersonal thinker, understood the universal struggle to be between a desire to remain embedded, safe, and free of tension and the pull to emerge as a separate, activity-seeking, and curious explorer. According to Schachtel, the main motivation for creative experience is man's need to relate to the world around him in an open way, going beyond the familiar and the routine. His definition of the creative person is one who tends to be more open, more receptive, and less tied to conventional ways of perceiving the world. He maintained that this relatively undirected and freely wandering play of perception, thought, and fantasy, rather than being regressive, actually tends to be progressive. He took serious issue with Kris's notion of regression in the service of the ego and wrote, "What distinguishes the creative process from regression to primary-process thought is that the freedom of the approach is due not to a drive discharge function but to the openness in the encounter with the object of the creative labor" (p. 245). Schachtel likens the artist's approach to the world to that of the young child fascinated by new objects. The creative process thus resembles the child's free play in its openness, its intensity of interest, and the repeated and varied approaches that characterize the play.

Another existentialist, Rollo May (1994), also took issue with Kris's formulation of creativity as regression in the service of the ego. While May agreed that creativity often draws on infantile unconscious parts of the artist's mind, which may seem regressive, it also has a progressive side. The powerful feelings evoked by the creative process include both ecstasy and anxiety. May saw "normal" anxiety as a source of creativity and emphasized that it takes courage to engage in creative action. Like Rank, who inspired his thinking, May linked creativity to the awareness of death and the desire to defy it by reaching beyond it through creative productions that live on. He distinguished between the creation of decorative and pretty objects and "real" creativity, by which he meant self-actualization and the giving birth to a new reality. He noted that when the creative process involves the fulfillment of potential, it results in great intensity and absorption, engaging the emotions and the unconscious. The creative act involves the emotions and the unconscious as well as reasoning, structure, and conscious thought. This conception of a dual creative process is consistent with Kris's view about the two phases of creativity—namely, the inspirational and the elaborational, where the latter focuses on problem-solving and evaluation.

The study of creativity was further advanced in the 1970s when George Klein (1976) systematically proposed a list of motivating factors in human behavior and identified the desire to use one's competence—or *effectance*, as he called it—as a powerful motivator for creative activities. The fact that many creative individuals tend to be different as children and may have difficulty fitting into conventional expectations makes it more likely that they suffer from vulnerabilities in self-esteem. The positive self-esteem derived from the use of one's talents is a powerful motivator, whether or not one has problems of self-esteem.

One of the most influential psychoanalysts who focused on creativity, particularly with regard to its evolution in the development of the individual, was Donald

Winnicott (1971/1990). Like Rank before him, he saw creativity as an essential life force and formulated a theory of development that makes creativity central and intrinsic to human nature, which he referred to as "creative living." He distinguished between creative living, a universal capability, and the artistic reactions of individuals with special talents. The roots of creative living are to be found in the infant's illusion of the creation of his world. The feeling of omnipotence, facilitated by the "good-enough-mother," which is gradually replaced by objective reality, still remains as a capability within each of us as a way of seeing; both as a personal view and a way of asserting the self.

Winnicott's astute understanding of childhood development was informed by his experience as a pediatrician rather than by theoretical speculations based on observations of adults, as was the case with most other theoreticians discussed. For example, Freud appreciated the connections between childhood play and creativity in the adult, but his theories on this subject were limited and somewhat vague. Freud wrote, "Every child at play behaves like an imaginative writer, in that he creates a world of his own or, more truly, he rearranges the things of his world and orders it in a new way that pleases him better" (1908/1958, p. 45). It is in daydreaming that Freud found the counterpart and continuation of play in adulthood. Imaginative creation, like daydreaming, is a continuation of and substitutes for the play of childhood. In contrast, Winnicott's understanding of the connection between childhood play and creativity was much more developed and elaborate, and was based on actual experiences with infants and mothers.

Unlike the experience-distant views of theorists like Melanie Klein, who also specialized in child analysis, Winnicott formulated his ideas from his direct observations of infants and children and their mothers. It is noteworthy that while Klein was not particularly interested in the reality of who the mother was and what she did, Winnicott, while never blaming the mother, understood that her subjectivity was crucial, as was the way that she interacted with the baby's emergent subjectivity. Taking issue with Klein's conceptualization of creativity as merely reparation, Winnicott saw creativity as bound up with a capacity for ruthlessness and aggressive assertion. Integral to both development and creativity is the search for an object that is resilient enough to withstand the force of the primitive love impulse (Phillips, 1988).

Winnicott (1953) perceived a direct development from the earliest transitional phenomena to playing and cultural experience. The concept of transitional space between the inner and outer world has been Winnicott's major contribution to our understanding of creativity, for it is in this space that he located creativity's beginning. He pointed out that written words of psychoanalytic literature do not tell us what we want to know about art or when we are engaged in playful activities:

> What for instance are we doing when we are listening to a Beethoven symphony or making a pilgrimage to a picture gallery or reading *Troilus and Cressida* in bed, or playing tennis? . . . We have used the concepts of inner and outer, and we want a third concept. (1971/1990, pp. 105–106)

Like Arieti (1976) and Balint (1968) who struggled to locate a place for creativity outside of the usual boundaries of experience, Winnicott also identified an intermediary area of experience located somewhere between fantasy and reality. His idea of the transitional space was a more highly developed concept than either the notion of tertiary process (Arieti) or the area of creation (Balint). As such, it became part of our psychoanalytic language. His concept of the transitional object has entered popular culture as well.

He introduced the concept of transitional objects—toys, words, music, or artistic objects—that come to represent the mother–child bond, threatened by the child's developmental growth into a separate being. In this developmental phase between psychic and external reality, the child is able to create what he needs and to maintain a fantasized bond with the mother. The transitional object represents a child's first original creative act; it is the earliest manifestation of creative play and symbol-making. The transitional object is the prototype of all later cultural activities, and the transitional space is the source of all art and culture.

Art, like religion and cultural phenomena, takes place in a zone, an intermediate area of experiencing that is partly internal world, partly external reality—a kind of third domain with permeable boundaries, a space that has both subjective and objective aspects, thereby allowing for the experience of temporarily merging. The space is a reparative one where mending can take place. I believe that it is this potential space that is represented by the concept of Muse or God.

The artist's journey from subjective imagery to the creation of an objective product has its parallel in the infant's journey from the purely subjective to objectivity, with a sojourn in the world in between—the transitional realm. Winnicott (1953) established this connection when he wrote,

> This intermediate area of experience, unchallenged in respect of its belonging to inner or external (shared) reality, constitutes the greater part of the infant's experience and throughout life is retained in the intense experiencing that belongs to the arts and to religion and to imaginative living, and to creative scientific work. (p. 97)

Winnicott's work has been influential and generative not only in the clinical and theoretical domain, where he has inspired major relational theorists (Benjamin, 1990, 1992; Ghent, 1990/1999, 1992; Pizer, 1998; Slochower, 2004), but also in current ideas about creativity.

One of the people inspired by Winnicott's work was Marion Milner. Like Winnicott, Milner emphasized the psychic growth aspects of creativity. Most of Milner's writing has a strong autobiographical element (1934/2011, 1937/1988, 1950, 1987/2011); she seems to move effortlessly from personal experience to psychoanalytic conceptualizations and back again. For Milner (1957/1987), creativity is about the creation of symbols. By creating symbols for the inner life of feeling, the artist organizes and gives form to feelings, making them knowable. According to her, we are "driven by the internal necessity for inner organization, pattern, coherence, the basic need to discover identity in difference without which experience becomes chaos" (1952/1987, p. 84). The artist strives for immortality in his work and, at the same time, expresses what he feels to be the most valuable moments of experience. The painter conceptualizes in non-verbal symbols the amazing experience known from the inside of how it feels to be alive: "What verbal concepts are to the conscious life of the intellect, what internal objects are to the unconscious life of instinct and phantasy, so works of art are to the conscious life of feeling, without them life would be only blindly lived, blindly endured" (1957/1987, p. 227).

In an attempt to understand the type of thinking that is associated with the creative process, Milner distinguished between the formal logical and what she called a reverie process or fantasy—both types of thinking alternating with and informing each other. The whole area of symbolic expression is irrational, since a symbol is both itself and something else. This non-logical type of thought depends on a willingness to forgo the usual sense of self as clear and separate and possessing a boundary. When engaged in reverie-like thinking, the ordinary sense of self temporarily disappears; there is a kind of blanking out of ordinary consciousness. These changes of consciousness have been described as an oceanic feeling or states of elation, blankness, or emptiness. This state of mind is akin to the infant's sense of oneness with the mother. Milner found that such states of mind can be a prelude to a new integration. Reflective thinking allows a merging of "me" and "not-me," thereby having an integrative effect on dissociated (my term) states. "May not those moments be an essential recurring phase if there is to be a new psychic creation? May they not be moments in which there is a plunge into no-differentiation, that results (if all goes well) in a re-emerging into a new division of the 'me-not-me,' one in which there is more of the 'me' in the 'not-me', and more of the 'not-me' in the 'me'?" (1957/1987, p. 223)

Milner acknowledged that her thinking was influenced by Ehrenzweig's concept of "creative surrender," a term which he used to describe the active surrendering of conscious ego control in the second stage of the creative process. Milner noted that his term provided her with a conceptual tool for thinking about boundaries and merging during the creative process (Kogan, 2012).

Like Ehrenzweig, Milner emphasized that, in the creative process, this oceanic state is in cyclic fluctuation with everyday conscious awareness. She believed that the two types or stages of thinking require a different atmosphere, with reverie or absent mindedness, as she sometimes called it, requiring a physical setting that feels safe and free of a need for immediate action. Such a setting, in which it is safe to indulge in reverie, is provided for the patient in analysis, as well as for the artist engaged in his craft, and even extends to the viewer of the art work.

A number of psychoanalysts, like Milner, arrived at insights about the creative process through their own personal experience with the arts. Alice Miller (1988), similar to Milner, learned more about herself from painting than she could have imagined, and concluded that non-verbal experience can circumvent defenses by shifting into an earlier mode of functioning. She wrote,

> Although I had undergone two complete analyses as part of my training, the analysts had been unable to shake my version of the happy childhood I was supposed to have had. It was only my spontaneous painting, which I took up in 1973, that gave me the first unadulterated access to my early reality. In my paintings I came face to face with the terrorism exerted by my mother, at the mercy of which I had lived for so many years. (pp. 6–7)

Such personal accounts communicate a sense of aliveness and vitality in the act of creation that is often missing from the theories and literature on creativity. While some theoretical formulations may be elegant and erudite, they often don't carry the energy and authenticity that one associates with creativity. We note that in recent years there seems to be a movement toward greater self-disclosure among psychoanalytic writers (Richman, 2006a). As a result, we have become more acquainted with the creative journeys of our fellow professionals.

Towards Radical Imagination: Contemporary Psychoanalytic Perspectives

At this juncture, I want to focus on two recent currents on the subject of creativity, as represented by contemporary Freudian psychoanalysts who continue to develop and update ideas that are influenced by the drive theory tripartite model of the mind but not limited to it, and to examine the writings of relational and intersubjective thinkers whose influence is growing dramatically and whose ideas tend to be most compatible with my own thinking.

One of the most significant developments in the last 25 years or so has been the appearance and expansion of the relational model of psychoanalysis, which includes within it interpersonal psychoanalysis, British object relations theories, self psychology, and the empirical traditions of infancy research and attachment models of development (Greenberg & Mitchell, 1983; Mitchell, 1988). The relational perspective, which maintains that the primacy of configurations of self and others, whether real or fantasized, is the motivating factor in human behavior, has been responsible for a veritable sea change in psychoanalysis (Mitchell & Aron, 1999; Orfanos, 2010, 2012). Yet, with a few exceptions that I will discuss below, there has been relatively little conceptualization or development of ideas about the creative process in the current literature; few works even make reference to it.

A shift in our conception of the unconscious, from a repository of repressed drives to the seat of unformulated experience, represents a major modification in our understanding of unconscious phenomena with implications for many aspects of cognitive functioning. Donnel Stern (1983/1999, 1997) dramatically altered our perspective by proposing that what eludes us is not repressed but rather unformulated. His explication and expansion of these ideas has great implications for our understanding of the creative process. According to Stern, the unformulated unconscious, composed of sensations, perceptions, and thoughts lacking in clarity and differentiation, is a rich source of creativity. The unformulated represents possibility and creative disorder; it is a welcome opportunity to give form to unformulated content, to create something new out of confusion and chaos. When we allow imagination free play, we court surprise. We cannot predict what form uncreated experience will ultimately take; the unformulated can organize itself and create something unexpected and new (Stern, 1997; see also Howell, 2005).

Initially, Stern limited the concept of unformulated experience to those experiences that can potentially be reflected on in verbal terms, but in recent years he has reconceptualized his theory to include nonverbal meanings as well. He uses the term *realization* to denote the formulation of non-verbal meanings and contrasts it with *articulation*, which is the formulation of verbal meaning (Stern, 2010a). Stern's extension of his theory is particularly relevant to my own thinking, for in my view, it is the arts that can give life and meaning to unformulated experiences, especially those that, due to the shock of trauma, have eluded verbal expression in its wake. Visual, auditory, and kinesthetic modalities, such as painting, music, and dance, lend themselves particularly well to the expression of inchoate and primitive feelings and imagery found in dreams and fantasies. Even when the art form features words, as in the case of poetry, creative prose, or words and phrases embedded in a painting or a collage, it is not verbal insight that is the essence of the experience but rather an emotional state. As Loewald (1978/1980c) has pointed out, words may be used to describe reality and logic, or they may express intense feelings in the form of evocative metaphors, such as can be found in poetry and prose. In most creative forms of language, there is an interweaving of primary and secondary process; it is the vitality of the primary process that infuses language with life and art. The secondary process must not become isolated from the primary process for it is contextualized by it. In those instances, language functions as a transitional mode binding abstract thought with bodily concreteness.

One of Loewald's most important contributions to psychoanalytic theory was his reconceptualization of the relationship between primary and secondary process. He took issue with the way that we tend to polarize these processes when in fact human mentation constantly moves between them. Although one or the other pole may be dominant at any one point, we all have the capacity to shift from secondary to primary process thinking and do so regularly when we dream or daydream or move from rational logical thought to free associations.

Gilbert Rose (1987, 1996) also reworked the concept of primary and secondary process. He contrasted the closed system paradigm of the 19th century, with its dichotomizing of reality/fantasy, reality/pleasure, intellect/emotion, and primary process/secondary process, with the more open model many of us subscribe to these days. Art forces us to rethink the customary subject/object dichotomy and to reconsider the fundamental principles that govern the primary and secondary processes. The sharp distinction between primary and secondary processes does not hold. "The imaginative, if nonlogical, perception and thought demanded by art are characterized by a temporary suspension and the reimpositions of the usual boundaries of subject-object, time and space." (Rose, 1996, p. 190). Presumably because of a greater ability to merge with reality and then to disengage from it, artists can immerse themselves in a regressive process in which they recover early fusion states. Creative imagination restructures reality and deepens and expands our understanding of the world, relating inner and outer in repeated fusion and separations. Central to the creative experience and to growth in general is a two-phase process of partial dissolution and reintegration in oscillating rhythm that can also be conceptualized as an alternating rhythm of regression and progression.

According to Rose (1987), the workings of imagination and rationality are inseparable; there is a continuum underlying all thought and perception. Primary and secondary processes are always working together in fine-tuned coordination in thought and perception. Rose also points out that the process of internalization and building of psychic structure is ongoing and not restricted to childhood. Arts promote the advancement of the primary process through objectification and by feedback from the outside.

An essential characteristic in the arts is that there exists a dynamic tension among elements that interact to form an organic unity, and that the nature of creative ability consists of the power to integrate many diverse elements into coherent patterns. Moreover, art facilitates emotional responsiveness; it is adaptive and inextricably intertwined with affect. For Rose (1996), all art is composed of mechanisms that catalyze experience of tension and release:

> For the artist, one may suppose that aesthetic form represents an externalization and a transformation of originally unmodified, emotional intensity into highly elaborated structures of interwoven tension and release . . . For the rest of us, the completed work of art may be used as an ambient context for creating an illusion of a witnessing presence to one's own emotions. (pp. 113–114)

Thus, art can stimulate and assimilate potentially dangerous degrees of affect, thereby extending the limits of what is bearable, allowing progressive integration within the safe holding presence of aesthetic structure.

Rose's emphasis on patterns of tension and release seems to bring back the concept of energy into creativity. But this is not instinctual or libidinal energy as defined by Freud. Rose's theory leans towards a relational view of creativity, in which the core of aesthetic experience contains a powerful interactive component (Hagman, 2010). Like some other contemporary Freudians, Rose appreciates the relational context of aesthetic experience and the role of relatedness and intersubjectivity, as well as the relevance of developmental issues. For many, the source of artistic experience is in the early mother–infant interaction. Through his art, the artist seeks to recover early experiences of fusion with the mother, and it is this early bond that is stimulated and recreated when the artist mutually engages with his artwork and his audience.

The growing literature on the empathic attunement between infant and care-taker and early sensory experience, along with recent infant development research, is changing our way of perceiving early development. It has come to light that babies experience some degree of separateness at birth, are object-directed from the start, and possess a preverbal information processing capacity in addition to self-regulation and mutual regulation processes (Beebe & Lachmann, 2002).

The contributions of Daniel Stern to our understanding of infant development have spanned over 30 years and continue to dazzle us. His most recent work on forms of vitality directly moves into the arts. Daniel Stern (2010) identified five basic components—movement, time, force, space, and intention/directionality—that give rise to the experience of vitality. The latter is a power manifested by all living things; it not only permeates daily life but is evident in the arts, particu-larly what he referred to as "time-based" arts, namely, music, dance, theater, and cinema. These are the art forms that Stern is particularly interested in and writes about, but I would add that all artistic expressions involve movement and can elicit a sense of vitality and aliveness for both the creator and the recipient of the artistic product.

Building on the work of developmental and object relations theorists, Marilyn Charles (2001, 2002) maintained that some of the earliest sensory experiences lead to fantasies that become integrated and remembered as non-verbal patterns of experience and ultimately come to have meaning. Charles elaborated on Milner's writings about the role of symbolization in the creative process. Symbol forma-tion and the creative act can be means for dealing with anxieties associated with object loss and the need for self-soothing. She pointed out that "symbolic func-tions enable us to play with that which might be too terrifying if it were to be per-ceived as too real" (Charles, 2001, p. 250).

As a psychoanalyst, poet, and visual artist, Charles is well-versed in the creative process and uses examples from her personal experience, illustrating how patterns are derived from basic sensory experience and how they can be used for healing and communication. By describing her drawings, collages, and poems, she illus-trates how patterned forms or sensations allow her to express complex and rela-tively unconscious affects that elude verbal expression:

> The creative act is born out of the basic patterns of meaning imprinted upon us by our experience, but not yet "known." Through the medium of choice, these patterns become elaborated into concrete symbols which can then be manipulated by the conscious mind into patterns that make sense. (Charles, 2001, p. 258)

The creative endeavor can function as a container for an intolerable awareness of separateness; the creative act becomes a link to the other in so far as it allows for communication in a form that can be received and mutually recognized. Charles wrote,

> The act of creation becomes the encoded tentative interpolation of the self toward the other in a fashion sufficiently cryptic that one might retreat, ostensibly unharmed, and yet containing enough of the essence of the self that one might, indeed, be "seen." (Charles, 2001, p. 249)

In many creative actions, one can see a repetitive engagement with a troubling or soothing theme, expressed through continually elaborated patterns that are attempts at self-soothing, working through, and communication.

Theorists who identify themselves as self psychologists have concerned themselves with questions of creativity and aesthetics since Heinz Kohut (1966, 1971) first developed his seminal ideas on the psychology of the self. Kohut perceived the artist as a relational being with fluid boundaries and more immersed in his surroundings than other people (Hagman, 2010). In Kohut's vocabulary, artistic objects are referred to as *self-objects* because they are experienced as part of the self. Self-objects perform important psychological curative functions; they are used to support the cohesion, vitality, and harmony of the self. The artist heals from the threat of fragmentation and restores a firm sense of self-cohesion as he merges with the self-object—the work of art (Kligerman, 1980; cited in Hagman, 2010). Similarly, Lachmann & Lachmann (1996) maintained that one function of the creative process is to transform a depleted, painful self-state deriving from a narcissistic injury. A creative endeavor is a means of transforming one's self-state, thereby mastering one's painful experience and enhancing the range of self-regulation.

George Hagman (2010), a self psychologist who writes about artists and the creative process, pointed out that most approaches to this subject have been focused exclusively on the intrapsychic dynamics of the individual artist while ignoring the relational context of aesthetic experience and the role of relatedness and intersubjectivity. He maintained that all aesthetic experiences and artistic efforts possess three dimensions of subjectivity: the intrasubjective, the intersubjective, and the metasubjective. Art is intersubjective in so far as there is always a sense of dialogue between subject and objects. Hagman wrote that once the artist embarks on creating a product, the boundaries of his mind expand, and he functions in "a transitional field within which there occurs a dialectic between the internal self and the emerging externalized self concretized in the artwork . . . the artist's mind now exists in the dynamic psychological space in which both inner and outer are contained, interact and affect each other" (p. 18).

Reviewing the extensive literature on the subject of creativity, I am reminded of Shakespeare's Hamlet, who says, "There are more things in heaven and earth Horatio than are dreamt of in your philosophy" (*Hamlet,* act 1, scene 5, pp. 166–167). Although we note that here and there in the literature we find bits of wisdom, thoughts that stimulate our thinking and resonate with us, none really capture the essence of the excitement of making art and creating something where nothing had been or where there had been chaos and confusion and sorrow. Perhaps it is in the nature of the creative endeavor that it is not amenable to theoretical analysis, particularly as traditionally approached by psychoanalysts. To quote my teacher, supervisor, and analyst Sabert Basescu (1967/2010):

> I think that the psychoanalytic attempts to understand artists are intrinsically limited by the very nature of psychoanalytic theory. It is essentially a theory that deals with the ways in which man is determined by his past experience, his social, cultural, physiological and genetic background. But the essence of art, the essence of artistic creativity, is precisely that which is not determined, namely the emergence of something new. The essence of art is freedom. Because of the psychoanalytic commitment to the deterministic view of man, it is invariably unable to deal with the essence of freedom in artistic creativity. However, psychoanalytic theory is eminently successful in at least throwing light on those aspects of the artistic product that are determined by the artist's personality. (p. 111)

I would add that when psychoanalysts focus on clinical material in its relation to the creation of art, their theoretical contributions tend to be less abstract and more experience-near. This is particularly the case when writing about the effects of trauma and the healing potential of art. The works of Bose (2005), Charles (2011), Glennon (2003), Knafo (2012), Orfanos (1997, 1999, 2010), and Ornstein (2010) are examples of the successful integration of theoretical insights with clinical material derived from psychoanalytic practice as well as from personal experiences with both trauma and the arts. In future chapters, the contributions of these writers will be discussed, and my own viewpoint on the creative process will be elucidated. I will introduce contemporary relational concepts of dissociation and witnessing into the discussion in order to further a better understanding of creativity and its healing properties.

Note

1. I thank Spyros D. Orfanos for these conceptualizations and references.

3

INSPIRATION, INSANITY, AND THE PARADOX OF DISSOCIATION

For much of human history, the idea that there is a relationship between creativity and psychopathology has been widely accepted despite the fact that there is no conclusive evidence to that effect. I will briefly review some of the psychoanalytic positions on this subject in order to show that there is in fact a relationship between inspiration and insanity based on the common factor of dissociation that they both share. I will then present my own theory of creativity that identifies dissociation as an integral part of the creative process.

Creativity and Psychopathology—Points of Intersection

The relationship between creativity and madness has been a subject of interest since the days of antiquity.[1] According to Aristotle there was "No great genius without a mixture of insanity" (in Rothenberg, 1990, p. 149). Despite considerable research and speculation on all sides of the issue, the growing literature does not lead to conclusive evidence that a relationship necessarily exists, and the subject continues to be debated (Chessick, 1999; Ludwig, 1995; Maher, 1993; Rothenberg, 1990; among others). There are many who believe that artists are prone to psychopathology (Jamison, 1995; Ludwig, 1995; Niederland, 1976, 1981; Storr, 1993), a few even going as far as to say that psychopathology is essential to true creativity (Lowenfeld, 1941), others who believe that psychopathology interferes with creativity (Arieti, 1976; Chessick, 1999; Kubie, 1958; Rothenberg, 1990), and some who point out that mental health actually enhances the functioning of the creative processes (Maslow, 1962; Noy, 1979; Rothenberg, 1990; Schachtel, 1984) and that it is the healthy part of the personality that allows the disturbed individual to create (McDougall, 1995). Some even take the position that artists are in a better place than so-called healthy people because of their capacity to be in touch with their primitive selves. (Winnicott, 1965)

A more interesting question for me is the one that concerns itself with creativity as a means of dealing with psychopathology and suffering. The notion that suffering hardships underlies creativity has featured prominently in our culture since antiquity (Haynal, 2003). There are numerous variations of this theme, including the use of the term *sublimation* when it is defined as the capacity to transform suffering into a creative product that is acknowledged by others. Related to this aspect of creativity is its role in the resolution of neurotic conflicts (Alexander, 1964) and its potential to alleviate and transform suffering (Bose, 2005; Charles, 2011; Haynal, 2003; Knafo, 2012; Ornstein, 2006a; Storr, 1993). This last theme, which is the subject of this book, will be explored throughout and in the chapters to follow. In this section, we will concentrate on some of the literature that relates to the points of intersection of creativity and psychopathology as understood by psychoanalysts who maintain that there is a connection based on common mental processes.

From early on in the history of psychoanalysis, the relationship among dreaming, the creative process, and psychosis was noted and led to the notion that the primary process is the link in all of these cases. In the mid 1800s, Moreau de Tours, a French psychiatrist, had anticipated some of Freud's ideas, particularly those relating to the primary and secondary processes. He noted the far-reaching similarity between dreams and neurotic and psychotic symptoms and referred to psychosis as "continuous dreaming in the waking state" (in Alexander, 1964, p. 119). Corresponding to Freud's differentiation between primary and secondary processes, Moreau identified two modes of existence within man: the first resulting from communication with the external world, the second a reflection of the self deriving from the internal subjective world. He located the dream in a kind of in-between land where the external life ends and the internal life begins.

The similarity between creative psychological processes and dreaming has been recognized and written about by many authors on the subject of creativity. According to Freud, both dreams and works of art provide imaginary satisfactions of unconscious wishes, and both rely on compromise formation in order to avoid repression. On the subject of art and neurosis, Freud (1935/1952) wrote: "The artist like the neurotic had withdrawn from an unsatisfying reality into this world of imagination; but, unlike the neurotic, he knew how to find a way back from it and once more to get a firm foothold in reality" (p. 73). This idea that the basic motivation for creativity is the same for artists as it is for neurotics, but that it is the ability to temporarily let go of reality and return to it when desired that ultimately distinguishes creativity from pathology, was commonly held and expounded by many psychoanalysts who followed and continues in some version to this day.

Kris (1952) believed as did Freud that the creative artist has a greater capacity to gain access to id material without being overwhelmed by it. He distinguished between the art produced by schizophrenics and the creations of healthy individuals on the basis of the strength of the ego and the capacity to regress in its service. He wrote that when it comes to artists, who are not psychotic,

> [t]he ego momentarily abandons its prerogatives: It can be considered a sign of the ego's strength if, occasionally and for a specific purpose, it is capable of tolerating the mechanisms of the id. But in the case of schizophrenic verbigerations and schizophrenic drawings, we meet with different conditions: The ego slips away from the processes of secondary elaboration and reality testing and indulges in plays on words and shapes. (p. 103)

For Kris, the primary function of art is communication—but not so with psychotic art, which primarily serves a restitutive function.

Like Kris, who saw ego strength in the artist's capacity to enter dark places within, Winnicott (1965) admired the artist's courage and ability to be in touch with primitive processes, a state that he declared neurotics fear and that healthy individuals miss out on to their detriment. His notion about the fact that healthy people are actually impoverished by their inability to reconnect with primitive processes adds a unique twist to the debate around creativity and psychopathology.

Historically, analysts have made connections between psychic trauma and artistic creativity (Kris, 1952; Lowenfeld, 1941; Niederland, 1976). Henry Lowenfeld (1941), writing within the classical tradition, maintained that artistically talented individuals possess greater accessibility to the unconscious and are more prone to trauma because of their innate sensitivity. In fact, Lowenfeld assumed that early traumatic experiences are one of the preconditions to artistic creativity. Artists feel the urge to give form to their fantasies and derive temporary satisfaction from the birth of their work. To the extent that artwork serves as an outlet and allows the artist to overcome conflicts through artistic sublimation, neurosis can be avoided. In the case of trauma, however, although the art serves as an outlet, the drive remains unaltered, so the artist is compelled to seek and overcome the trauma in continual repetition.

Lowenfeld's (1941) analysis of artists, ostensibly based on his clinical work, seems quite extreme in its pathological tone. He states, "Artistically talented persons almost without exception are subject to neurotic conflicts. They suffer periods of neurotic inhibition in their work, periods of depression and hypochondria, fear of insanity, tendencies towards paranoid reactions, and, relatively frequently, schizophrenia" (p. 120). He identified narcissism as a basic issue in the artist's life and linked it to a strong bisexual element. He explained both the frequency of neurosis and the artist's drive to artistic accomplishment as the result of a heightened bisexuality.

A totally different view was put forth by Kubie, a contemporary of Lowenfeld. Kubie (1958) took issue with the idea that there are any similarities between creativity and neurosis. He posited an inverse relationship between creativity and neurosis, with the latter acting as a disturbing influence on the creative process, interfering with it and distorting it. According to Kubie, man's symbolic processes constitute the instrument of both his creativity and his psychological illness. It is the interplay among various aspects of the symbolic process that determines the form and fate of both the neurotic and the creative processes.

In an extensive review of the psychoanalytic literature on creativity and neurosis, Franz Alexander (1964) found that while many psychoanalytic authors posit a relationship between neurosis and artistic productivity, substantial controversies exist with regard to the motivational powers behind artistic creation and symptom formation and the nature of psychological processes underlying them. Alexander concluded that these controversies are the result of dichotomous thinking, the use of global terminology, the setting up of an antithesis between normal and healthy mentation, and a tendency to draw sharp structural lines between the actually more fluid transitions among conscious, preconscious, and unconscious processes. He maintained that whether the sources of creativity are unconscious or preconscious has no meaning, for it is not the structural localization of a conflict but rather the way it is expressed and resolved that ultimately determines the value of a creative act.

The theory of creativity that Alexander (1964) offered is one of conflict. For Alexander, the source of all creative acts is a state of frustration or tension created by internal and external conflicts that the individual can only resolve by finding new solutions. He wrote,

> Frustration is the source of all creative acts, that is, of all efforts to find new solutions no matter whether for practical purposes, self-expression, communication or satisfaction of the urge to understand the world around us, or simply to do something better, express something more effectively than it was possible before. (p. 127)

Like the creative process, dreaming and neurotic symptoms are also motivated by internal tension or conflict with external reality. Thus, all three are attempts at resolving conflict, but creativity involves a highly developed ability for creating new and worthwhile combinations of perceptions and ideas, as well as a special capacity for representation and communication.

In a more recent review of the literature on creativity and psychopathology, Chessick (1999) concluded that the creative process is metapsychologically similar to any other form of conflict resolution. Rather than finding a neurotic solution for unconscious conflicts, the artist transforms them into a socially and artistically acceptable symbolic form. He cited Noy (1979), who had stated that creativity and neurosis both represent attempts to solve the same underlying problems, but the solution found by the artist is exactly the opposite of the neurotic solution. The neurotic tends to resist change, whereas the creative individual "is characterized by never-ending attempts to originate new and daring patterns of adaptation" (Chessick, 1999, p. 282). Noy viewed the creative act as an attempt to resolve fragmentation and therefore saw it as a movement toward mental health.

Noy (1979) made the interesting observation that, as a general rule when it comes to creativity and mental health, the perspective of psychoanalysts is quite different from that of academic psychologists. Psychoanalysts, who are primarily interested in latent motives, tend to highlight psychopathology, while psychologists in academia, who focus on the creative process, tend to be impressed with the flexibility and productivity of the creative mind; they see ego strength and integrity where psychoanalysts see psychopathology.

While some theorists like Lowenfeld arrived at their conclusions about artists from interpretation of clinical material, many studies linking creativity and psychopathology have been based on the analyses of the works of various eminent creative personalities, or they represent an attempt to relate certain diagnostic categories (such as mood disorders) to artistic productivity (Andreason, 1987; Jamison, 1989; Ludwig, 1995; Rothenberg, 1990; Storr, 1993). Kay Redfield Jamison (1989) made a powerful case for a connection between affective illness and creativity based on her professional as well as her personal experience with a bipolar condition. Although she has been accused of flawed research methodology (Rothenberg, 1990), and one may not necessarily agree with her generalizations, her case is quite compelling as presented in her memoir, which provides an intimate look at her struggle with this illness.

Some of the characteristics of creative people have been identified as rendering them particularly vulnerable to pathological states. Knafo (2008) described creative individuals as sensitive, shy, insecure, and often isolated. She wrote, "sensitivity involves a greater capacity for feeling, emotional reactions, and tolerance of extreme affective states; it is the artists' inordinate sensitivity that provides the link between creativity and mood disorder" (p. 575).

Anthony Storr (1985) believed that a tendency toward depression can actually be a spur to creative achievement. Since one of the main characteristics of those who are prone to depression is fragile self-esteem, when an individual has the talent to use art as a way of coping with their depression, they have within them the means to have a greater sense of self-worth. I would add that not only does artistic creation allow them to feel good about themselves and to achieve some recognition from others, but it also facilitates communication with the outside world.

Another version of the link between creativity and pathology derives from the often-made observation that artists as a group tend to become substance abusers (Arieti, 1976; Knafo, 2008). The history of this connection dates back to the 19th century, when opium was the drug of choice for many writers and poets. Arieti recognized that while certain substances may remove excessive anxiety and inhibitions, they do not promote innovative ideas. Primary-process mechanisms may be enhanced, but the use of the secondary-process also necessary for creative production is impaired. In a well-researched article, Knafo (2008) examined the relationship between creativity and addiction, citing countless cases to illustrate her point that artists often turn to drugs or alcohol in an attempt to stimulate creative inspiration and allay their anxiety about the creative process. The disinhibiting effect of alcohol and the heightened emotional responsiveness of drugs is part of the allure of substances, which eventually become addictive and destructive to their users.

Storr (1993) also acknowledged that while drugs can temporarily give access to the unconscious and thus be experienced as a source of inspiration, ultimately their habitual use is destructive to creativity because, like insanity, they impair the functions of the ego: "For creative work, access to the inner realm of the psyche is essential. But so is a strongly functioning ego, capable of judgment, inhibition of immediate impulse, persistence and control" (p. 297).

Another way of understanding the reliance of creative individuals on various mood- and cognitive-altering substances is that they may facilitate a shift into altered states of consciousness, states that are associated with the production of unique and self-expressive works of art. While drugs can facilitate these states, it is also a fact that many individuals have the capacity to shift into altered states without the help of drugs. My experience with hypnotic phenomena indicates that in order to achieve an altered state, or what has been referred to as a "regressed" state, drug usage is unnecessary for most individuals and certainly unnecessary for those creative individuals who tend to have greater facility with shifting states.

Albert Rothenberg has extensively investigated the relationship of creativity to psychosis; in fact he has written an entire book on the subject—*Creativity and Madness* (1990). In it, he exposed the myths about the supposed relationship between creativity and psychopathology and attempted to give the basis for these longstanding myths. Rothenberg concluded that creative thinking transcends the usual modes of logical thought, and in that respect there are some similarities to psychotic thinking, but he cautioned these are superficial, because according to him creative thinking generally occurs in a rational and conscious state of mind.

He coined the term *translogical* for the thought processes of creative people engaged in the process of creation in order to distinguish this type of thinking from ordinary logical thought. For instance, translogical thinking involves the ability to place paradoxical and antagonistic ideas into a single entity, creating unique, unexpected, and interesting patterns of thought. Another term coined by Rothenberg is *Janusian* process, which describes a creative cognitive sequence in which multiple opposites are conceived simultaneously and experienced as coexistent. Presumably, the creative individual is aware of these contradictions while the psychotic is not. Like Kubie, Rothenberg also believed that mental illness is actually a hindrance to creative work.

Rothenberg's assumption was that creative thinking is healthy thinking, while psychotic thinking is pathological and impoverished. Even when there is an overlap—that is, when a creative person is also psychotic—the presence of a creative process is a sign of his capacity for healthier functioning. I have some difficulty with Rothenberg's conceptualizations about two types of thinking as being either advanced/healthy thinking (i.e., creative thinking) or impoverished/pathological thinking (primitive primary process); I take issue with the split that implies that these are mutually exclusive categories rather than different possibilities that could shift depending on life circumstances and on internal states. I think the split between healthy and pathological is a sweeping generalization that is not helpful and does not take into consideration the fact that multiple states of self exist and that there are areas of functioning that vary within any individual. For instance, seriously disturbed individuals who have special talents can use them in the service of expressing themselves and communicating their suffering to others, and in that process are able to achieve a higher level of functioning.

Rothenberg denied that translogical thinking has any similarities to trance states or altered states of consciousness; apparently, he anticipated that some readers might wonder about this—as I have. Having worked with hypnosis for over 35 years, I am very familiar with the kind of thinking process that is called *trance logic* (Orne, 1959), which occurs when someone is in an altered state. Trance logic refers to the suspension of critical judgment and a tolerance of inconsistencies and logical incongruities—a common state of mind for a hypnotized individual. In that state, ideas can emerge that transcend the usual modes of ordinary logical thought, and one would be hard-pressed to distinguish them from what Rothenberg called translogical thinking. There seems to be a certain circularity of thinking in Rothenberg's theory. His definitions of terms seem arbitrary, and his designations of health or pathology appear to follow from the way he has defined his terms.

The data from hypnosis provides an interesting corroboration for the observation that there are similarities between creative and psychotic thinking in the context of trance phenomena. It has been noted (Spiegel & Spiegel, 2004) that while artists and psychotics may both show a positive biological potential for trance, the most severally disturbed patients generally cannot be hypnotized because they tend to be so distractible and disorganized and are unable to maintain the level of concentration necessary to enter, follow instructions in, remain in, and exit from a trance state. The Hypnotic Induction Profile (HIP), a measure of hypnotizability developed by Spiegel (1974), identifies the ability to enter the trance state. The "decrement" profile is a designation that indicates a positive biological potential for trance without the ability to actually enter it because of impairment in focal concentration. Clinical research indicates that hypnotizability as measured by the HIP is a function of relative mental health characterized by integrated concentration, and that an impairment or collapse in hypnotizability as represented by a decrement profile indicates a high probability of the presence of serious psychopathology (Spiegel & Spiegel, 2004).

In my experience, people who have an artistic temperament and people who suffer from psychotic features do share certain characteristics, such as greater access to primitive ideation and intense affect. Their ideas tend to be more fluid, their associations looser and more unusual, and their emotions more labile. However, those who function well are able to play with ideas and feelings but do not get lost in them. Studies of creative people indicate that they show a greater tolerance for the chaotic, the conflicting, and the disordered, and a respect for the irrational forces in themselves and in others (Basescu, 1967/2010). Because they are not overwhelmed by their associations or feelings, they are able to return to a rational place when the play is over. Regression is not a frightening state for those who can move in and out of it at will; it represents a freedom and a potential to grow.

That's not to say that artists, particularly if they suffer from mood disorders or are trauma survivors, don't enter dark places from which they sometimes cannot find their way out. The literature is replete with examples of artists who have taken their own lives (Ludwig, 1995). The question of suicide, however, is a complicated one; elsewhere, I have written about this in relation to Holocaust survivors (Richman, 2002). It seems to be a common idea that artist survivors are more prone than others to end their life, and it is assumed that the horrors they endured in the past came back inevitably to haunt them in their later years (Gerson, 2009).[2] While I don't deny the possibility that depression can lead to suicide and that many survivors suffer with depression throughout their lives, it is also true that people who have experienced trauma at the hands of others know what it's like to be helpless and to have no control over one's life. Being able to take control over one's death becomes a form of freedom.

Freud's physician-assisted suicide is another example of an assertive individual's choice to determine his own life and death in the face of suffering (McCue & Cohen, 1999). It is believed that his cancer of the mouth and the pain of countless surgical procedures ultimately led Freud to the decision to die (Molnar, 1992; Schur, 1972). This does not negate the possibility of a depression, but we generally don't think of his suicide as a sign of depression or an avoidance of pain but rather as an assertion of autonomy to choose his own exit from life. Why would we automatically assume that a Holocaust survivor who ends his life is doing so because of Holocaust-related trauma?

It is my impression that creative action and a sense of empowerment are intertwined in such a way that an artist in the act of creating has a heightened sense of personal agency. Creativity encourages the enhancement of the self, the increased understanding of the self, and the resultant sense of agency (Oppenheim, 2013). At the same time, the artist's need for control is sometimes challenged by the fact that she can't always count on her talent to produce works of art. It is a commonly held notion by artists that creative inspiration comes from outside and visits them like a muse. The latter can be fickle and unpredictable; it can come and go and is not within one's control. The anxiety and insecurity about being able to produce at will is probably another factor that contributes to the reputation of artists as mentally unstable individuals (Gilbert, 2009).

It is likely that the alleged connection between creativity and madness has affected the way that artists relate to analysis. Many are reluctant to expose themselves to analytic scrutiny, fearing the potential inhibiting effects of psychoanalysis on their creativity. Their concern is that the act of analyzing thinking and emotional processes could cause undue self-consciousness and interfere with creative expression.

Perhaps there is some validity to such fears when artists end up in the offices of psychoanalysts who subscribe to a reductionistic model of mind. The authoritarian, reductionistic attitude of the profession, so common in the past, likely contributed to the suspicions of artists. Lowenfeld's (1941) assertion that mental illness is inevitably "almost without exception" the lot of the artistically talented is an example of such stereotyping. Nevertheless, even with a potentially good therapy experience, artists may hold on to the commonly held notion that personal suffering gives depth to their creative work and may fear that if they become better adjusted as a result of psychotherapy or psychoanalysis, they will lose their creative edge or their motivation to create. It is as if they needed some level of disturbance in order to create.

On the contrary, it seems that "psychotherapy overall serves to improve mental health and thereby enhances the functioning of the creative processes" (Rothenberg, 1990, p. 171). According to Kohut, one of the criteria for termination of an analysis and thus a sign of mental health is the general liberation of creative energy and the emergence of "the urge to create" (in Strozier, 2001).

At the same time, we know that the reverse is also true; engagement in the creative process has a positive effect on mental health. It has long been known that artistic endeavors have the power to heal the artist. The basic premise is that engagement in the creative process, whether in the form of writing, painting, or composing, is a means to self-understanding and a way to work through conflict and pain, thereby helping to regain a sense of equilibrium in the aftermath of trauma. The urge to create in circumstances of pain is a powerful force for self-healing, regardless of whether or not the artist is seriously disturbed or especially talented. Graham Greene says it eloquently in his 1980 memoir, *Ways of Escape*: "Writing is a form of therapy; sometimes I wonder how all those who do not write, compose or paint can manage to escape the madness, melancholia, the panic fear which is inherent in the human situation" (p. 10).

For some, psychoanalysis does not feel like a viable option for self-discovery. Those include individuals who cannot afford analysis, people who are more comfortable with nonverbal forms of communication, or those who have difficulty trusting others. If we speculate that highly creative individuals have an innate tendency toward introspection and the ability to access hidden dimensions of consciousness, but at the same time are less likely to trust or defer to authority, then we can understand why self-analysis might be a safer way to know oneself than entrusting one's psyche to a psychoanalyst. In those cases, art becomes a way to work through one's pain and gain insight. When creative individuals are also trauma survivors, there is a double incentive to try to heal oneself rather than turning to a psychoanalyst/stranger (Richman, 2009). The reverberations of trauma are long-reaching and have great implications for creative healing.

Surrender, Trance, and Dissociation

One of the major shifts from the drive model to the relational model has been a change of focus from a pathological perspective on creativity to one in which creativity represents a striving for growth, transcendence, and transformation. This view, found in the earlier writings of Rank, the interpersonalists, and Winnicott, has been further developed in the work of Emmanuel Ghent, one of the founders of the relational movement. Like his predecessors, Ghent viewed liberation and expansion of the self as a fundamental human need. In that context, he put forth the concept of "surrender" as a controlled dissolution of self-boundaries, the expression of a healthy wish to let go of defensive barriers, a yearning to be known and recognized.

Although Ghent, a composer himself, makes numerous references to the creative process, he does not make its relationship to surrender explicit except to quote the work of Marion Milner (1950), an artist and psychoanalyst. As noted in chapter 2, Milner wrote about art as a force for growth that is expressed as an impulse to break down false inner organizations—a kind of creative fury that gives birth to a new integration. In describing her own creative process, she wrote: "The process always seemed to be accompanied by a feeling that the ordinary sense of self had temporarily disappeared, there had been a kind of blanking out of ordinary consciousness" (1950, p. 154). This process of breaking free from the familiar allowed a new unexpected entity to emerge.

Both Milner (1950) and Ghent (1990/1999) recognized that the creative moment in art is the surrender of the conventional view of an object, and that this experience means a period of chaos before a new reality can be expressed. A sense of safety is therefore a prerequisite to the ability to let go, to temporarily set aside conscious logic and allow oneself to plunge into a state of uncertainty. When the artist cannot bear the uncertainty of what is emerging, she is likely to interfere with the process of creation. Presumably, there are considerable differences among people with regard to their willingness and/or anxiety about surrendering to the experience.

Deeply influenced by Ghent, Jessica Benjamin (2005), writing about her own creative process, distinguished between two states of consciousness: "the one in which we immerse or float or allow ourselves to be carried by association of ideas and one in which we have a definite intention" (pp. 188–189). She pointed out that the state of surrender paradoxically involves the loss of self in order to find oneself. From her description of her own writing process, Benjamin appeared to delight in the temporary letting go of self-consciousness and of control: "Maybe that is why I write, to find my way into the state of receptivity" (p. 191).

In contrast, Bollas (2011), who developed his own artistic talents relatively late in his life, wrote, "An artist does not go easily into this altered state of unconsciousness. They feel the boundary between ordinary psychic life and the artistic workspace, as one that is always difficult to cross and sometimes unbearably so" (p. 200).

The state of surrender as described by these authors has a similarity to what Mihaly Csikszentmihalyi (1990, 1996, 2004) has called the "flow" state, which he defined as an almost automatic, effortless, yet highly focused state of consciousness. Csikszentmihalyi has done extensive research on the subject. He has studied creative individuals from different disciplines, including artists, scientists, business CEOs, and other highly successful professionals, over many years. He found that what these people in diverse fields had in common was the capacity to become deeply immersed and involved to the point where they could enter an ecstatic state in which their sense of self seemed to disappear. Along with this state usually came a lack of awareness of bodily needs, a distorted sense of time, and a transcendence of normal awareness.

A quote from one of Csikszentmihalyi's subjects, a leading composer he studied in the 1970s, illustrates the state he enters when the composing is going well in the following way:

> You are in an ecstatic state to such a point that you feel as though you almost don't exist. I have experienced this time and again. My hand seems devoid of myself, and I have nothing to do with what is happening. I just sit there watching it in a state of awe and wonderment, and the music just flows out of itself. (Csikszentmihalyi, 2004)

This description is reminiscent of the trance-like state that I associate with hypnotic phenomena. For many years, I have studied and used hypnosis as an adjunct technique in my analytic work, as mentioned in the previous section. This state of consciousness, which can be referred to as an altered state, is quite familiar to me, both experientially and from my work with patients. The hypnotic experience is characterized by heightened attentiveness, receptivity, intense focal concentration, and diminished peripheral attention (Spiegel & Spiegel, 2004). In trance, one is able to temporarily put aside evaluative judgment and rational concerns and allow emotionality and imagination to hold sway. It is a state of freedom, willingly chosen and anticipated.

Although the hypnotically induced trance is in itself a pleasurable and relaxing state, it may or may not bring with it a state of ecstasy depending on the purpose for its use. When an artist is deeply immersed in the creative process, under the spell of a passionate idea, working at a fever pitch, affect is intensified and more accessible, resulting in a heightened sense of aliveness. When engaged in trauma work, this same emotional availability can propel the artist into reexperiencing the intense affect associated with the original traumatic event. In trance, the individual is more open and receptive to suggestions from inside and out, and can relive the traumatic experience so that ultimately it is possible to find alternative creative ways to cope with its aftereffects.

There are substantial individual differences in the capacity for trance; some people are unable to experience it, others are highly responsive to it, and most people are able to enter it with varying degrees of depth. It is also notable that creative and imaginative individuals are more likely to be hypnotizable (Hilgard, 1970; Krippner, 1999; Spiegel & Spiegel, 2004). Hypnotizable people are capable of a deep involvement and almost total immersion in an activity in one or more imaginative feeling areas of experience.

An interesting example of the use of hypnosis to enhance creative expression is reported in the work of Viktor Frankl (1967), an existential psychoanalyst. His patient, a middle-aged professional female artist, had been struggling with intense self-criticism. She experienced both an obsessive drive to paint and a fear of immersing herself deeply into her art work. In her words, "I want to find the picture to which I can say 'yes' with all my heart . . . I have to bring up to consciousness those form creations that dwell within me" (p. 167). She wondered if under hypnosis she could free her own experiences and shape them into works of art. Frankl taught her what he called a "relaxation" exercise, which is another way of referring to a trance state. Immediately afterward, the patient described her experience: "A feeling of great clarity, one is less conscious of oneself—but all objects are much more distinct. A feeling of freshness, as though a veil had been removed from my eyes. This is quite new" (p. 168).

For several months the patient used the trance on and off during sessions and occasionally on her own. She noted that the hypnotic exercises provided her with immediate relief from tension—she described the experience of floating. The result in the artwork was greater productivity; the painting style became more forceful and personal and showed greater depth. Eventually, she was able to achieve this change even without inducing a trance state. She felt that her ability to work had been restored.

Marion Milner (1934/2011), using herself as the subject, described a similar experience after being taught a "relaxation exercise." The technique as she described it involved total muscle relaxation along with visual imagery and suggestions for arm levitation. This procedure is identical to frequently used hypnotic induction techniques. Milner found that using this technique enabled her to shift her center of awareness where she chose to focus, with beneficial effects for both body and mind. Her drawing and her singing greatly improved as she used this newfound skill. She wrote, "The automatic widening of mental focus which seemed to follow muscular relaxing brought a twofold deepening of experience, a flooding in of overtones both from present bodily awareness and also from the past, in wave after wave of memories" (p. 137).

When we consider altered mental states, such as those referred to as surrender, flow, or trance, we are moving into the area of dissociation—a much-discussed phenomenon in recent literature. In fact, hypnosis can be considered a form of structured and controllable dissociation (Butler, 2006; Frankel, 1994; Hilgard, 1977; Spiegel & Cardeña, 1990, 1991). The dissociated state is another kind of trance in which consciousness is divided and the person is functioning on several mental tracks at the same time. In that context, dissociation involves a disruption of a normal state of consciousness and perception that can vary from minor lapses of attention to alterations in the sense of self. Like hypnosis, dissociative experience can be conceptualized as a general mental state different from one's ordinary mode of experiencing, to which some individuals are more predisposed than others, and which may be elicited by different processes, including the person's deliberate intentions (Cardeña, 1994).

Originally, the concept of dissociation developed in a pathological context. Pierre Janet, in the 19th century, observed a relationship between narrowing of attention and dissociation when working with patients who had experienced overwhelming trauma (Van der Hart & Horst, 1989). Today, we understand dissociation in a broader context. In fact, theoreticians like Elizabeth Howell (2007) see the new focus on trauma and dissociation as a paradigm shift that reorganizes our view of consciousness, of the unconscious, and of human motivation. In much of the psychoanalytic literature, dissociation continues to be viewed and associated with psychopathology, but in fact, most dissociative experiences are not pathological. A large proportion of the stream of consciousness can be characterized as "normative dissociation" (Butler, 2006). Dissociation is a characteristic of everyday life; we see it in absorption in daily activities, in daydreaming and night dreaming, in fantasy, and in the performance of activities that require deep concentration and engagement; we also see it in the consulting room in projective identification and enactments (Howell, 2005).

Philip Bromberg has written extensively about the subject of dissociation, both its pathological and normal aspects. Normal dissociation, according to him, involves the natural hypnoid capacity of the mind, which works in the service of creative adaptation. The dream for instance, is the most familiar special case of the more general phenomenon of dissociation. He wrote, "Dreaming can be considered among the most routine day-to-day dissociative activities of the mind" (1998, p. 298). The hallmark of the experience, whether pathological or not, is a telescoping of the attentional field and concentration on a narrow range of experience, with simultaneous exclusion of internal and external material from both awareness and accessibility (Butler, 2006).

Thus, with hypnotic states, as well as with dissociation, we note a high level of absorption or full engagement, intense focal concentration, a loss of awareness of surroundings and imperviousness to normally distracting events, time distortion, a suspension of reality constraints, and deferral of critical judgment. Along with an altered sense of reality, there is a suspension of self-evaluation and a reduction in self-consciousness. At the same time, there may be a heightened sense of enjoyment attendant to the experience of being deeply engaged. In my interviews of artists (see chapter 6) and my personal experiences with painting and writing, I have noted that when fully engaged in the creative process, a prominent aspect of the experience is dissociation, as described above. It is my contention here that dissociation is an integral part of the creative process, an essential aspect of making art, and is sometimes also experienced by the observer viewing artistic products and performances.

As indicated in the previous chapter, Weissman (1968) also believed that the capacity for dissociation is a predominant feature in the creative process. According to him, it is the dissociative function, rather than ego regression, that is the optimal state for creative inspiration. The artist has both a creative self and a conventional self; it is the dissociative function that liberates the artist from his usual way of operating.

Regardless of whether there is psychopathology, the dissociative function enables the creative person to temporarily detach his creative self from his personal or conventional self. If the creative self is derived from a pathological personal self-image, the product produced may reveal this rather than being a sign of psychopathology. Weissman believes that, in the creative activities of psychotics, the dissociative and synthetic functions operate as they do with other creative persons, and that psychotics may actually achieve a respite from psychotic regression during creative activity because of the positive (synthetic) effects of the dissociative function.

In more recent years, the relationship between dissociative experiences and creativity has been noted and researched by academic psychologists, whose perspective is quite different from that of psychoanalysts interested in the clinical manifestations of dissociation, yet they have arrived at similar conclusions about artists and dissociative experiences (Pérez-Fabello & Campos, 2011; Sapp & Hitchock, 2003). For instance, it has been observed that artists as a group tend to have a greater capacity for dissociation, which may be related to an innate ability to tolerate paradox and ambiguity and the capacity to entertain contradictory ideas simultaneously (Pérez-Fabello & Campos, 2011).

Butler (2006), writing about normative dissociation, says,

> The benefit of dissociating, particularly in the case of flow experiences, is that absorption allows for the full commitment of attention to the activity and a reduction in distractibility and self-consciousness and may therefore, enhance performance in skilled activities (such as sports or performing) or enhance the flow of creativity. (p. 56)

Given the variations in the concept of dissociation and the broad range of level of pathology that characterizes it, some theorists (Davies, 1998; Davies & Frawley, 1994; Hilgard, 1977) have proposed the notion of a dissociative continuum, ranging from transient normal everyday events involving absorption to relatively rare pathological states such as Dissociative Disorder or Dissociative Identity Disorder. Others, like Butler (2006), have maintained that pathological dissociation is not part of a continuum, but rather represents a disorder of normative dissociative processes.

Cardeña (1994) has proposed that the term *dissociation* be restricted to significant departures from ordinary modes of experiencing in which there is a sense of being disconnected from one's surroundings and oneself. This is compatible with the way that I use the term here and also consistent with the way that psychoanalysts tend to think of it.

Another perspective on dissociation comes from current work in cognitive science and in neuroscience. The multiple code theory (Bucci, 2002, 2007) offers a broad understanding of dissociative processes as they operate both in adaptive functioning and in psychopathology. Wilma Bucci (2007) wrote,

> Humans have evolved as complex organisms, with multiple states, multiple functions, multiple ways of processing information, and substantial but limited integration of systems. We are all more dissociated than not. The dissociation among systems is the basis for our vulnerability and also, in some respects, our strength in negotiating our worlds. (p. 166)

Among Bucci's examples of the adaptive capacity for encompassing multiple and shifting states are the absorption of a scientist in his creative ideas, the capacity of an athlete to enter a zone state, and a jazz musician in the flow state of improvisation.

The subject of dissociation has been at the center of relational theories for the last couple of decades (Bromberg, 1998, 2006; Davies, 1996, 1998; Howell, 2005; Stern 1997, 2010a; among others). These theorists view the mind as a configuration of shifting, nonlinear, discontinuous states of consciousness best described as multiple selves. According to Bromberg (1998), normal multiplicity is a loose configuration of multiple self-states that are experienced as a unitary self.

Jody Davies (1998) distinguished between dissociation as a predominant dynamic aspect of mind and traumatic dissociation with its fragmentation of experience. Through her clinical material, she highlighted the difference between an experience of discontinuity resulting from the temporary suspension of cohesive levels of psychic organization and the profound disruptions that are the result of traumatic experience. She proposed the use of the term *therapeutic dissociation* to describe the clinical process of working with multiple self-organizations, a process that she finds integral to analytic treatment.

The healthy individual, according to Bromberg (1993/1998), is the one who is able to "stand in the spaces between realities without losing any of them. This is what I believe self-acceptance means and what creativity is really all about—the capacity to feel like one self while being many" (p. 186). According to Bromberg, the human capacity for creative living is based on the intrinsic multiplicity of the self. He provided an example of a performing artist who, when playing a character on stage, can for a brief moment escape from herself. She can lose herself in a character and find the character in herself, allowing a different aspect of her own personality to dominate and take center stage—so to speak.

The way in which the concept of dissociation will be used here is similar to what Bromberg (1998) has referred to as "healthy dissociation"—as an adaptive function of the human mind that allows individual self-states to function optimally "when full immersion in a single reality, a single strong affect and a suspension of one's self-reflective capacity is exactly what is called for or wished for" (p. 273).

I don't, however, share the view that it is only "healthy dissociation" that is adaptive. In my thinking, the psychological state of dissociation is basically a neutral phenomenon that can be viewed from either a healthy or a pathological perspective and has different connotations depending on its context. Regardless of context, however, I see this state as ultimately adaptive, for even when deemed pathological, it is a way of coping with life's assaults.

More specifically, in a clinical context, I see dissociation as a defensive process involving the separation or compartmentalization of experience, thoughts, or feelings in order to cope with an impossible situation. It involves a split in consciousness that is experienced as both knowing and not knowing simultaneously. This process was beautifully described in the novel *1984*, written by George Orwell in 1949. He called this phenomenon "doublethink":

> *Doublethink* means the power of holding two contradictory beliefs in one's mind simultaneously, and accepting both of them. The Party intellectual knows in which direction his memories must be altered; he therefore knows that he is playing tricks with reality; but by the exercise of doublethink he also satisfies himself that reality is not violated. The process has to be conscious, or it would not be carried out with sufficient precision, but it also has to be unconscious, or it would bring with it a feeling of falsity and hence of guilt. (p. 176)

Orwell did not use the term *dissociation*, but his description of this phenomenon and his example captures the paradox at the heart of dissociation—a process that allows the mind to compartmentalize and split off incompatible thoughts or troubling feelings from consciousness. While he describes the phenomenon brilliantly in his futuristic novel, he doesn't attempt to explain the workings of the mind—this is left to the analysts and researchers. Orwell viewed the unconscious and conscious in linear terms, a model of mind that fails to explain the shifting states of consciousness, which our current theory of multiplicity succeeds in doing.

The nature of dissociation is such that one can't know that one is engaged in it for it to work effectively, yet on some level one has to recognize it. I have referred to this phenomenon as "remembering to forget to remember" (Richman, 2002, 2006c). Through a trick of mind, like a sleight of hand, we find a way out of an impossible situation by altering our consciousness.

My understanding of this process comes from personal experiences in childhood. When I was very young and living in hiding during the Holocaust, I had some awareness of what was happening around me, while at the same time I was beset by confusion—my mother's terror was palpable, yet she smiled when we were out in public; my father kept appearing and disappearing from the attic, his hiding place. No one felt it necessary to explain anything to me about these strange goings-on. In their eagerness to believe that, because of my young age, I wouldn't be affected by the horrors we had lived through, my parents insisted that I was too young to remember what had transpired during the war years. Hence, they never helped me to integrate or make sense of what I had seen and heard when I was 2 and 3 and 4 years of age. I interpreted their denial of my experience as an injunction against talking about my memories, thoughts, or feelings. So the few fragments of memory that I did have of the years in hiding remained private isolated images without a context to give them meaning. The stage was set for dissociation.

How I handled the memories of my little sister born in hiding provides an illustration of the ability to hold contradictory beliefs simultaneously—a characteristic of dissociation and of trance states. One of my clear memories of childhood involves my little sister born when I was 3 years old: I remember the circumstances around her birth, I remember playing with her, and I remember the day of her death when I was 4 years old; I even remember the conflicting feelings I had about her throughout her brief life. Years later, when asked if I had any siblings, I always responded, "No, I'm an only child"—a designation my parents used for me frequently, as if to obliterate my sister's brief presence in our lives. I never questioned the discrepancy; I accepted both realities as true despite the contradiction—I had vivid memories of my sister *and* I was an only child.

Another Holocaust survivor, who at the age of 9 had to pass as a Catholic, eloquently describes how she was able to alter her consciousness in order to survive without experiencing the conflict that could have betrayed her. In her memoir, *Dry Tears,* Nechama Tec (1982) wrote,

A slow transformation was taking place in me. It was as if in certain circumstances I lost track of who I really was and began to see myself as a Pole. I became a double person, one private and one public. When I was away from my family I became so engrossed in my public self that I did not have to act the part; I actually felt like the person that I was supposed to be. There were times when I believed myself to be truly Stefa's niece, as Polish as any of her blood relations. It was not that I really forgot who I was, only that I became able to push my true self into the background. (p. 144)

In this brief description, Dr. Tec provided a dramatic example of dissociation at work. According to her, she did not feel that she was lying or playing a part. As it became necessary, and for the moment, she could shift into an "as if" state and experience herself as another person. Once she forgot about her Jewish self, she was able to keep that self safe within. Had she remembered her Jewish self or kept her in mind, she might have been less convincing and in greater danger of being found out. It is noteworthy that when Tec was not in the dissociated state described above (when she was "standing in the spaces" as Bromberg [1996] would say), she experienced a mixture of emotions: "I felt an odd confusion of emotions—fear because I was losing touch with my real self, but a kind of pleasure too because it was so easy to give up and become my newer, safe self" (p. 197). She also reported experiencing the guilt of separating from her Jewish family when dissociation took over.

Tec's description of the process is very similar to what I have observed in hypnotically induced trance states when there is an alteration in consciousness for a specific intended purpose. In response to a suggestion from either outside or inside (in the case of self-hypnosis), aspects of self that normally coexist as separate self-states can become disconnected or disengaged from one another and a suggested self can take center stage; the shift seems effortless and dramatic. I would guess that Tec had an innate capacity to shift from one state to another that was heightened by her motivation for survival.

When does dissociation become pathological and not work as well as it did in Nechama Tec's case to help her to survive her ordeal? I think there are several factors involved in determining the efficacy of the process. When the assault on the psyche is massive and unrelenting, when the individual is constitutionally particularly vulnerable, and when the defenses are strained to the max—then trauma becomes overwhelming. In those cases, the individual is unable to make use of the human capacity for dissociation in the service of survival.

Even when the dissociative process is successful during a time of crisis, it can have negative sequelae in its aftermath. A blessing under traumatic circumstances, it can ultimately narrow one's consciousness in a more permanent way, limiting one's freedom to develop. Sometimes, it becomes a rigid way of functioning, a way of being in the world that limits one's options and choices. The traumatized survivor behaves as if the traumatic situation still exists, or at least is a constant possibility. Much energy is devoted to the avoidance of retraumatization. Split-off aspects of self contribute to a state of fragmentation and interfere with a sense of wholeness and continuity.

As Donnel Stern (2010a) puts it, dissociation is a constraint on the freedom of thought and the freedom to feel. Our recollections of traumatic events—whether hazy or clear—tend to be flat, factual, and lacking in affective nuance. My personal experience validates Stern's observation. When, after years of therapy, I finally became more open about my childhood history and spoke about my experiences more freely, I found my speech to be hollow, awkward, and affectless. When I told my story, it seemed as if I were describing someone else's life. During that same period, strong affect in the form of tears would suddenly erupt when least expected, triggered by a film, a line in a book, or a random thought.

The Paradox of Dissociation

When Emmanuel Ghent (1990/1999) wrote about his belief in the fundamental human need for self-expansion expressed in a yearning to surrender, he reminded us of Winnicott's view of regression as part of a healing process. In that context, Ghent told us that "regression and surrender are close relatives" (p. 214).

In general, the concept of regression has not received much recognition or appreciation from contemporary relational thinkers, presumably because of its association with the classical drive model. Traditionally, regression had the connotation of pathology because of its potential to bring about disequilibrium, irrationality, and heightened emotional vulnerability. More recently, Balint (1968) made a distinction between benign and malignant regression, and Winnicott and Ghent emphasized that there are circumstances when regression carries the hope of new opportunity, particularly when it takes place more or less voluntarily and is in the service of expanding and enlightening the self. It has also been recognized that the reorganization of the self brings with it the potential for maturational growth, self-actualization, mastery, and effectance.

This view is similarly expressed by Bromberg (1979) when he distinguishes between the regressive state in psychosis and regression as a benign state actively pursued with intention and enlisted in the service of growth. In the case of the latter, the individual can allow the emergence of regressed states of experience and primitive modes of thinking, feeling, and behaving by partially relinquishing the function of protecting his own ego stability. In those cases, Bromberg wrote, "The deeper the regression that can be safely allowed by the patient, the richer the experience and the greater its reverberation on the total organization of the self" (p. 654). Here he recognized that the emergence of regressed states of experience, with their intense reenactment of early and sometimes primitive modes of functioning, can actually encourage changes in self-representation—changes that are at the heart of what psychoanalysis aims for. In fact, he saw regression as an inevitable process that will automatically take place unless it is discouraged in the treatment. When he maintained that the self (or ego), in order to grow, must voluntarily allow itself to regress, he gave a nod to Kris's concept of regression in the service of the ego. Thus, he wrote, "The ego (or self), in order to grow, must voluntarily allow itself to become less than intact—to regress. Empirically this is one way of defining regression in the service of the ego" (p. 653).

To paraphrase Ghent, dissociation and regression are also relatives. The close relationship between regression and dissociation is particularly evident in altered states. Age regression is a common phenomenon in trance states, as anyone who does hypnosis work knows. In response to a suggestion, the hypnotized subject returns to an earlier time and place in order to face and explore troublesome issues and work though them. In so far as surrender, dissociation, and regression are part of the same family, we see their relationships unfold in the creative process. When artists are making art, they are prone to enter a creative space where the lines between dissociation and regression may be blurred.

Kris's recognition that the artist is able to regress in order to create may be another way of referring to the dissociative phenomenon that facilitates imaginative productions. In both phases of the creative process—the inspirational and the elaborational, as defined by Kris—the trance state plays a facilitative role; in the inspirational phase, it facilitates regression, and during the elaborational period, it enhances focused concentration.

Knafo (2012) discussed Kris's concept of regression in the service of the ego from a contemporary object relations perspective. She is in favor of retaining this concept despite its limitations—such as its connotation of pathology and its exclusive association with drive and ego psychology. She redefined the concept as "the ability to maintain contact with early body and self-states and with early forms of object relationships as well as with different modes of thinking" (p. 28). Although I appreciate the way that Knafo updated the term, and I agree that regression does take place in the inspirational phase of artistic activity with positive consequences, my own thinking takes me somewhere else. I believe that the concept of dissociation is closer to a description of what actually takes place during the creative process.

It is my contention that dissociation is an essential feature of the creative process. Regardless of the motivational aspects of making art—whether to communicate, to repair one's losses, to express one's suffering, to heal from trauma, to assert oneself in the world, or to reach for immortality—dissociation is an essential aspect of creativity.

The dissociative or altered state renders the contents of the mind more readily accessible. There is more vivid imagery, a lessening of anxiety and tension, and a greater receptivity to new ideas. Defenses are relaxed; logical thinking and critical judgment are deferred. I maintain that in a dissociated state, regression is only one of a number of possible behavioral options. The individual in this state of mind is not only able to regress into earlier more primitive modes of functioning, but also can move forward into a world of future fantasies. During the creative process, both regression and progression are in the service of healthy development. I conceptualize it as a movement in either direction along a vertical axis, which is made possible by loosened boundaries and greater fluidity of associations.

In addition to the potential movement along the vertical axis, I envision a movement along a horizontal axis into different self-states that have become more accessible as a result of altered awareness. I believe that the normal need for the unity of self is set aside during states of altered consciousness, allowing for greater access to a range of self-states, more fluid communication between them, and a greater freedom to explore the different voices coming from within.

Thus, what I propose is that in a dissociated state, there is greater potential for fluidity of movement in all directions—up and down and side to side—with the result that regression, progression, and shifts into multiple self-states are all possibilities, dependent on self-suggestions or expectations. In the case of the artist, all of these potential movements are meant to develop the themes the artist is focused on at any given time and ultimately serve to foster psychological growth and healing.

To my knowledge, the conceptualization that the dissociative state allows for both vertical and horizontal shifts in psychic levels is new, and it is not to be confused with Kohut's (1971) terminology of vertical and horizontal splits in the psyche, referring to the defensive maneuvers of repression and denial.

To summarize, the artist during the inspirational phase surrenders to the creative process and enters an altered state of mind that facilitates the imaginative capacity, the expression of visual or auditory imagery that had heretofore not been verbally accessible. Just as dreamwork makes use of the mind's capacity to enter hypnogogic states (Bromberg, 2003), artwork also makes use of this capacity and facilitates the act of holding multiple disparate self-states at the same time. In a state of double consciousness (Bosnak, 2003), one can fully experience different states of awareness that correspond to various subjectivities without having to exclusively identify with each.

Presumably, these shifts in psychic states can facilitate psychological growth regardless of the direction taken. When individuals are engaged in the creative process, whether they are regressing, progressing, or moving from one self-state to another, they enter a place where they have more access to internal problematic material and have an opportunity for working through the material towards self-continuity. We can say that in those moments, individuals are "standing in the spaces," to borrow Bromberg's (1998) felicitous phrase.

Trauma complicates the picture. The human capacity for dissociation plays a particularly powerful role in the case of trauma, and it is here that we encounter the paradox of dissociation. Bromberg (1998) defines psychological trauma as, "the precipitous disruption of self-continuity through invalidation of the internalized self-other patterns of meaning that constitute the experience of "me-ness" (p. 11). He distinguishes between "normal dissociation"—the natural hypnoid capacity of the mind that works in the service of creative adaptation—and "pathological dissociation"—a pathological mental structure developed as a defense against trauma.

I find Bromberg's dichotomy between normal and pathological dissociation unnecessarily complicated and prefer to view dissociation as a unitary capacity of mind whose efficacy is determined by the circumstances that elicit it. Similar to regression, dissociation has great potential as long as it is used with purpose and intention rather than being out of the subject's control. So, for instance, when the person becomes immersed in a creative endeavor, the mind's capacity to dissociate facilitates surrender, enriches self-expression, and enhances self-knowledge, in contrast to a toxic situation in which the primary motivation is avoidance and the need to not know. In the latter case, the person can use this same capacity for dissociation in the service of blocking out what is intolerable and irreconcilable; in this scenario, the state of dissociation impedes knowing while it facilitates coping. The price for coping may be disintegration, which can be considered pathological, but it is not dissociation that is the culprit here.

As Bromberg (1998) states, dissociation developed as a defense against trauma is a pathological mental structure, yet paradoxically, at the same time, the capacity to dissociate may hold the key to healing. In essence, when it comes to trauma, dissociation can play a dual role: It can be used in the service of defense, in the service of healing, or both. In dissociative illnesses, such as Dissociative Identity Disorder, its role is primarily a protective one, whereas in the creative experience, its role as a potential healer is highlighted.

When art is employed in the service of self-repair, it facilitates integration of aspects of self that have been touched by trauma and transforms them into artistic products. In the protected transitional space between fantasy and reality where creative play resides, the survivor can meet and recognize aspects of self that have been hurt and hidden—both from self and from others. Similar to the dream state, in which a multiplicity of states can be experienced simultaneously, in the process of making art, the survivor may face different self-representations, such as the "victim self," the "hidden self," and the "artist self." At first, these representations coexist, but gradually, with a growing sense of mastery and empowerment, self-representation shifts from "victim" to "artist." Art creates the connection between consciousness and the traumatized self.

Loewald also understands trauma as an event that cannot be integrated or absorbed until the event is relived and the passive state of trauma is turned into the active process of representation. The artist who relives her trauma in her work over and over again, with each new painting or each new poem that evokes a different aspect of the traumatized experience, has an opportunity to work through and absorb what happened to her when she was in a passive, helpless state. Working through in that context involves the recreation of a traumatic experience on a higher level of more dimensions and further differentiated and integrated functioning.

In contemplating different aspects of dissociation, an interesting paradox emerges. On the one hand, dissociation refers to a pathological process, and on the other, it refers to its potential resolution. In other words, in artwork, one enters a dissociated state in order to mend a dissociated state.

When Stern (2010a) talks about dissociation as a failure to allow one's imagination free play, he highlights one aspect of the paradox. When Ghent (1990/1999) refers to self-surrender in the creative process leading to the expansion of self, he highlights the opposite, namely, that a state of total absorption can lead to the freeing of imagination. These are the two paradoxical aspects of dissociation. Dissociation is a kind of talent that, like intelligence, falls on a continuum, a bell curve in terms of people's capacity to enter this state. It is always adaptive, but in any given circumstance it can facilitate or it can impede one's functioning.

Altered States and the Transient Hypofrontality Hypothesis

Neuropsychologists and neuroscientists generally do not talk about dissociation, but some have done research on what happens in the brain during altered states of consciousness, such as dreaming, daydreaming, meditation, flow, and hypnosis, states in which imagination reigns supreme and which can be seen as dissociative in nature. Many neuroscientists are also interested in creativity and the brain mechanisms that underlie original thinking. New techniques of brain imaging have revolutionized research possibilities; now it is possible to correlate brain traits like tissue volume, chemistry, and connectivity with aspects of the creative process.

One of the prominent researchers in this area is Arne Dietrich, a neuropsychologist with research interests in the neural basis of altered states of consciousness and neurocognitive mechanisms of creativity and the flow state. Since 2003, he has written extensively on these subjects (Dietrich, 2003, 2004a, 2004b, 2007; Dietrich & Kanso, 2010).

Going well beyond the neuroscientific explanations of creativity based on hemispheric asymmetry, which highlight the distinctions between right and left brain functions, Dietrich proposed a broader neuroscientific approach, identifying discrete circuits involved in specific aspects of higher brain function. He coined the term *transient hypofrontality* to refer to what happens in altered states of consciousness. His thesis was that the neural mechanism that explains the phenomenology of altered states of consciousness is the temporary downregulation or deactivation of prefrontal areas of the brain (Dietrich, 2003).

The prefrontal cortex controls the higher-level mental functions, such as executive attention and working memory, and accounts for a sense of time, a sense of self, and a sense of willed action. As a result of a temporary hold on the workings of the frontal lobes, thinking becomes more meandering and less directed, and the thinking person is able to make creative connections. The individual experiences cognitive and emotional changes, such as drifting attention, decreased awareness of surroundings, a sense of timelessness, and oceanic feelings of oneness with the universe—all states of altered awareness.

Researchers have observed that the hypofrontal state can be induced by meditation or other activities that involve flow when the brain is not engaged in ongoing cognitive activity like active problem-solving. This downtime leaves space to meander around and put ideas together, often in a playful way (R. Jung, 2012).

It is striking how similar this description of the effects of frontal hypofunction is to the phenomenon of altered attention, which characterizes the state of dissociation and has been described by those who write about the experience of flow (Csikszentmihalyi, 1990, 1996). Dietrich (2004a) examined the neurocognitive mechanisms underlying the experience of flow—the almost automatic, effortless, highly focused state of consciousness in which people report the disappearance of self-consciousness, a lack of concern about failure, and a sense of timelessness. He applied the concept of explicit–implicit thought processes and proposed that "a necessary prerequisite to the experience of flow is a state of transient hypofrontality that enables the temporary suppression of the analytical and meta-conscious capacities of the explicit system" (p. 746).

Additionally, Dietrich (2004b) developed a complex theory of creativity based on functional neuroanatomy. He maintained that there are four basic types of creative insights, each mediated by a distinctive neural circuit terminating in the prefrontal cortex. According to Dietrich, processing modes can be *deliberate* or *spontaneous* and can occur in *emotional* or in *cognitive* structures, each leading to different types of creativity. Creative behavior is ultimately the result of a combination of these four basic psychological processes. While deliberate searches for insight are instigated by circuits in the prefrontal cortex and result in structured, rational productions, spontaneous insights occur when unconscious thoughts are not bound by the attentional system and therefore result in random, unfiltered, and unusual connections. The spontaneous processing mode is the underlying mechanism for intuition or inspiration—a state in which one arrives at a solution while the frontal attentional system is deactivated and therefore does not control the content of consciousness. In this mental state, knowing occurs without intentional reasoning. The finding that creativity can be the result of defocused attention has been corroborated by other researchers (Martindale, 1999) and is supported by anecdotal evidence (Knafo, 2012).

It is important to keep in mind that creativity is not a unitary process and that the executive functions of the prefrontal cortex are involved as well; cognitive abilities, such as working memory, sustained attention, and cognitive flexibility, are required to implement the creative insights discovered during the intuitive phase: "To that end, prefrontal circuits are involved in making novelty fully conscious, evaluating its appropriateness and ultimately implementing its creative expression" (Dietrich, 2004a, p. 1023).

The different phases of the creative process as explicated by the neurophysiologists are reminiscent of Ernst Kris's early theories. What he observed more than 60 years ago about the different phases of the creative process—the inspirational and the elaborational—is now being validated in the laboratory. After the inspirational phase, which takes place during the down regulation of prefrontal circuits, the frontal lobes take over in order to evaluate these ideas and to develop them.

Similarly, Dietrich's transient hypofrontality hypothesis is totally consistent with Weissman's psychoanalytic speculations about the ego's dissociative function during the phases of creativity. Forty-five years ago, Weissman (1968) wrote,

> Creative imagination flourishes in a transient state of dissolution of the supremacy of the reality principle over the pleasure principle and a transient state of disregard for the superiority of secondary over primary thought processes. Under such modifiable conditions of the ego, brought about by the dissociative function new and original syntheses are created. (p. 468)

The language and methodology may be quite different, but the essence of the ideas is the same. Both the neuroscientist and the psychoanalyst deal with the question of whether or not creativity and psychopathology are related by emphasizing transience. Dietrich (2003) wrote, "Unlike most cases of mental illness and brain damage, altered states of consciousness can be characterized as transient in nature" (p. 238). This is also in keeping with Freud's view that the artist, like the neurotic, enters the world of imagination, but that unlike the neurotic, the artist finds his way back into reality.

The field of neuroscience is still young and developing, and investigations tend to lead to correlational findings rather than to causal explanations. Although I find the propositions of Dietrich and his colleagues quite compelling, it must be remembered that the transient hypofrontality hypothesis is still a hypothesis. Nevertheless, we can speculate that when the artist is totally engaged in the creative process, she enters an altered state of consciousness that has both phenomenological and neurological manifestations.

In conclusion, it is proposed here that in the process of making art, when the artist is in the inspirational phase, she is in a somewhat dissociated state characterized by heightened imaginative productions, the loosening of cognitive inhibitions, and an absence of critical self-evaluation. Rather than seeing this state as regressive, it is better described as a place of potential growth and productivity. It is a normal occurrence and universal experience, but some individuals have more capacity than others to enter such altered states, and some have more talent to render aesthetically pleasing and universally meaningful creations. Later in the process, when the artist brings critical judgment to bear on the product that was conceived during the phase of inspiration, then individual differences in the capacity for integration and communication also play a role in the final artistic product.

From time immemorial, we have tried to make sense of this mysterious phenomenon of dissociation; in it, we find a link to both inspiration and insanity. The same dissociative process that is responsible for moments of inspiration when the artist is deeply immersed in creative work is also responsible for fragmentation of the self when the individual is beset by trauma. This is the paradox: This same universal capacity to altered consciousness may disrupt our lives or help us heal.

Notes

1. In this section I use terms like *neurosis, psychopathology, madness*, and *insanity* interchangeably. I do not mean to imply that they are in fact interchangeable or have the same meaning. Some of these terms are literary; others are not in current use but are part of the historical context of which I write. All of these terms when used here are meant to communicate some form of mental anguish and impaired functioning.
2. See chapter 5 for a discussion of the presumed suicide of Primo Levi.

4

THE SURVIVOR AND THE MUSE

The Muse as Witnessing Presence

In Greek mythology, *Mnemosyne* (Memory) is the mother of the Muses, the nine Greek goddesses whose role it is to inspire artists to create. The personification of inspiration and its connection with memory is in keeping with the theme of this work, and a fitting beginning to the chapter on witnessing. The Muse as conceptualized here is an imaginary other who exists in the space between inner and outer experience; it is an embodied image that serves a mirroring, echoing, and admiring function for the creator of works of art. Usually the Muse is seen as a female, which is the likely connection with the early mother who has the power to inspire and admire.

Stolorow and Atwood (1979), discussing Rank's analysis of the artist, highlighted the narcissistic aspects of the artist's relationships. The artist, according to Rank, has a great need for mirroring affirmation from others that takes the form of a desire for public approbation, as well as the need for a single person—a love object or a Muse—who functions as a narcissistically sustaining presence (Stolorow & Atwood, p. 148). Rank also attributed to the Muse the power to relieve the artist of guilt feelings originally derived from his assertion of will in the process of creation (Rank, 1932/1989).

The ancient Greeks also had their *Chorus*, a group of performers in classical Greek drama who in unison, in one voice, narrated and commented on the action taking place on stage in the external as well as the internal world of the protagonist. The Chorus served a number of functions, including offering background information on the play, providing a commentary about the unfolding drama, and sometimes verbalizing the character's secrets and fears. The Chorus members usually wore masks, and hence had no recognizable identity or motivation of their own. This faceless, identityless group can be seen as a generic witness who sees and understands the essence of what is being enacted on stage and merely comments on it without actually participating in the drama. This generic witness occupies a transitional space between the reality of the audience and the fantasy of the play acted out on stage.

As I see it, the Muse and the Chorus are both imaginative representations of aspects of self and other that come into play when creativity is viewed from a relational perspective. In this context, the Muse is akin to Winnicott's (1967) original formulation of the *third*—an area of experience where play, artistic creativity, culture, and imagination dwell:

> This third area has been contrasted with inner or personal psychic reality and with the actual world in which the individual lives and that can be objectively perceived. I have located this important area of experience in the potential space between the individual and the environment. (p. 372)

The Muse, like an imaginary friend, is a not-me subjective object (Winnicott, 1967) that exists in that intermediate area of experience—the potential space between psychic reality and the outside world. The symbol of the Muse is conjured up when the artist is engaged in making art; in that state he is alone in the presence of the other, an unconscious representation of the early mother who was totally devoted to her infant's care and well-being.

A version of this idea was expressed by Balint (1968) in his description of the *area of creation*, a level of the mind where creativity takes place: "We know that there are no 'objects' in the area of creation, but we know also that for most—or some—of the time the subject is not entirely alone there" (p. 25). Although the person is on his own in that space, he is not truly alone. Balint invoked Winnicott's (1958) concept of the capacity to be alone when he described what happens when the person is almost entirely absorbed in the area of creation (Balint, p. 130), a state that Balint considered regressive in a benign sense. In order to capture the primitive quality and lack of organization that characterizes the object in the area of creation, Balint proposed the term *pre-object*. In my view, the notion of the Muse, which is universal and associated with the arts, better describes this idea of the other, particularly when the term *Muse* identifies an amorphous presence rather than a specific person in the life of an artist.

We generally think of the creative process as a solitary activity; but, in fact, one can make the case that the presence of the other is always implied since most artistic products are meant for an audience—a viewer, a listener, or a reader. Even when there is no actual audience present, an image of an external other may exist in the form of a projected other who will react to the creation and the individual creating. Kris (1952) wrote, "Wherever artistic creation takes place, the idea of a public exists, though the artist may attribute this role only to one real or imaginary person" (p. 60). The response of others, according to Kris, is essential to confirm the artist's belief in his work and to restore a balance that the creative process may have disturbed. While Kris did not see the striving for recognition and success as the major goal of the artist's labor, he did feel that there is a need for some response nevertheless. I would agree that some form of recognition is necessary, whether verbal or nonverbal—recognition in the sense of being known, not necessarily admired.

Intrinsic to the concept of Muse is the sense that inspiration comes from outside oneself, and one may or may not count on her presence. The notion that the Muse is fickle and has to be courted is related to the difficulties in the process of creation. One can't count on inspiration. I noted in the previous chapter that in the inspirational phase of creativity, when the artist is in a somewhat dissociated state, he may have the sense that he lacks volitional control. In that state, sometimes thoughts and emotions seem to come out of nowhere, and one may find oneself carrying out an action as if it were controlled by an outside force. The sense of agency returns in the elaboration phase of the creative process when executive control reigns supreme. In relation to the final artistic product, I have heard artists exclaim, with a hint of surprise and pride, "I have done that?"

The phrase attributed to the writer Jean Malaquais, "the only time I know the truth is when it reveals itself at the point of my pen" (in Blythe, 1998, p. 4), communicates a similar idea—the sense that the creative process seems to unfold without conscious intervention. Benjamin (2005) put it this way: "I write in order to know myself . . . At the start, I simply reflect that I can be in a self-forgetful state when I start writing, waiting to see what the writing itself will reveal" (p. 188, 190).

Stern (1983/1999) used the term *allow* to describe this phenomenon: "One allows the things that are there to impress themselves on one's consciousness" (p. 100). This applies both to the psychoanalytic process and the creative process. In both cases the process is emergent and not necessarily predictable; occasionally it can be threatening and overwhelming. At those times having a witness and guide on the journey may facilitate our exploration and provide us with a holding environment. When such a witness is not available, then sometimes one is created. During both phases of the creative process, the presence of the Muse is conjured up to provide the essential function of witnessing the artistic creation.

The need for witness is universal and ever-present. It begins early in life and is essential to the organization of our experience and the development of a sense of who we are.[1] Stern (2010a) wrote, "We construct what we know of ourselves by identifying with the other and 'listening' through his ears to the story we are telling" (p. 112). We need a witness, a partner in thought and feeling, as Stern puts it, in order to make sense of events in our lives. Being known and being kept in mind by another is what allows us to organize our experience into meaningful patterns or coherent narratives.

Initially, it is parents or caretakers who serve this witnessing function and elucidate the meaning of our experience, but later that same function is provided by others, even imaginary others, in which we witness ourselves. The choice of witness depends on the context of the situation as well as our state of mind. In my opinion, the ubiquitous concept of God found in most cultures reflects the human need for witness and its creation in order to meet that need. The quintessential witness, the one we evoke when we exclaim, "As God is my witness!" conveys the need to appeal to an ultimate authority who can serve as witness to our actions and intentions. The concept of God provides us with the comforting sense that "someone" is watching over us, listening to our prayers, caring about what we think and feel, and aware of everything that happens to us. The concept organizes our world and gives meaning to an arbitrary, neutral universe. Prayer in that context can be seen as a dialogue with an imagined, powerful, all-knowing other.

While the need for witnessing is ubiquitous, it is in the area of trauma where it becomes most essential and yet profoundly complicated. For the trauma survivor, whose experience has been chaotic and disorganizing, the witness can serve a holding function as well as a validating and integrating one. The ability to step outside of oneself and see one's narrative or the product that one has created through the eyes of another (i.e., the witness) allows a person to shift perspective and achieve some distance—a state that is helpful to gain mastery over the chaotic feelings that follow in the wake of trauma. Yet trusting others sufficiently to reveal the vulnerability that attends trauma does not come readily to survivors. How can anyone understand the depths of what has been suffered? And why would one want to revisit what has been so painful in the first place? It is with this population that imaginary witnessing is particularly common.

Stern (2010a) used some interesting examples from film and literature to illustrate the concept of imaginary witness. Among those examples, he described the movie *Cast Away* in which the character is marooned on a deserted island for over four years. With little hope of rescue, he is in a state of despair until he creates an imaginary companion with whom he develops a powerful relationship. I, too, have been fascinated by this story and would like to add some reflections of my own.

The character in the film, Chuck Noland, is a FedEx agent who survives a plane crash and is washed ashore along with some of the packages in his care. In one of the packages, he finds a volleyball. One day, in a desperate attempt to create fire, Chuck wounds his hand and in a rage he throws the ball leaving his bloody handprint on it. When he calms down, he notices that it looks like a face and draws some features on it. He then gives the ball a name—Wilson, the brand name printed on the volleyball. He places Wilson nearby on a surface where he can keep an eye on him at all times and soon he begins to talk to Wilson as if he were a real person and a friend. His first words to Wilson are, "You wouldn't have a match by any chance would you?" as he resumes the struggle to make fire, and when he finally succeeds, he dances around and joyfully calls out to Wilson, "Look what I have created—I have made fire!"

Wilson becomes a witness to the ordeal. Chuck is always aware of Wilson's presence, watches him from the corner of his eye, has conversations with him, jokes with him, argues with him, and shares his concerns with him. He says, "They may never find us." From the moment he designates him as a companion, it is no longer *me* or *I*, but *us* and *we*. With the creation of Wilson, Chuck is no longer alone. On the night before embarking on his escape from the island he says to Wilson, "You're still awake? Me too. You scared? Me too."

As he leaves the island on a raft that he has put together from branches and assorted bits of materials he found in the FedEx packages, Chuck ties Wilson down carefully but a great storm loosens the ball from its mooring and it drifts away. When Chuck realizes that Wilson is adrift, he panics. He cries out desperately,

"Wilson, I'm coming!" Chuck puts his own life in jeopardy as he swims out to save his friend. But he is unable to reach him and, in his grief, keeps repeating, "I'm sorry, Wilson, I'm sorry, Wilson." He wails and is inconsolable until he drifts into a deep sleep from which he is finally woken by the ship that ultimately rescues him.

In the early part of the film, Chuck has a significant relationship with Kelly Frears, a girlfriend whom he leaves behind to go on the doomed flight. Kelly gives him a pocket watch with her photo in it as a gift before he leaves. This is the only possession that survives the crash. Chuck keeps her photo in view at all times and looks at it longingly, but does not relate to it in the way that he does to Wilson. He does not speak to it or interact with it. The photo is not a companion, but rather a memento that reminds him of Kelly's presence in her absence. Perhaps his girlfriend's image is too painful a reminder of what he has lost, while Wilson is a more neutral object on whom he can project his thoughts and feelings—a transitional object that brings him comfort.

Just before his escape, Chuck engraves a statement into a rock—a kind of testimony left behind for a potential witness. It reads:

> Chuck Noland was here 1500 days
> Escaped to sea
> Tell Kelly Frears
> Memphis TN
> I love her

In the last frame of the film, after Chuck is rescued and returns to civilization suffering a profound sense of dislocation, we see him in his car and note that on the seat next to him sits a brand new Wilson volleyball, still in its original packaging. We wonder if his connection with Wilson has transcended time and space to help him once again through this psychologically difficult juncture.

Imaginary friends don't always have a shape and form; they can be an object, an animal, or a human being. Laub (1992) wrote about a child survivor during the Holocaust separated from his parents who clung to a photograph of his mother, maintaining his relationship with her by praying and talking to her image. The photo served as a transitional object, an internal witness. When at the end of the war, the real mother appeared, the child was distraught because of the great discrepancy between the person who came to get him and the symbol that had represented her.

The creation of imaginary companions is fairly common in childhood particularly among only or first-born children. Imaginary companions serve a number of functions, such as mentoring, giving comfort and company, and bolstering self-regulation and motivation (Hoff, 2004), among other benefits. This type of imaginative play has been associated with early language development (Kidd, Rogers, & Rogers, 2010) and creativity in childhood (Hoff, 2005), as well as in adulthood (Myers, 1979). According to Myers, imaginary companions allow traumatized children to creatively master a variety of narcissistic blows, and to displace unacceptable affects. In creative adults who had imaginary companions in childhood, the early fantasies served as an organizing schema in memory for the childhood trauma (p. 292). In his book *Solitude,* Anthony Storr (1988) cited examples of creative people who coped with childhood loneliness and suffering by creating their own imaginary worlds; among them were the writers Beatrix Potter, Anthony Trollope, and Rudyard Kipling.

My own childhood experience of living with traumatized parents who had barely survived the Holocaust and had lost beloved family members made it difficult for me to turn to them for relational needs. We moved from place to place, and my parents were preoccupied with the struggle to adapt to new lands, new cultures, new languages, and ways to make a living. It was in my imagination that I could find solace and satisfaction. There I was in full control and did not have to depend on others for emotional sustenance and support. I have written about my personal experience with imaginary friends in childhood and discussed the witnessing function that they served for me (Richman, 2002, 2006b, 2012). My first memories of such experiences date back to a time after the war when we were living in Paris. Although I was never lacking in real friendships, I seemed to have a powerful need for another with whom I could share private moments.

When I lived in Paris, I invented a little girl named Francoise who was exactly my age and who shared identical interests to mine. The way that we were different was that while I was a foreigner trying to fit in, Francoise was obviously from France. I aspired to be a little French girl just like her. She was my witness; I conjured her up when I was alone and wanted to share something with someone who knew me intimately and who accepted me unconditionally. My desire to share the joys of my life with her was as strong as my need to share my frustrations.

The fact that I most often conjured up my friend Francoise during the times when I visited the public bathroom outside of our apartment suggests another function served by this imaginary relationship. This bathroom, like many others in the tenements of post-war Paris, was basically a large hole in the ground with footholds on either side. I lived in fear of the possibility of slipping and falling into the disgusting cavernous hole, and I'm sure that having a companion during this private time was a great comfort to me.

Similarly, around the same period of life, I created an imaginary horse to ride whenever I went outside of the apartment. The horse was tied to the banister at the bottom of the staircase—adjacent to a particularly dark and frightening area of the building where someone could be lurking unnoticed. Thus these imaginary companions functioned as supports and distractions from the fears of childhood.

These companions also provided an ingenious way of dealing with the loneliness of being an only child. This is particularly evident in a brief fantasy that I had when we first came to America. Here I created an entire family of brothers and sisters for myself. If I remember correctly, there were about seven of us in this family, a lively bunch with different personalities. Talking with them allowed me to practice my English as well as my social skills, both which were quite necessary in adapting to this new world.

In retrospect I believe that my imaginary friendships were a solution to my loneliness and, even more importantly, they were a way of dealing with my need to be recognized. A hidden child who had to be on guard much of the time could not readily trust others to share intimate thoughts and feelings. These fantasy relationships met my need to be known without jeopardizing my security needs. Only in imagination does one have full control over the response of the other; there is no risk of disappointment or danger of having one's perception tampered with, as had been the case for me in my early years. A witness of one's creation is totally safe because it is an aspect of oneself. I believe that the imaginary witness is a dissociated self-state serving the crucial function of mirroring, affirming, and validating our experience. It is a healthy and positive coping strategy, a way of using a self-state for therapeutic purposes. As such, the creation of an imaginary witness is an achievement, particularly when it is not a substitute for real relationships, but merely a transitional space providing a bridge to connection with significant others.

Eventually, imaginary friends disappeared from my life—at least in their original forms. I believe that they continued to have an indirect presence in creative activities. Although activities like writing are generally thought of as solitary, there are relational components present insofar as we anticipate certain reactions from an audience—an imagined listener, viewer, or reader. Will our artistic product be received with admiration or with a critical review?, we wonder as we work or when we look at the final product that we have created. Sometimes it is difficult to identify a specific person as the potential reader; perhaps it is a stand in for a parental figure we want to convince, impress, or reach in some way. As I wrote my autobiographical narrative, I found myself in dialogue with a projected reader, an interested observer, someone who wanted to know more about me and my life. This imaginary other is a version of my imaginary childhood friends and family.

Memory, Mourning, and Memorial Spaces

In Greek mythology the Muses are the daughters of Memory. What are we to make of this lineage? Memory gives birth to the arts. André Haynal (2003) saw it this way: "The Arts were born—as the offspring or elaboration of memory, of the memory of our losses, of what we lack, a creation stemming from something we have introjected, and perhaps at the same time, a transformation of that introject" (p. 34). Haynal linked memory and the arts to our universal concern about death and to the many losses we endure throughout our life. Art is our attempt to restore what we have lost. Through the creative process, what is absent is symbolized and thus survives, is restored, and attains immortality.

The relationship between mourning and the arts has been explored by a number of psychoanalysts (Aberbach, 1989; Ogden, 2000a, 2000b; Orfanos, 2006; Ornstein, 2010; Pollock, 1989a, b; among others). George Pollock (1989a) wrote extensively on the creative arts and expressions of mourning, particularly among recognized artists, musicians, poets, and writers. According to him, the successful completion of the mourning process results in a creative outcome that can include a restoration of personal vitality and growth, as well as the actual creation of an artistic work. The creative work may reflect the mourning process in its content or theme, and may represent a memorial to the lost object.

Pollock distinguished between those with talent and others in terms of the quality of the work, but maintained that regardless of talent, the product represents a creative achievement. Pollock acknowledged that in certain instances creativity following a loss may express either incomplete mourning or even attempts to deny the loss, but more often than not, mourning enriches creative endeavors. Even when the creative product is not the end result of the mourning process, or when there is no final creative product, it represents an effort to mourn through the creative process. Under those circumstances, there is an attempt at completing the work of mourning through the process of restitution, reparation, discharge, or sublimation. In these formulations, Pollock was influenced by Klein's theory that the basis of creativity and sublimation is the attempt to restore the loved and lost internal and external objects, which begins in infancy during the depressive position. Klein postulated a reparative drive and as early as 1929 noted that drawing and painting could be used to restore and repair a psychological injury.

Pollock (1989a) understood mourning to be an adaptive response to any significant loss or transition, and saw the work of mourning as the establishment of a new intrapsychic homeostasis in the face of an altered external and psychic reality. Successful mourning according to him is conceptualized as decathexis of energy from lost objects to new ones. He coined the term *mourning-liberation process* to describe this freeing of psychic energy allowing the restoration of psychic equilibrium. An art product that emerges from the mourning process actually maintains the connection to the lost object and gives it life and immortality. Although I don't conceptualize this process as Pollock does, I find his biographical studies helpful in illustrating the ways in which successful mourning can enrich creative endeavors.

Pollock's idea of mourning as a time-limited process and his notion that complete mourning is possible are both open to question. Although he did acknowledge that some losses, such as the loss of a child, can never be integrated and totally accepted by the mother or father, I would add that when it comes to the catastrophic losses of genocide, the possibility of a resolution to mourning is similarly unlikely. As Hagman (1995) has pointed out, the standard theory of mourning based on Freud's original ideas about mourning as an intrapsychic process leads to the notion that an ending to mourning is possible and desirable. When the central task of mourning is decathexis rather than continuity, then it follows that normal mourning leads to a point of resolution. Once we depart from the classical view of the mind as a private, closed system that regulates an inner world of energies and defenses, and move into a more relational perspective on mourning, a continued tie to the lost object can be seen as a desirable outcome.

It seems to me that Pollock is caught between two paradigms—the traditional view of mourning that he was trained in, and the changes in perspective brought about by the relational model that has influenced our thinking in recent years. When he wrote about mourning as a biologically based process that unfolds in predictable stages, he viewed the process from within a traditional psychoanalytic model; in contrast, when he wrote about the function of mourning as a creative and transformative one, rather than a restorative one (in the sense of restoring psychic equilibrium), he was viewing the process from a different conceptual position.

Contemporary psychoanalysts, particularly those whose theory base is the relational model, recognize the important role of others in mourning (Bassin, 2011; Hagman, 1995; Slochower, 1993, 2011). The traditional emphasis on the need to detach from lost objects has obscured the importance of creating continuity (Gaines, 1997) through the repair of disruption to the self–other relationship. Mourning, as a social and relational process, emphasizes the importance of individual meaning assigned to the loss of a significant other. The relationship to the lost other continues to evolve and change.

It is my contention that through the creation of art it is possible to maintain an attachment to the lost object and preserve meaning and dialogue that has been threatened with rupture. The communicative function of grief also plays a role in art-making; the artist has an opportunity for connecting with others and creating witnesses for his grief and his devotion.

Thomas Ogden's (2000a) formulation of creativity and its role in the act of mourning is compatible with the idea that the mourner has a need to reestablish connection with the lost object and struggles to maintain integrity of self-experience. Ogden believed that mourning is a process that involves the experience of creating something from within ourselves that captures the essence of what the loss means to us. He wrote,

> I suggest that successful mourning centrally involves a demand that we make on ourselves to create something—whether it be a memory, a dream, a story, a poem, a response to a poem—that begins to meet, to be equal to, the full complexity of our relationship to what has been lost and to the experience of loss itself. Paradoxically, in this process, we are enlivened by the experience of loss and death, even when what is given up or is taken from us is an aspect of ourselves. (p. 65)

Ogden used some of the writing of Jorge Luis Borges as an illustration of "mourning art," but he pointed out that the creativity involved in the art of mourning does not necessarily only refer to the work of the talented artist, since it is the experience of making something relating to the loss that is the essence of the mourning process. While Ogden's interest lies primarily in verbal artistic expressions, my own inclination is to take a broader perspective on all the arts in relation to grief and mourning. Memory and dreams come in images and sensations as well as words, and often visual images, dance movements, or sounds of music are just as powerful if not more so in communicating lament and the experience of loss. Sometimes film, which combines and integrates various forms of artistic expression into a story, can be an act of mourning as well as a fitting memorial to what has been lost.

A most poignant example of the use of art as a way to mourn is offered by Marilyn Charles, a psychoanalyst, graphic artist, and poet. Charles, who has lived through personal traumatic losses, has written specifically and eloquently on the subject. In a moving chapter entitled "Remembering, Repeating, and Working Through; Piecing Together the Fragments of Traumatic Memory" (2011), she took up the issue of creativity in relation to trauma and mourning, and illustrated how artistic activities allow unformulated experiences of pain and loss to be given form, thereby providing a means of repair. Charles used her own art work—poems and collages—as examples of how artistic expression can facilitate the working through of traumatic experience.

After her 3-year-old son was killed, Charles turned to poetry as a way to process and work through the momentous loss. She reported that not only was the experience of writing cathartic, but also it was a means for reconnecting with others, a way to create something that would communicate to others the enormity of the overwhelming feelings within her. She explained that she was drawn to the medium of poetry as an expressive vehicle because it provided a bridge between words and experience, allowing the expression in language of non-verbal moments of inspiration and intuition.

Another form of non-verbal expression to which Charles had turned was collage because of its capacity to illustrate the fragmentation and reintegration that is so important to the working through of trauma. Of the collages, she has written,

> The creative act provides a means for articulating unformulated experience, for playing with it, and giving it form. This process itself can be healing, as I found in my poetry, drawings and collages, where the elaboration of affective meanings seemed to smooth over the harsh edges of traumatic experiences. (2011, p. 9)

The most personal of her collages, titled *Mother and Child* (see Figure 4.1), also movingly memorialized the catastrophic loss of her son. In this collage her little son's face is clearly represented in the place where one would expect the mother's face to be, thereby communicating a merging experience of mother and child. This image also captures a precious moment in time when the baby was in the womb and the mother's maternal preoccupation was able to keep the outside world from intruding—a time remembered and cherished.[2]

Even prior to the death of her son, Charles had been no stranger to trauma; her family history was marked by the Holocaust, and its shadows had permeated her childhood. She was acutely aware of the intergenerational transmission of trauma passed down through the generations as unspoken memories. Since early on, she found herself interested in the transformation of traumatic memory. Trauma, she

Figure 4.1 Marilyn Charles, *Mother and Child* (2007). Collage: ink and paper 11 × 14 inches. Copyright, 2007. Courtesy of the artist.

wrote, is elusive and by its nature fragmented; traumatic moments are stored not only as images, but also in the body and speak their truths in patterned forms. "Nonverbal meanings that may not be consciously known can be worked through and communicated implicitly in creative products" (2011, p. 7).

The concrete product—a poem, a collage, or a photograph—becomes a memorial to what was lost. In some cases, memorials exist on a grand scale. The work of Shimon Attie, a young American photographer, exemplifies such a memorial to the Nazi Holocaust. Attie (1994), who does not think of himself as a "Holocaust artist," described his experience of walking through the streets of East Berlin, wondering,

> Where are all the missing people? What has become of the Jewish culture and community which had once been at home here? *The Writing on the Wall* grew out of my response to the discrepancy between what I felt and what I did not see. I wanted to give this invisible past a voice, to bring it to light, if only for some brief moments. (p. 9)

Making slides of historical photographs of Berlin's Jewish quarter during the 1920s and 1930s, Attie superimposed these images of pre-war Jewish life in Berlin onto the same neighborhood buildings in present-day Berlin—thus rebuilding the ruined world of Jewish Berlin on the site of its ruin. Despite the fact that it was only possible in about 25% of the installations to project the image onto its original site, through his photography he was able to achieve a powerful effect, calling attention to the striking presence of absence (Hirsch, 1996).

Jeanne Wolff Bernstein (2000) introduced the work of Attie to a psychoanalytic audience through her fine paper about how the exhibition titled *The Writing on the Wall* created a memorial place for the loss of an entire culture in Germany. Through his photography, Attie created a memorial place in which the past is remembered and actively mourned by him and his viewers. Bernstein defined a memorial place as a potential space created in which the viewer, reader, or listener has an opportunity to create his own response. The spectator is drawn into this potential space or intermediate field where he can exist between the two worlds of past and present, enter into it with his own imagination, and draw his own connections between the buried past and the present. In the case of the photographs, the memorializing place is a cocreation of the photographer and viewer. This series of live projections functions as testimony and memorial. The memorial activity is a powerful linking mechanism that both recasts the past as it is remembered and reshapes the present. The work evokes a psychological space to allow recognition of loss in the present and remembrance.

Bernstein (2000) contrasted this artwork with a purely documentary work in which a past can be portrayed in detail but without engaging the spectator in an enlivening way. Unlike other Holocaust monuments and memorials that commemorate past atrocities, this work of art allows a glimpse into how the Jews lived, rather than how they died. Bernstein reminded us that mourning involves remembering not just the death but also the life of the one who is mourned:

> Monuments commemorating the Jews' barbaric deaths tend to trivialize their prewar quotidian existences by emphasizing their destruction

rather than their lives. In glossing over the Jews' prewar individual lives and merely paying tribute to their deaths, Holocaust monuments eventually encourage what they were designed to combat—that is, forgetting. (p. 352)

Trauma and Creativity: A Healing Alliance

The existence of a relationship between the experience of adversity and creativity has been assumed for many years based on the observation that creative individuals seem to be able to channel their negative experiences as sources of inspiration. It has been theorized that increased creativity is a component of post-traumatic growth—the positive psychological changes that often take place following traumatic circumstances (Tedeschi & Calhoun, 2004). Anecdotal reports suggest that the experience of adversity is a recurrent theme in the lives of highly creative individuals, implying an intimate connection between adversity and creative thinking. Currently, empirical studies are providing preliminary scientific support for the existence of a link between adversity (in its various forms of life events, physical illness, and psychological disorders) and subsequent creativity. In an intriguing and elegant study, Forgeard (2013) enlisted 373 research participants and tested whether scores on a measure of post-traumatic growth related to scores on self-reported measures of creativity in the aftermath of adverse life circumstances. Her results confirmed her hypothesis that a link exists between self-reported distress and creativity outcomes. Her conclusion was that given that a majority of human beings experience adverse events at some point in their life, they may be able to use their experiences to heal, grow, and fulfill their creative potential (p. 257). It is important to highlight that she stated that these results do not imply that suffering is necessary for creativity.

These scientific findings are in alignment with the psychoanalytic notion that the artist can transform psychic pain into works of art and thereby achieve some mastery over the effect of trauma (Bollas, 2011). Psychoanalysts interested in the interface of trauma and creativity, have written about well-known artists like Egon Schiele (Knafo, 1991a & 1991b), Frida Kahlo (Bose, 2005; Knafo, 1993), Francis Bacon (Bose, 2005), and Francisco Goya (Wolfenstein, 1966), among others. There are countless excellent examples of artists who have used their craft in order to work through their personal traumatic experience, and it is only the limits of time and space that necessitate choosing a few as illustrations here.

The art work of Frida Kahlo provides an excellent example of the use of artistic creativity to deal with tragic experiences. Faced with a series of traumatic events in childhood and adolescence—polio at the age of 6, a severe accident at the age of 18 with resulting chronic and escalating pain, countless surgical procedures with eventual amputation of her leg—Kahlo turned to painting as a means of regaining some sense of wholeness and control. She began shortly after her accident and seemed preoccupied with replicating her own image—a mask-like countenance with a tortured, damaged body expressing unbearable pain.

Danielle Knafo, a psychologist/psychoanalyst, has written about Kahlo's pro-lific self-portraits, understanding them as an expression of a narcissistic distur-bance. She saw these works of art functioning as mirroring objects, aiding in self-consolidation and identity maintenance (Knafo, 1991b, 1993). Focusing on narcissistic issues and how they were dealt with creatively, Knafo pointed out that similar to the search for self that takes place in the mirroring reciprocity between mother and infant, the self-portrait is a means by which the artist transforms the canvas into a mirror, reflecting both the need and its fulfillment of self-definition.

In addition to the physical traumas that Kahlo endured, Knafo points out that Khalo's relationship with her mother was a failing and ambivalent one. Preoccu-pied with her own needs, Khalo's mother was unavailable and rejecting. Through her self-portraits, Kahlo strove to obtain what was missing from her mother's eyes, the validation of self that she needed, thereby replacing the mother and becoming her own mirror. Another way in which Kahlo replaced the mother through her art-work was by giving birth to herself through the creation of a "double" that serves several functions, such as denying the idea of death, protecting against the loss of self, alleviating loneliness and expressing different aspects of self in an attempt to unify opposite images.

Joerg Bose (2005), another psychoanalyst interested in the work of Kahlo, wrote about the way that Khalo's art helped her to come to terms with devastating traumatic experiences. His theoretical understanding is very similar to my own, which will be formulated and elaborated in the next section. Bose saw the creative product both as a witnessing presence and as a kind of messenger between disso-ciated self-states and consciousness that can be used by the artist for expressive as well as protective purposes.

In his formulation, Bose used a different terminology from Knafo, but in many ways the conceptual understanding is similar. Although he didn't describe the issues in terms of underlying narcissistic difficulties, he did believe that the art-work served self-supporting and self-constitutive functions. Witnessing (Bose) and mirroring (Knafo) seem to address a similar phenomenon—the art becomes an external presence, like an imaginary companion. Personally, I prefer the term *witnessing* since it has more of an intersubjective feel than *mirroring*, which has traditionally been associated with a one-person model—that is, a therapist who supposedly keeps his/her own subjectivity out of the clinical encounter function-ing as a self-object for the patient.

In painting, the image in its concreteness conveys the sudden impact of trauma and has a testimonial quality for the viewer—who, I would add, also becomes a witness to trauma. It is striking to note that Kahlo's family did not want to acknowl-edge her suffering and that she manages to create witnesses for herself on a world-wide scale. Kahlo was intent on communicating her pain and presented the viewer with shocking, horrifying scenes that others might be tempted to dissociate.

In the same article, Bose (2005) also considered the work of Francis Bacon, another visual artist whose work represents a less direct way of dealing with trau-matic experience than Kahlo's forthright acknowledgment of her suffering. In the

92

case of Bacon, the creative product is used for protective purposes—he did not acknowledge that the brutal abuse he experienced as a child had any relationship to the monstrous and horrifying images that he portrayed on canvas. He denied that his intent was to express personal suffering or terror, yet it is evident from his artwork that he was preoccupied with destructiveness and death. Bose concluded that "artistic work can serve the cause of defense as much as the cause of expression" (p. 68). Although Bose did not conceptualize Bacon's reaction to his art as one of dissociated affect, it seems to me that this is what his denial of the affective impact of his work indicates. He visually and symbolically presented the terrors he had endured for the viewer to see, but his feelings were disconnected so that he could not imagine that the viewer might feel assaulted and horrified. Nevertheless, we assume that the very process of creating the images and sharing them with others allowed him to represent and give voice to the brutality he experienced in childhood when he was a passive victim. Without feeling the connection himself, or taking responsibility for what he evoked, he could elicit the horror in the viewer of his art, thereby making the viewer a witness.

"The process of representation is crucial for contending with potentially overwhelming and unbearable experiences of trauma," said Bose (2005, p. 67). He was interested in the question of the synthesizing capacity of the individual who is a victim of trauma. He wrote, "The act itself of finding and of making expressive forms at the time of traumatic experience is a remarkable assertion of the human capability to synthesize and to counteract fragmenting dissociative processes" (p. 51). This quote is in direct contradiction with another statement that he made several pages later: "severe traumatic experience abolishes one's self-synthesizing, creative and integrative abilities" (p. 67). In an apparent effort to resolve the contradiction, Bose ended up saying, "And yet sometimes a powerful talent may allow for the survival of the ability in times of disastrous experience to synthesize a rearranged personal gestalt that can be experienced as me or myself" (p.68). The problem with the widespread assumption (Laub & Auerhahn, 1989, and others) that catastrophic trauma destroys the ability to represent, symbolize, and integrate experience is that it does not hold up to scrutiny, particularly when we note that symbol formation is the very essence of artistic creativity (Segal, 1991) and that it is through artistic expression that trauma can be symbolically represented. If one abandons the assumption that trauma destroys the ability to symbolize, then one does not have to conjure up a "powerful talent" to explain creative endeavors as a means toward healing, for it is this very capacity to create that is most often enlisted at times of trauma or in its aftermath in order to cope with devastating circumstances.[3]

The Therapeutic Action of Art

In treatment, the patient uses both verbal and non-verbal modes of communication, but according to Bucci (2001) emotional experiences are best expressed through non-verbal channels: "One cannot directly verbalize the subsymbolic components of the affective core; their nature like the art of the sculptor or dancer is such that they cannot be expressed directly in words. To describe a feeling in verbal form, one describes an image or tells a story" (p. 51). Writing from the perspective of multiple code theory, Bucci (2002) stated that the goal of psychological treatment is integration of dissociated schemas, which requires activation of subsymbolic representations, in relation to symbolic representations of present and past experience. Change, she wrote, ultimately requires connection to bodily experience that has been dissociated and redirection of such experience. She made the important point, for our thesis, that verbal interventions may actually not be the optimal therapeutic vehicle for change to take place:

> Music, dance, and art therapies are all designed to access the subsymbolic system directly; on a different level, so is the currently popular eye-movement therapy, and on still another level, so is yoga and meditation. If we take seriously the endogenous organization of the subsymbolic and symbolic nonverbal systems, we need to examine the degree to which the multiple nonverbal modes of communication themselves may be sufficient to bring about therapeutic change. (2002, p. 789)

Bucci characterized the non-verbal mode of functioning as aesthetic and creative.

When Bucci wrote about the therapeutic process in this context, she was not referring to working with traumatized individuals specifically. We know that in the case of trauma, the difficulty in finding the words to describe one's experience presents an even greater challenge. Traumatic memories generally lack verbal narrative and context; they are encoded in the form of vivid sensations and images, often in fragmented form. Wordless registration becomes embodied and enacted, finding expression through movement and action. In this context, art can be conceptualized as the symbolic representation of traumatic experience.

Although trauma may elude linguistic, symbolic forms of articulation and meaning making (Caruth, 1996), through creative action the survivor strives to articulate what has been endured, to organize it, and to make some sense of it. Trauma breaks up the continuity of life, leaving the self in a state of fragmentation and dissociation; making art is an attempt to restore continuity and facilitate integration of dissociated self-states and splits in experience by reuniting affect, cognition, and perception torn asunder by traumatic experience.

Greenberg and van der Kolk (1987) reported on a case in which art was used therapeutically for the retrieval and integration of traumatic memories. They referred to this treatment as the "painting cure." Their premise was that since traumatic experiences are encoded in sensorimotor or iconic form, they cannot be readily translated into language. The traumatized person is overcome by troubling emotions, dreadful images, and bodily sensations that are dissociated from all semantic linguistic and verbal representation; therefore such images or memories may only be retrievable by non-verbal means. They made a parallel between the altered state of dreaming, with its pictorial, emotional, and alogical quality, and the capacity of art to facilitate the generation of eidetic images in order to retrieve and integrate traumatic memories.

Greenberg and van der Kolk provided an interesting case example with drawings to illustrate how various memories are pictorially represented and then later verbally explored with the patient. Although the authors did not mention the significance of the witnessing function for successful treatment, I believe it is an essential component of the treatment that they describe. Memories of trauma are often unmentalized and concrete, and cannot be contextualized in the present; it is witnessing that holds the possibility for affectively charged memories of trauma to emerge (D. B. Stern, 2012). When a patient brings in her artwork to her therapist, she creates the possibility of being deeply known and recognized. Additionally, in the process of making art, she often comes to recognize aspects of herself that may not have been formulated prior to the drawing exercise. For instance, in the case presented by Greenberg and van der Kolk, the authors reported that the therapist suggested to the patient that she visualize her "bad me" and attempt to draw it. Through this suggestion, the therapist is in effect helping one self-state to witness the experience created within another self-state. In response to this suggestion, the patient produced a symbol that graphically expressed her feelings—she drew "The Ogre," a half-woman, half-bug image being attacked by other insects. Her artwork was replete with such symbols and metaphors, which pictorially represented various memories and fantasies that were later explored in the verbal mode. The authors concluded that conceptual verbal insight was made possible by the concrete visual representation of her inner world.

As I noted in the previous chapter, when the artist is immersed in the creative process, she enters an altered state of consciousness in which a sense of relaxed concentration prevails. In the privacy of her studio, working at her own pace, the artist who feels safe enough to surrender to the creative process enters a psychic transitional space that encourages the emergence of traumatic memories, associations, and feelings in manageable form. In that transitional safe space, painful memories and agonizing emotional states can be externalized and transformed into a creative product; previously unarticulated thoughts and feelings are given form; affects are contained. The emotional distance helps the survivor face the raw material that is emerging. As one is involved in creating, one is both participant and observer. In that process, the passive victim of trauma has become the creator of a work of art. She has control over her medium and chooses the way in which she expresses her ideas, feelings, and message. Many of the creative arts, like painting, sculpture, drama, and dance, have physical components and thus provide an opportunity for catharsis and for the release of kinesthetic tensions and body memories.

As discussed in the previous chapter, and highlighted in Greenberg and van der Kolk's case, making art is a two-part process of expression and reflection. In the second phase, which sometimes occurs when the patient brings the artistic product into the analytic session, there is an opportunity to elaborate and reflect on what has emerged during the inspirational phase. At that point the person's relation to the trauma experience can shift as new perspectives open up in the dialogue with the analyst. Through reflection and collaboration, connections can be made, and insights can emerge and be integrated into a coherent co-constructed narrative.

The vitalizing function of art counteracts the deadening effects of trauma, resulting in a sense of vitality and aliveness. Earlier we noted that Ogden (2000a) wrote about the paradoxical effect of being enlivened by the process of creating something out of our confrontation with loss and death. The mourner has a need to create something that expresses the loss and reestablishes a connection with the lost object, and by taking such an action, he is enlivened. With mourning comes the potential for healing.

The artistic product serves various crucial functions in addition to its organizing role: It stands as a witness to the traumatic experience; it can be known by others; it can be admired by them; and it restores self-esteem damaged by the humiliation and shame attending victimization. One of trauma's most devastating effects is on human relationships. The sense of safety in the world is shaken and, as a consequence, disconnection and alienation pervade relationships. Art as a means of communication has the potential to reconnect the trauma survivor to others. It is immensely curative to feel known and recognized when one has felt alone and isolated.

For many years I have noted a curious phenomenon. When I write deeply personal, affect- laden material in solitude, I rarely react emotionally in the process of writing. Yet if I read the same piece of writing out loud in the presence of an audience or even just imagining one, I find myself often reacting with unexpected tears. The crucial variable seems to be the knowledge of being witnessed. This reminds me of Stern's (2012) astute observation that "as we listen to ourselves (in imagination) through the ears of the other, and see ourselves (in imagination) through the eyes of the other, we hear and see ourselves in a way we simply cannot manage in isolation" (p. 60). In the presence of the other, even when imagined, when our sorrow is recognized, we know that we are not alone. Shared memories and experiences have a cathartic effect (Ornstein, 2006a, 2010). Having a witness to our suffering provides us with a holding environment that facilitates a fuller integration of the experience—both affective and cognitive.

Whether painting, journaling, or making music, making art is a repetitive process and as such encourages the working through of significant themes in one's life. Each painting deals with a different aspect, each piece of writing builds on the previous one, and each musical piece has the composer's signature but touches a different chord. Loewald (1973/1980b) distinguished between repetition as a compulsive and passive act, and repetition in the form of action and affect, which he sees as a kind of remembering. In my view, the artist engages in active and re-creative repetition that ultimately can allow something new to emerge.

Undoubtedly, there is much to be gained from enlisting the artistic process in the service of recovery, but in my view, it is artistic expression in conjunction with psychoanalysis that makes for a most effective combination. Self-analysis has its limitations; there are blind spots when one is exploring one's own psyche. The presence of another (in the flesh) as witness to one's journey can be an invaluable companion, particularly when one stumbles across road blocks along the way. To be truly known by a significant other and to enter an ongoing therapeutic relationship where one is accepted, has an opportunity to work through relational conflicts and enactments, and see oneself through the eyes of another is of great value. The analyst's witnessing of the patient's self-inquiry is an essential aspect of the analytic process (Poland, 2000; Reis, 2009; Seiden, 1996; Ullman, 2006).

Clinical Illustration

The working through process, whether it unfolds collaboratively in analysis or outside of the consulting room at a desk or at an easel, can be experienced as creative engagement. As Levenson (2012) points out, under conditions where the patient brings in "her own contributions into play, then working-through assumes all the attributes of a creative process—hard work, persistence, confusion and despair, leavened by flashes of originality and discovery" (p. 3).

I will now illustrate my work with a woman who spontaneously turned to creative writing as a form of adjunctive therapy during and following our analytic work.[4] I will discuss how the combination of writing between sessions, sharing the writing with me, and psychoanalytic psychotherapy enriched and complemented our work. Marnie, a 50-year-old woman, came to see me at the recommendation of her friend who had a brief successful hypnosis experience with me for smoking cessation. In that first session with Marnie, I discovered that six months earlier she had undergone surgery for a benign stomach tumor in which one third of her stomach had been removed. Although the procedure had been deemed successful, her recovery was not going so well. In addition to numerous debilitating symptoms, such as nausea and vomiting, she was having flashbacks and nightmares. She had never considered or sought treatment for these post-traumatic stress disorder (PTSD)-like symptoms, but it soon became clear that she welcomed the opportunity to go beyond hypnotherapy for smoking cessation. In fact, I soon realized that she had known that I am a psychoanalyst and had used the hypnosis referral as a way to check me out.

As part of my assessment for hypnotizability, I learned that Marnie was capable of entering a deep trance state and had a good capacity for dissociation. We would later learn how she had been able to use this capacity, spontaneously, to cope with surgery and its aftermath. On the other hand, I could also see that a certain level of non-compliance—and perhaps fear of losing control—kept her from fully entering the state of trance and using it for her own benefit. She never did stop smoking.

Most people found Marnie to be intimidatingly beautiful, and her beauty had provided a kind of shield, a distance between herself and others. She had married early, and her successful and dominant husband provided safety from the outside world. In many ways he parented her. She had lost her father to cancer many years before when, as a young woman, she was pregnant with her first child. Her father had been the loving nurturing parent and had tried to compensate for her narcissistic mother, who was neglectful and highly critical. Her mother was preoccupied with physical appearances—her own and those of her three daughters. As the most attractive and wealthy of the three, Marnie was her favorite.

Marnie's beauty was her identity in the world but it was also a source of conflict as she recognized the superficiality of it. She had contempt for her mother's values and resentment that she was judged for something so superficial. She was aware of people's gaze and had very mixed feelings about being looked at and admired. Even as she aged, she seemed to maintain her beauty, but when illness struck in her 50th year, the blow was catastrophic. Her body had betrayed her.

In therapy she struggled with the pervasive effects of the surgery on her daily life, and at the same time, she mourned the profound loss of the innocent person she had been before trauma struck. She described her old self as a Pollyanna who did not take things too seriously or delve too deeply into anything. When things would get uncomfortable, she would mentally leave and float away somewhere else in her mind. Despite the fact that she had a relatively successful career in design, her dissociated manner gave people the impression that she was "ditzy" or "flighty," as she put it. But now her illness forced her to be constantly aware of her digestive system. The pretty and perfectly put-together woman was repeatedly vomiting her guts out, with her head in the toilet. An unrecognizable and irreconcilable self had taken over. Her defenses were no longer working,

Our relationship grew deeper with time, but I noted a cautious quality, some reluctance to trust me—not surprising given the kind of mothering she had had. Then, one day, our relationship changed dramatically. About two years into the treatment, I learned that Marnie was writing the story of what had happened to her when the tumor was discovered. I had known that Marnie, who had undiagnosed learning disabilities, had never done well in school and had dropped out of college prematurely, but until that day, I had not known that she was a gifted writer.

I must have lit up when she mentioned her writing, and of course she noticed. When she said that she was amazed at how readily the words flowed and how healing it felt to write her story, I smiled and nodded, "Yes, I know." She picked up on it and said, "Do you really know? How do you know?" I then told her that I had had a similar experience with writing and that I had written a memoir. My memoir had just been published two months prior to this conversation. I had not consciously intended to disclose this information, but under her watchful eye, it had inadvertently slipped out. She became greatly excited, ordered the book online when she got home, had it delivered by Federal Express, and by the next session, five days later, had read it twice.

The memoir opened a door in the treatment. It brought us closer together and deepened our work. Initially, she had experienced me as very different from her and wondered if I could possibly understand her. Now that she learned more about me, she focused on how much we had in common, including a trauma history, and that knowledge was reassuring to her. She felt that she could trust me. My appreciation for her writing encouraged her to write more and to share her writing with me.

The first pieces that she brought in specifically dealt with her trauma story. They involved minute details about what had happened to her: time and place of medical consultations, diagnoses, surgical procedures, and most importantly observations about the feelings she experienced or failed to experience as she revisited the events. She had created a coherent narrative that put the entire experience in chronological order, and I felt as if I had been present during the trauma experience, witnessing everything from her perspective. She probably could have told me her trauma story instead of writing it, but I understood from personal experience that it was just not the same. Marnie was a very private person who found writing this kind of emotionally charged material easier than speaking about it to another. I, too, find that writing comes more easily to me, presumably for different reasons, but similarly I find myself better able to express my complex emotional state in writing than in spoken words.

When Marnie brought her writing into our therapy sessions, the experiential space we shared became alive with energy. Like a dream brought into analysis, Marnie's writing was something we could both look at together and discuss. We co-created a narrative of what had happened to her and how she had been coping with it. Between sessions she held me in mind as she continued to work through and make sense of her reactions to the trauma experience, and as a result of the self-analytic work of autobiographical writing, she brought new associations, memories, and dreams into the sessions. She rewrote and refined her story as memories and feelings returned. She allowed me to be witness in a unique way—both to her creative process and to the intimate details of her reactions to trauma.

Much of Marnie's writing expressed the sense of herself as altered by the trauma experience. In describing her self-experience in the aftermath of surgery she wrote,

> I was no longer the old Marnie. It seemed like the *before-surgery me* and the *after-surgery me*. Once again, through therapy, I learned that those feelings are typical of a person who was traumatized, and that I was experiencing Post Traumatic Stress. I felt totally different from the old me. I felt vulnerable. If this could happen to me, what else could?

Once the trauma story was told and further explored in our sessions, from time to time, Marnie continued to bring in pieces incorporating what she was working on in therapy; her pieces were concise and always relevant to the themes that we were exploring.

Her writing served different functions at different times. Some seemed addressed to me in the hope of my better understanding her. For instance when we talked about her tendency to dissociate and its significance in her life, she wrote a piece on dissociation describing how as a school child when she didn't understand the teacher,

> I simply went somewhere else in my mind . . . Sometimes the thoughts
> were like daydreams, but sometimes periods of time would pass, and I
> didn't know where I went in my mind . . . When I was traumatized by
> my surgery and illness, I disassociated automatically. That is scarier not
> feeling in control and not feeling emotions that I know intellectually that
> anyone with common sense would feel. I would like to walk through that
> stage of my life again, and feel the pain, rather than know that I didn't
> experience it in my mind, only in my body.

Other writing captured a stream of consciousness resembling free association, and still other pieces represented a kind of integration of what she had learned over time about herself and the analytic process. Her writing was spontaneous, she tended not to review or edit, and she was honest and funny—a pleasure to read. Her wry humor was meant to lighten her despair—"I have a scar from my breast-bone to my navel and look as if I had been filleted."

At first, she was processing the trauma that had taken place months earlier, but as our work continued she was faced with additional medical crises. Yearly follow-up medical examinations were difficult because they brought back the trauma memories, but even more troublesome were her continued symptoms, like pain and vomiting, which led to additional procedures to remove scar tissue from the original surgery that was interfering with her digestive functioning. The procedures turned out to be only temporarily successful; the scar tissue was strangling her stomach, and it began to appear that a second surgery might be necessary—a possibility that filled her with terror. Eventually Marnie mustered her courage and underwent a second surgery. She wrote,

> To me, having another surgery was facing my biggest fear. It had been
> so tough the first time. I let my feelings control me for years, avoiding
> surgery and not seeing the facts clearly. But clearly something changed
> internally in me. The biggest difference this time around is that I was pre-
> pared for it, felt in control, and did not fall apart after. One of my biggest
> fears is that I would be traumatized again from the experience. I wasn't,
> I got through it sanely.

Over the next few years, Marnie continued to put her thoughts and feelings on paper and proudly brought these pieces into the treatment; each felt to me like a gift. Even after our work together ended, she continued to send me material that she wrote from time to time as new challenges emerged and as she gained new insights into herself. As her dearest friend was struggling with the final stages of cancer, Marnie wrote a series of pieces, among them "Suspended in Time," anticipating her friend's death:

> Time makes the pain lessen but it does leave a scar. I don't believe in closure . . . There are a lot of feelings after the death of a loved one, but closure is not one of them. I think the best one can hope for is acceptance, sadness, tinged with a little bit of anger now and then.

Immediately following her friend's death, she wrote "Life Again" acknowledging the loss and the void, but reaffirming her own commitment to living life fully and meaningfully. She determined to explore another talent that had been dormant for many years as she returned to art classes and studied drawing and painting.

Writing served many functions for Marnie: It was a way to make sense of what she experienced and to solidify her understanding of herself, and a way to communicate with me. It provided her with a safe outlet for her rage at what she had suffered and her bitter resentment about having to be constantly vigilant about her body state, and it allowed her to mourn for the self she had lost. Sometimes it helped her self-regulate intolerable feeling states, and finally it was an important source of self-esteem. Feeling recognized and appreciated for what was in her mind was a wonderful experience for someone who in the past had felt primarily valued for her appearance. Integrating analytic therapy with expressive autobiographical writing is not my typical way of working. In this case, Marnie led the way and I followed; we both recognized the potential for greater depth that this combination could offer. When we began working together, she had some dim awareness of a creative self longing for expression. Finding someone who could hear her muted voices and reflect them back to her allowed her to integrate the different aspects of herself into a meaningful narrative. As these multiple voices found expression in her writing, she gained confidence and felt more complete. It was my privilege to be Marnie's Muse during a time of crisis in her life.

Notes

1. For a detailed account of the role of witness in early development, see Donnel Stern's book *Partners in Thought: Working With Unformulated Experience, Dissociation and Enactment* (Routledge, 2010).
2. M. Charles, personal communication, July 16, 2013.
3. This idea will be further elaborated in chapter 5.
4. Different aspects of my treatment with this patient are discussed in chapter 8, where she is identified as Mrs. E.

5

ART BORN OF GENOCIDE

Few people seem to be aware that the often quoted statement by Theodor Adorno, "To write poetry after Auschwitz is barbaric," was revised by him in a later essay to read,

> I have no wish to soften the saying that to write lyric poetry after Auschwitz is barbaric . . . Yet this suffering, what Hegel called consciousness of adversity, also demands the continued existence of art while it prohibits it; it is now virtually in art alone that suffering can still find its own voice, consolation, without immediately being betrayed by it. (1962/1982, p. 313)

In this last statement, Adorno called our attention to the dialectic—the impossibility and, at the same time, the necessity of representing traumatic experience. It is this theme that we often encounter when we examine the art from the ashes of genocide. Each work of art is a window into the soul of the survivor and reflects this struggle to express what feels both impossible and imperative to communicate. The need to communicate, which is another version of the need for witness, requires that the witnessing other be open to surprise, free of preconceptions and misconceptions about the survivor experience. It is my contention here that this is often not the case.

With the evolution of the relational perspective in psychoanalysis, we have come to increasingly value the uniqueness of the self and self–other configurations, but when it comes to the trauma of genocide, this principle is often abandoned. In this chapter, I will examine some of the theoretical formulations put forth by psychoanalysts who are considered experts on Holocaust trauma and who have been widely quoted in the literature. It has generally been my experience that such formulations about survivors, which are based on highly abstract theoretical ideas, tend to gloss over vast individual differences in the capacity of human beings to cope with traumatic circumstances. The one-sided view of survivors as irreparably damaged has been perpetuated by theories that seem to have totalized the psychoanalytic field of trauma studies.

My intention here is to expose the basic assumptions underlying these unwarranted hypotheses that have been presented as facts. Several vignettes of actual survivors of genocide will illustrate the complexity and diversity of potential responses to massive psychic trauma. Each of these individuals has demonstrated the ability to effectively cope with traumatic events through artistic expression. Their life and art is a testament to a creative life force that refuses to be extinguished by adversity.

Dichotomous Thinking and Sweeping Generalizations

It has been said, and it would seem to be true, that survivors of massacres such as the Holocaust and the atomic explosion of Hiroshima inevitably become so disturbed that in their mental states they are like people from another planet.
—Psychoanalysts Leon and Rebecca Grinberg (1989, p. 155)

When it comes to theories about the impact of catastrophic trauma on the survivor, we note a number of widespread assumptions that need to be addressed because, in my opinion, they lead to stereotypic notions and ultimately do a disservice to survivors of genocide. Those who have worked with survivors and studied our testimonies maintain that the major consequence of Holocaust trauma is the destruction of empathy, which leaves the individual unable to establish a link between self and other (Auerhahn, Laub, & Peskin, 1993; Laub & Auerhahn, 1989). According to Laub and his associates, the massive failure of the environment to mediate needs resulted in erasure of the primary empathic bond and the destruction of the internal representation of the relationship between self and other. They presented this theoretical hypothesis as an indisputable fact, and their beliefs have been widely quoted in the trauma literature.

I take issue with the categorical nature of some of their theoretical formulations and assertions, which do not take into account the complexity and diversity of individual responses to trauma, which, in my experience, are highly variable. I strongly disagree with the idea expressed by Laub and Auerhahn (1989) that there is "a generic" Holocaust survivor experience:

We do however, postulate a *generic* [emphasis added] survivor experience, common to all those who were directly affected by the Nazi persecution, whether in hiding, ghettos, labor camps, or extermination camps. The essence of Holocaust trauma is the breakdown of the communicative dyad in the internal representational world of the victim . . . With the trauma-induced loss of the empathic communicative dyad, both self and object are thus subject to annihilation. (p. 380)

Laub and Auerhahn went further to postulate that, in the wake of massive psychic trauma, there is a shutdown of processes of association, symbolization, integration, and narrative formation due to the annihilation of an internalized good object. This loss means a cessation of inner dialogue and an inevitable suspension of reflection and self-reflection. These presumed effects of massive trauma have been widely and unquestionably cited in the literature, even by those who don't accept the concept of the death instinct—a construct that is at the heart of Laub's highly abstract theoretical formulations. According to Laub and his associates, the concept of the death instinct is indispensable to the understanding and treatment of trauma (Laub, 2005; Laub & Lee, 2003). In a 2005 paper, Laub wrote,

> I contend that it is the traumatic loss of the (internal) good object and the libidinal ties to it that release the hitherto libidinally neutralized forces of the death instinct and intensifies these clinical manifestations of its derivatives, in the aftermath of massive trauma. (p. 316)

The notion that "death instinct derivatives are unleashed once the binding libidinal forces of object cathexis are abolished" (p. 307) is neither part of my vocabulary, nor my conceptual framework, but more importantly, these theoretical constructions do not resonate with my understanding of survivors. I agree that empathic failure is certainly part of the trauma experience, but to say categorically that the primary empathic bond is erased and the internal representation of the relationship between self and other is destroyed seems to me a sweeping generalization that contradicts the many reports of survivors that it was their relationships with significant others—whether internalized or in real life—that kept them alive through their ordeal. Knowing that there was a loved one waiting for them somewhere kept many survivors going, despite their wish to end their suffering.

It is noteworthy that when Laub and Auerhahn (1989) observed some higher level functioning among Holocaust survivors, they were surprised by it. "The character structures of many survivors show a *surprising* [emphasis added] mosaic of areas of high level psychological functioning coexisting with the potential for severe regression" (p. 391). I personally do not find it surprising that areas of high-level functioning coexist with moments of confusion or dissociation in the lives of most survivors. It is only surprising to the theoretician when the survivor is exclusively viewed through a pathological lens.

I acknowledge that it is possible that at the time of the traumatic event there might be a temporary disruption in the ability to reflect on or to integrate one's experience, but the notion that, in the aftermath of trauma, there is unequivocally, a shut-down of cognitive processes such as self-reflection, symbolization, and narrative formation does not make sense to me. In fact, I think that it is those very functions that allowed many survivors to hold on to their sanity and to begin the long road toward recovery in the aftermath of the Holocaust. The creative self that emerges in desperate circumstances to help the individual survive, as well as to cope in the wake of trauma, is a testament to the presence of the capacity for such cognitive functions as representation, symbolization, and reflection. We have much evidence of the fact that creative self-expression went on even under the worst of circumstances in some of the concentration camps—places like Theresienstadt and even Auschwitz. Also, the plethora of creative production in the wake of the Holocaust attests to the survival of self-reflection, the ability to represent traumatic experience, and the capacity to create a coherent narrative, as will be illustrated in this chapter.

Most of the survivors I have known personally, or whose work I have read, certainly do not fit the description of the victim who has suffered severe and lasting impairment in cognitive functions. Ironically, some of the theoreticians who maintain and perpetuate these ideas are themselves survivors whose great intellectual achievements belie their own theories. It has been difficult for me to reconcile the great respect that I have for Laub's important and invaluable contributions in the area of Holocaust testimony with some of his dogmatic theories about survivors. The contradiction may have to do with a theoretical framework that limits his perspective; he attempts to fit every survivor into his procrustean bed of theory. In my view, the survivor is both damaged and resilient, at different times, in different ways, and in different situations. The traumatic state in which thinking is impaired and there is a break between self and other is but one of the multiple states in which we survivors live in the aftermath of trauma. There are times and circumstances that trigger a state of mind that can be characterized as despairing and hopeless—when there is a felt loss of empathic connection, a sense of abandonment, and the dread of retraumatization. But there are other times as well, times when the zest for living prevails. We are complex individuals who are not affected in the same way by our diverse experiences. What we have in common is that we all have scars from wounds that are forever in the process of healing. These scars, which may fade with time and sometimes may be invisible to others, are permanent reminders of what we have lived through, but they don't necessarily prevent us from living productive, meaningful lives.

Of course there have been cases where the experience of trauma results in irreparable damage, but those cases are extreme. An example we're familiar with from the concentration camps was the *muselmann*—the living dead who had lost all hope, who was apathetic and totally unresponsive to his surroundings. To say that the muselmann had lost the capacity to think productively, to symbolize, or to self-reflect would probably be accurate. But how can one possibly describe the likes of Elie Wiesel, Charlotte Delbo, Viktor Frankl, Primo Levi, or Anna Ornstein, among others, all concentration camp inmates, as having lost their self-reflective capacity or their ability to narrate and symbolize? The idea that the internal other is destroyed in situations of terror makes it difficult to reconcile the fact that so many survivors, like my father, found meaning and purpose in their determination to survive in order to tell the world about the atrocities they had witnessed. The decision to bear witness and the abundance of autobiographical writing in the aftermath of trauma imply the existence of an internalized, receptive other in the form of a reader who wants to know the story (Richman, 2006b).

It is of note that my father chose the word *Why* as the title for his memoir. To me, it reflects his struggle to make sense of the incomprehensible tragedy of the Holocaust and suggests that his capacity for reflection and self-reflection was intact. Writing, which he did in hiding, after his escape, provided the antidote to the poison of trauma; it kept him sane; it stimulated his associations and his memory as he struggled to create a coherent narrative.

Those looking through the lens of pathology will see disturbance, while those more inclined to view behavior in the context of adaptation will see resilience. It is unfortunate that the prevailing view in the field of trauma psychology is weighted toward psychopathology rather than a more balanced understanding of the human capacity to cope with tragedy. In my view, those writing about massive psychic trauma, including Auerhahn, Laub, and Peskin (1993); Boulanger (2007); Gerson (2009); Krystal (1988); Laub and Auerhahn (1989, 1993); Laub and Podell (1995); and Niederland (1968), among others, unwittingly minimize the capacity for self-healing. A few dissenting voices have been heard, such as Ornstein (1985, 2010); Parens (2004); Tedeschi, Park, and Calhoun (1998); and Whiteman (1993), but they sometimes go to the other extreme and overemphasize the capacity for resilience. It may be that these few voices highlight what is usually minimized in an attempt to redress the wrongs of those who have pathologized survivors. The problem is that both extremes are instances of dichotomous thinking, ignoring the complexity and diversity of emotional reactions in general and to trauma specifically. For me, the concept of shifting multiple states of mind better describes the complicated and nuanced behavior and affects that characterize human beings in distress.

Trauma and Transcendence

From the memoirs of survivors who have lived through the most unimaginable horrors, we are able to see how many were able to cope effectively with the worst conditions of camp life. For example, an excerpt from Frankl's (1946/1984) memoir, *Man's Search for Meaning*, illustrates the way in which he was able to use his imaginative and dissociative capacities in the concentration camp to cope with the desperate situation that he found himself in:

> I forced my thoughts to turn to another subject. Suddenly I saw myself standing on the platform of a well-lit, warm and pleasant lecture room. In front of me sat an attentive audience on comfortable upholstered seats. I was giving a lecture on the psychology of the concentration camp! All that oppressed me at that moment became objective, seen and described from the remote viewpoint of science. By this method I succeeded somehow in rising above the situation, above the sufferings of the moment, and I observed them as if they were already of the past. (p. 95)

Through fantasy, Frankl created imaginary witnesses who would know what he was going through. In his daydream he was making an important contribution to the field of psychology, and he was bringing himself back to a position of power.

A similar use of imaginative, dissociative capacity can be found in Anna Ornstein's autobiographical narrative (2004). She described how as a 17-year-old, when standing on the interminable lines in Auschwitz, she and her fellow inmates would try to recover lines of a poem or piece together the plot of a novel. These mental games took her away from her awful situation and brought her into a world of fantasy that made her situation more bearable. She created an elaborate fantasy about a small house that she passed every day on the march out of the camp on a work detail. As she returned from hours of labor, exhausted and hungry, in shoes that didn't fit because they had belonged to someone else, she found a way with her creative mind to transport herself to another world. In a trance-like state, she focused on the small, lace-curtained window of the house and in her mind's eye she imagined the most intricate details of a room behind the window. She furnished the room with glowing lamps, books piled high on a night table next to an imaginary bed with clean sheets smelling of soap; she even imagined the drawers of a dresser filled with clean underwear, warm sweaters, and wool socks. Every day she looked forward to the fantasy, which she savored and used to make her life a little easier to bear.[1]

I will now give several illustrations of survivors of genocide who have used their imaginative capacities and their artistic talents in the service of working through their tragedy. These cases highlight the questionable status of the frequently held assumption that catastrophic trauma destroys the capacity for creative synthesis and integration.

Anna Ornstein

The life of Anna Ornstein, an immensely creative individual, challenges those proponents of the view that catastrophic trauma inevitably destroys various cognitive functions and results in disengagement from life. As a young woman who survived Auschwitz, Ornstein returned with the fullness of her love of life undamaged, and her dreams and ambitions intact, according to her husband Paul Ornstein, who wrote the preface to her memoir (Ornstein, 2004). With great energy, she concentrated on rebuilding her life and planning for the future, marrying her childhood sweetheart, becoming a parent, completing her interrupted schooling, studying medicine, becoming a physician, a psychiatrist, and a psychoanalyst. She and her husband, Paul, also a survivor and psychiatrist, eventually became the leading figures in the self psychology movement developed by Heinz Kohut.

With good reason, Ornstein (2010) took issue with the view that survivors are irreparably damaged by their trauma experience. Her views on recovery and the establishment of psychic continuity differed radically from most psychoanalysts who have written extensively about survivors of the Holocaust. She believed that the nature of early attachments (secure rather than disorganized or avoidant), the capacity to regulate affect, which is acquired early in life, and the internalized values and ideals of the survivor can all serve the individual to reestablish psychic continuity in the aftermath of devastating experiences.

With a special interest in creativity and its healing potential, Ornstein (2006a) wrote about artistic transformation of individual suffering and the transformation of traumatic memories into works of art. She maintained that art can serve a vitalizing self-object function for the survivor, as well as for those who are the consumers of the artwork. She postulated a complex relationship between the work of art and its audience, a shared experiential space between the subjective reality of the viewer/reader/listener and the artist.

Within the self psychology theoretical perspective, Ornstein understood artistic creativity as an attempt to ward off or repair fragmentation and to facilitate the reintegration of thought, emotion, and perceptions that have been torn asunder by trauma. She described how this happens by referring to Rotenberg's (1988) formulation: "Unarticulated feelings and ideas are externalized and in the process of their articulation (whether in words, or visually in form and color, or in music) the creative work itself is supposed to validate the artist's not fully conscious intentions" (p. 387).

Examining the art created in concentration camps and ghettos, Ornstein concluded that the inmates who engaged in artistic activities were more likely to emotionally survive the ordeal and to eventually recover. Art under those circumstances served numerous crucial functions, such as providing evidence for what was going on, functioning as a form of resistance against the effects of humiliation, creating mental escape routes for the individual, serving as memorials for the dead, and preserving the memory of the Holocaust.

Ornstein noted that in the aftermath of the Holocaust there has been a plethora of creative works by survivors, particularly in memoir form. Survivors of trauma have a deep need to articulate what has been experienced as unspeakable and to overcome the sense of isolation. That, along with a drive for catharsis and the desire to communicate with a real or imagined audience, has been a motivator for those with or without literary gifts to write about their life experiences. Although she recognized that the benefits of creative activities are not limited to those who have great talent, she did point out that the work of those who are gifted can serve as a mirror, able to reflect and resonate with feelings and experiences that most survivors are not able to adequately articulate.

According to Ornstein, art and literature are one of the most successful methods by which memories are preserved and transmitted to future generations, and it is with this in mind that she wrote a memoir about her experiences during the war. In 2004, she published an account of her survival, titled *My Mother's Eyes*. It is a powerful and moving collection of stories based on her memories of events that took place in 1944, when as a young girl of 17 she was imprisoned in Auschwitz along with her mother.

In writing her memoir, Ornstein lived out what she wrote about, namely, the creation of memorial art that serves memory and facilitates mourning. She added her own perspective to the literature on the relationship between mourning and creativity, a perspective informed by self psychology as well as by her personal experience of catastrophic loss. Memorial art and literature, according to her, provide opportunities for belated mourning by creating "memorial spaces" for the artist as well as for the consumer of art (Ornstein, 2013). In this memorial space, grief

108

that has been dormant can be awakened but also contained. She maintained that creative activities serve mourning functions by imposing a structure on the art-ist's chaotic experience, much as well-articulated interpretations impose structure in analysis on a patient's not fully conscious experiences. Feeling understood, she writes, enhances self-cohesion, which in turn facilitates the undoing of disavowal and permits painful affects to enter consciousness.

Marian Kołodziej

A most fascinating instance of delayed mourning in the wake of catastrophic trauma is to be found in the life and art of Holocaust survivor Marian Kołodziej.[2] Kołodziej was a Polish Catholic who was deported to Auschwitz at 17 years of age, when he was caught working for the Polish resistance. He arrived there in the first transport and managed to stay alive until the end of the war. He was liberated by the Americans from the Mauthausen concentration camp, where he had been taken during the Nazi death march from Auschwitz. He then returned to Poland, where he had a brilliant career as a set and costume designer in theater and film.

Kołodziej never spoke about his concentration camp experience until 1993, at the age of 72, when, after a stroke resulted in paralysis of his hands and limbs, he began to draw as a form of rehabilitation. In his words,

> For almost fifty years I did not speak about it but nevertheless throughout the whole time Auschwitz was present in everything I did. I do not know if I would have ever gone back to Auschwitz if it hadn't been for my stroke. My drawings stem from my illness. During my rehabilitation I asked to be given a pencil and I started to draw. Drawing became a battle for life; I wanted to get away from the illness; there was no great plan, just an attempt to save myself . . . Afterwards a sense of duty came into play. It was a chance to do what I promised my friends in the camp; my friends who died and who . . . obliged me to tell people what happened there. (*The Labirinths. Passing 2*, p. 15)[3]

In his early seventies, after this new encounter with death, Kołodziej finally decided to face his demons head on and give testimony through his art. Appar-ently the stroke that had brought him near death also enabled him to reach into the depths of his memory. As we will see in chapter 10, in some cases, neurologi-cal trauma may actually enhance one's ability to express oneself artistically. Cre-ativity involves the removal of inhibition, and in the case of a brain injury like a stroke, the result can be disinhibition and enhancement of specific functions. After a brain injury, many artists have shown progressive interest in fine details, often recalling images from earlier years, and have become intensely preoccupied with their art (Kandel, 2012). In Kołodziej's case, a combination of the neurological trauma in his current life and the psychological trauma of his young adulthood resulted in an outpouring of amazing works of art. In a state of frenzy, Kołodziej was driven to record his memories in detailed pen-and-ink drawings done in a realistic style filled with the symbolism of death and destruction.[4] Some have likened his work to the nightmarish details and fantastic imagery of Hieronymus Bosch's drawings. Along with throngs of ghostly figures with black holes for eyes and mouths, Kołodziej depicts hundreds of skeletal bodies, with distinct features that capture the faces of friends and tormentors alike, and that function as documents and memorials. Among them his drawings are numerous self-portraits in which his concentration camp identity—number *432*—appears prominently displayed on his forehead or on other parts of his body. In some of his works, one can see a rendition of his current self carrying his former emaciated self on his shoulders; other times the young inmate Marian guides the hand of the old survivor Marian in drawing his memories (see Figure 5.1). In one piece the two faces are in close proximity, the camp image presented as a mask in contrast to the real face of the aging artist; Kołodziej refers to this as a "double self-portrait" (see Figure 5.2). Through this technique, Kołodziej conveys how life in the camp meant pretending and hiding, and now "In the picture, I uncover myself." (Kołodziej, 2009, p. 17) he writes. Here we meet the "double"—the two selves in juxtaposition, the current self and the past self, side by side. In this case the need for continuity is served by this technique, a continuity that has been severed by the walling off of the wounded self for so many years.

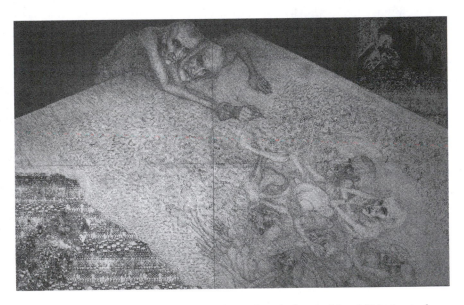

Figure 5.1 Marian Kołodziej, *Young Marian guiding the hand of the old Marian in drawing his memories.* Drawing: pen and ink on paper. Photo: Jason Al Schmidt and Christof Wolf, S.J., as seen in the documentary, *The Labyrinth: The Testimony of Marian Kołodziej.*

Figure 5.2 Marian Kołodziej, *Double Self-Portrait*. Drawing: pen and ink on paper. Photo: Jason Al Schmidt and Christof Wolf, S.J., as seen in the documentary, *The Labyrinth*: *The Testimony of Marian Kołodziej*.

It is interesting to learn that Marian Kołodziej is actually not his birth name. *Kołodziej* is the name of another prisoner who was executed and whose identity Marian took over when he himself was sentenced to die because of his subversive drawings. The person in the camp who had the power to switch his identity, and thereby save his life, turned out to be the very same man whom he had once befriended and given extra soup to. Such was life in the camps; inmates were interchangeable and chance encounters could make the difference between life and death. What is most interesting to me is that he never went back to his birth name; it highlights the splits so characteristic of trauma—the "me" before the trauma no longer exists; it is forever lost.

Kołodziej's rehabilitation began with a few drawings, but once he started, it took on a momentum of its own, and he could not stop drawing until he had completed 300 drawings. Early drawings were done with a pencil taped to his hand on small scraps of paper that he would eventually combine into larger works. The exhibition of his drawings that he calls *Memory Images: Labyrinths* fills the entire basement of a Franciscan convent in Harmeze, near the town of Oświęcim (Auschwitz), Poland, the current site of the exhibit. The installation is designed to look like the interior of a concentration camp bunker; it is underground and dark, and the walls are covered with gigantic, mostly black-and-white murals depicting piles of skeletons with black cavernous eyes and gaping mouths—a chilling sight. Along with the images, there are signs bearing verbal messages from the artist to the viewer. The artwork is magnificent and horrifying at the same time, eliciting a sense of awe at the talent of the artist and at the magnitude of the tragedy that he depicts. Kołodziej did not consider his work "art." In that regard, he stated,

> Art is helpless in the face of what man did to man . . . I believe that I do not do art. Art always goes in the direction of aestheticism, and all of this is quite brutal and quite cruel. That is why I thought about how to present it, especially since there was no photographer during these events and I have the obligation of memory. All of us that were in the camp have such an obligation. You cannot call this art. I thought about how to begin this; and started with my own growing up and rescuing my own humanity. (in Sawicki, 2009)

Kołodziej acknowledged that he held a conversation with the history of art and the artists whose work he admired, particularly with Durer and Memling,[5] taking certain postures from them to express suffering, pain, and despair and to place these themes within 20th-century experiences. He wrote: "I very much want my drawings to be understood today" (2009, p.16). At one point he considered using a more contemporary style with abstract forms of expression, but ultimately he decided that the realistic renditions were more suited to what he was trying to accomplish, namely, "to fulfill the duty I had to photograph memory . . . Out of respect for those who had been with me in the camp, I tried hard to reproduce those remembered faces as faithfully as possible; like a photographer" (2009,

p. 16). Rather than use new means of expressing suffering, he decided it was necessary to speak in a language that people were familiar with: "After all, I wanted to speak to them." At another point he said, "I wanted to make them expressive enough so that the viewer could also feel what was going on inside me." Witnessing in this case can be observed on several levels; he functioned as a witness for those who perished in the camp, but at the same time he expressed his desire to be known and witnessed by those who came to see his work. He was both witness and witnessed simultaneously, and both aspects of witnessing were essential to his healing process.

Even in Auschwitz, apparently there was art. Kołodziej tells us that among the inmates there were actors and theater directors and musicians who managed to meet secretly on a regular basis to recite poetry or give performances "to keep up our hearts" (2009, p. 19). He attributed these precious moments to his ultimate future profession in the theater. After Auschwitz, he succeeded in creating a life for himself by compartmentalizing his traumatic experiences. It seems that one of the ways he coped with his trauma was to isolate it, perhaps to dissociate from it, and to channel it into his work. He returned to school, graduated from the Academy of Fine Arts in Cracow, took a position in the theater, and married.

In the text of the album that features the exhibition (Kołodziej, 2009), Kołodziej made some references to how the Auschwitz experience infiltrated his professional life. He saw Auschwitz as a constant presence, in the sense that he was determined to create an atmosphere in his work that was in direct opposition to what he had experienced there. The camp was chaos and disorder, while in the theater he always took great care to make the stage arrangements and layouts meaningful. Although he tried to be faithful to the text and to the stage directions, he attached great importance to light and made sure to open up the space on the stage in an attempt to counter the closed physical space of the camp. Most of all, he was drawn to the Gothic style in stage design, which he felt could express the magnitude of suffering. What for some critics was a sign of excessive décor in his stage designs, according to Nowosielski (2009), revealed an attempt to bridge the inner emptiness and darkness that he kept secret from the public. The implication is that he used his work both as a means to hide and to reveal, a way of working through his trauma. Apparently, he did not deny the impact of the Holocaust in his life, but made a conscious decision to remain silent on the subject until his stroke resulted in a confrontation with death. It was then that he reentered the world of Auschwitz, this time on his terms. The task of giving testimony and witnessing became a passionate goal for the remainder of his life.

An examination of the life and work of Kołodziej challenges the assumptions of theoreticians who believe that the inevitable consequence of massive psychic trauma is the loss of the internal, empathic other. Through his art, we become witnesses, not only to the horrors of concentration camp life, but also to some of the acts of kindness, dignity, and courage that he memorialized in his art and in his writing. For example, he remembered Father Kolbe, the Catholic priest who voluntarily took the place of a prisoner condemned to death. This event had a great impact for prisoners, and they clung to such inspiring acts as a way of maintaining the good in the midst of overwhelming evil. Kołodziej described another instance of a valiant attempt to hold on to his dignity. At one point he was given the job of bringing corpses to the crematorium and recognized the body of his closest friend. Refusing to throw the body on a pile, he carried him on his hands, "as a mother carrying her child, directly to the hole of the gas chamber" (Kołodziej, 2009, p. 62) (see Figure 5.3). In such a small but meaningful gesture, he found a way to express his respect for the memory of his friend. It seems that he maintained his connections with both the living and the dead.

The notion of the "dead third" (Gerson, 2009) and the death instinct theories (Laub, 2005; Laub & Lee, 2003) do not account for the fact that many survivors, despite their inability to take assertive action, maintained a strong sense of defiance and refused to allow their spirit to be broken. Kołodziej wrote that the camp was not just beatings, constant hunger, and death, but "it is also a silent interior NO, a rebellion with the limits set, an endurance to spite them all" (in Sobel, 2003, p. 13). I believe that this statement speaks to his vitality, strength, and determination, which served him well in the camp and in its aftermath.

In his last words to the reader, Kołodziej told us that the experience of the camps have made him what he is today:

> I learned and I taught myself how to live—in loneliness and in a community, and for the community, to live honestly and with dignity, to have conscience. Maybe it was worth going through? [Then he added with more pessimism] Looking at this 20th century of ours at the end of my life, I can see that nothing has changed in this earth after Auschwitz—and it was to have changed—but it is worse. The laws of a camp still rule the world. The death factory—modernized, computerized. The monster Apocalypse from my drawing—continues to exist. (Kołodziej, 2009, p. 20)

Primo Levi

We are reminded of the vast individual differences in the response to trauma when we note that there are survivors like Marian Kołodziej, who could not directly face their trauma until decades had passed, and others like Primo Levi, who could barely contain themselves at the time of their release from the concentration camp, who had a desperate need to tell anyone and everyone about what they had endured. Levi, an Italian Jew born in Turin, Italy, was 25 years old when he was sent to Auschwitz. A chemist by training, Levi had been a member of the anti-Fascist resistance until 1944, when he was arrested and deported. His first memoir, *Survival in Auschwitz*, originally titled *If This Is a Man* (1947/1996), poetically described his 11-month imprisonment.

Ian Thomson (2005, 2012), Levi's biographer, tells us that Levi's need to express himself was so intense that following his return to Italy in the fall of

Figure 5.3 Marian Kołodziej, *Marian carrying friend to the gas chamber.* Drawing: pen and ink on paper. Photo: Jason Al Schmidt and Christof Wolf, S.J., as seen in the documentary, *The Labyrinth: The Testimony of Marian Kołodziej.* For additional images, visit: www.thelabyrinthdocumentary.com.

1945, he talked to strangers on the street, on trains, and on buses, telling his story to anyone who was willing to listen. He seemed to have a compulsion to unburden himself; it was a cathartic release and a way of finding consolation. Later, the moral duty to bear witness became important as well. In preparation for his book, which he completed within 10 months, he recorded thoughts, events, and conversations about what he had seen in Auschwitz on anything within reach— scraps of paper, the backs of train tickets, flattened cigarette packets. The frantic energy with which he worked on the manuscript is described by Thomson: "And he wrote, if not in a trance-like state, then with extreme facility, the words pouring out of him ceaselessly, he said [in Levi's words] 'like a flood which has been damned up and suddenly rushes forth'" (2005, p. 47). It is interesting to note that at the same time as he was writing *If This Is a Man* he was also writing poetry that was not intended for publication. Thomson saw this poetry as a private ritual cleansing, which Levi had to undertake before he could chronicle the story of his persecution in prose because the rage had to be excised first in poetry. In contrast to the emotions of the poetry, the prose narration seemed oddly lacking in affect. When Levi told his story, he seemed to be talking about someone else's life (Thomson, 2005)—a common characteristic of a dissociated state.

In his introduction to *Survival in Auschwitz*, Levi let the reader know that this urgent need to tell, which began in the camp, was like a violent impulse competing with other basic needs. Writing was the fulfillment of that need and represented "an interior liberation" (Levi, 1947/1996, p. 9).

The passion with which Levi struggled to exorcise the demons that had overtaken him during his year in the hell of the Lager reminds me of my father's attempts to deal with his imprisonment in Janowska Concentration Camp, which also lasted about a year (see chapter 1). The drive to survive in order to tell what had transpired there, the determination to create a document featuring names and situations, with authentic terminology—such as German phrases and expressions—is similar in both memoirs, as is the narrative form. This motivation and style of expression can be found in numerous other autobiographical narratives of camp survivors, but Levi's remarkable talent and astute observational capacities are unique, and his work is not only an important document but a literary masterpiece.

Levi's psychological astuteness was profound; he had an intense drive to understand and a powerful curiosity. He was acutely aware of his environment and determined to record the world and people around him. He referred to this period of his life as one of "exalted receptivity" and "exceptional spiritedness." (Levi, 1987, p. 11) In view of the theories we have encountered earlier in this chapter about the supposed shutdown of reflection and self-reflection and the lack of curiosity in the wake of massive psychic trauma (Laub, 2005), it is striking to learn that Levi actually found mental functions such as thinking, observation, and curiosity to intensify during his Auschwitz experience. Thus he wrote, "It might be surprising that in the Camps one of the most frequent states of mind was curiosity. And yet, besides being frightened, humiliated, and desperate, we were curious: hungry for bread and also to understand" (Levi, 1987, p. 99).

In a conversation with Philip Roth (1986) toward the end of his life, Levi acknowledged that while luck played a central role in his survival, he also considered his capacity for reflection, thinking, and observation as survival factors. He reported having a heightened awareness during that period of his life that was helpful in his physical and spiritual survival. As a deep thinker, Levi was aware of the multiplicity of feelings and the shifts in emotional states in his experience and how these were expressed in his writing. Thus he told Roth, "Please grant me the right to inconsistency: in the camp our state of mind was unstable, it oscillated from hour to hour between hope and despair. The coherence I think one notes in my books is an artifact, a rationalization a posteriori" (Levi, 1947/1996, pp. 180/181).

What remained constant for Levi was the significance and importance of relationships for both physical and psychological survival. He credited these with the ability to hold on to his humanity in the face of massive physical and psychological assaults. Occasional unexpected acts of kindness reminded him that humanity could prevail over the bestiality of the Lager. For example, his relationship with Lorenzo, an Italian civilian worker who provided him with extra food regularly during the last six months of his imprisonment, was a constant reminder of the existence of a just world outside, for which it was worth surviving. Levi wrote, "Lorenzo was a man, his humanity was pure and uncontaminated, he was outside this world of negation. Thanks to Lorenzo I managed not to forget that I myself was a man" (Levi, 1947/1996, p. 122).

The concept of "man" was central in Levi's writing as the original title of his memoir attests. This concept was used synonymously with humankind and placed in juxtaposition with the barbarism of Auschwitz. In the final chapter of *Survival in Auschwitz*, which dealt with the last 10 days in Auschwitz, we observe another instance of the triumph of humanity over the laws of the Lager, which were "eat your own bread, and if you can, that of your neighbour" (p. 160). Levi and a dozen other severely ill inmates had been left to die in the makeshift infirmary when the Germans retreated from Auschwitz along with the remainder of the prisoners, setting out on the notorious death marches. In the chaos that followed, Levi and two other prisoners, all sick with scarlet fever, managed through a herculean effort to save themselves and the others suffering from more debilitating illnesses. This act of generosity and its recognition by the other inmates represented for Levi the beginning of the transformation from prisoner to man.

It is noteworthy that, even before liberation, Levi felt himself returning from the dead to the living. Despite the horrific subject matter of the book, Levi, according to Thomson, did not dwell on the mechanics of mass murder, but managed to hold on to and convey a sense of humanity and hope. Much like Kołodziej, Levi did not lose sight of a future beyond Auschwitz. Thomson (2005) tells us that the optimism that Levi felt about life and his impending marriage impacted significantly on the writing of *If This Is a Man*. Levi told Thomson that after he had written the book he felt himself to be a true "man" again—a man in the sense of the title of his book.

Thomson believed that Auschwitz was the catalyst that turned Levi into a writer. After the war, Levi returned to his work as a chemist but he also continued to write. Eventually writing became his primary career. He had initially believed that, after his first two memoirs about Auschwitz and his return home to Turin, he was done with testifying and writing about that period of his life, but found himself 40 years later compelled to return there, as memories clamored for expression. The new memoir, titled *Moments of Reprieve* (1987), focused on "men" he remembered who stood out for their will and capacity to react and not to be defeated by the inhumanity around them.

Levi's early death at the age of 67 is presumed by many to have been a result of suicide. This presumption, however, has been challenged by Diego Gambetta (1999), the eminent Italian sociologist who extensively researched Levi's death. He gathered evidence and the testimonies of people on both sides of the issue, and concluded that there is no proof of suicide—no witnesses, no suicide note, and no direct physical evidence. If Levi wanted to kill himself, he would have known or had access to better ways than jumping into a narrow stairwell with the risk of becoming paralyzed. On the basis of his research, Gambetta concluded that there is overwhelming evidence that Levi's supposed suicide was actually an accident. He goes on to say, what I myself believe, that there is a general bias that if one survives Auschwitz, everything that happens subsequently tends to be interpreted in the light of that experience. The readiness with which people assumed that Levi's death was suicide driven by bad memories reflects the stereotype that survivors are forever and irreparably damaged by their trauma experience.

Hannelore Baron

For Hannelore Baron, another visual artist who was deeply affected by the Holocaust, we note that a commitment to bring a message to her viewers was a powerful motivator. Baron, as a child of 12, escaped Nazi Germany with her parents shortly after Kristallnacht, when her father was brutally beaten and their small fabric shop destroyed. After a number of separations from her parents, near escapes from the Nazis, and desperate attempts to find a country that would take them in, eventually the family found refuge in America in 1941. Throughout her adult life, Baron suffered from bouts of anxiety and depression and battled cancer, eventually losing that battle at the age of 61. But what kept her hopeful and engaged in life was her art: "Art enabled Baron to act beyond her fears, as well as to journey into life and engage with its people and places, and with the past" (Schaffner, 2001, p. 2).

Baron worked in a unique abstract style, putting together small-scale, mixed-media collages and boxed assemblages. Her identification with her work was powerfully expressed in her comment, "The work is very small in dimensions and big in feeling and that's, I think, exactly how I am."[6] She used many different types of materials found at flea markets and in nature, such as wood, scraps of fabric, thread, string, torn paper, pieces from children's games, paints, ink, glass, and nails. These materials were placed in what appear to be whimsical arrangements featuring childlike figures, birds, patterns, and blocks of color—mostly muted or earth tones—and rich, varied textures. She developed her own iconography and hieroglyphics; occasionally scribbled words can be discerned on pieces of torn paper. A common motif was an abstract child figure boxed in or bound with twine or crossed out, communicating a sense of entrapment and fragility (see Figure 5.4). In the boxed assemblages, the theme of imprisonment and restriction similarly prevailed. "Her ability to suggest both the condition of entrapment and the possibility of release is remarkable" (Brenson, 1989). Most works are untitled, which gives viewers an opportunity to enter the space without preconceptions and to have their own associations with the material.

Figure 5.4 Hannelore Baron, *Untitled* (1983). Paper, ink, cloth, 9¾ × 10 inches. Photo credit: The Estate of Hannelore Baron. The original in color can be seen at www.hannelorebaron.net.

Baron acknowledged that some of the elements that she used in her art, such as the strings and the black boxes, were symbols of imprisonment and mourning. Her black boxes were memorials, providing evidence of some kind of disaster. She worked and reworked the box constructions, trying to strip away all extraneous matter and to convey a sense of urgency and total sincerity. About the string or wire around the boxes, she said, it is like a "finishing off of a memory that can now be put away. It's as if a feeling or a sentiment has been put in the box and it's tied up and that's it."

> The string does have to do with imprisonment. You see a lot of the work is done on a totally subconscious level and then I try to think up later why I might have done that and I can't really tell how much of it is subconscious and how much of it is conscious . . . I am very concerned about the political prisoners all over the world and of course it had to do with my own past experiences . . . As I've experienced for myself, you can be in prison without being in a locked room. You are imprisoned by your own fears, inhibitions, phobias. It's the same effect as if you're tied up with ropes.

Baron was struck by the contradictions within herself. She described herself as timid and constricted in her outlooks, with a great fear of the unknown, yet at the same time in her artwork she loved unpredictable results and appreciated accidents. I personally don't see this as a contradiction, but rather as the capacity to use art as a place where she could give expression to dissociated self-states.

Although she didn't seem to explicitly make the connection between her passion for old cloth and her father's textile business in pre-war Germany, it seems evident to me that her incorporation of fabrics in her art was a way of bringing her childhood past into the present in an attempt to work through what she had lost as a result of the war and the displacement that followed. It is also noteworthy that Baron's passion for fabrics in earlier years was expressed in her choice of textile design as a course of study. What she said about using old textiles in her artwork, rather than new ones, was that she preferred the fragility of the old, finding that new material lacked the sentiment and the emotional connections.

The message of her work was immensely important to Baron, both on a personal and on a political level:

> Everything I've done is a statement on the human condition . . . The way other people marched to Washington, or set themselves on fire, or write protest letters, or go to assassinate someone, well, I've had all the same feelings that these people have had about various things and my way out, because of my inability to do anything else for various reasons, has been to make the protest through my artwork hoping that it will reach the same ends.

Then she added wryly,

> And it probably will have the same effect which means nothing at all!
> But it clears my conscience. I feel that as long as I know all the things that
> have happened and are happening which I consider totally terrible, I feel
> that if I keep silent I am part of this terribleness and if I make a statement
> I've done my share.

Ogden (2000b) believed that art is inevitably part of the cultural milieu and that
the artist is not only responsible for the integrity of her art as a creative event in
its own right, but that she is also responsible for her art as part of the moment in
the history of mankind in which she lives. Baron's art fulfills both of those functions. She was deeply affected by the events of her time; many of her collages
were expressions of protest against the war in Vietnam, civil rights violations, and
other injustices of her time. Preservation and protest, the past and the present, the
personal and the political were all intertwined in her work.

For Baron, the strong desire to communicate a message about the human condition also included a more personal aspect—she wanted the viewer to know her
feelings. She said,

> For some reason in my family nobody understood what it is all about and
> I would like to somehow through the collages explain myself to everyone
> as if to say 'this is it, this is what was behind it, this is what was bothering
> me, this is how I feel.'

At the same time as she wanted to be known, she also had a need to hide a part
of her:

> I always wanted to keep some of myself back because I was afraid that
> there would be nothing left. The small part that I wanted to keep had to
> be sort of a secret part of myself. I always felt the work, the collages were
> my own and like the secret part of myself. At first, I was very reluctant
> to show them because I felt the minute I gave them to the public they'd
> no longer be my own, but I also wanted official approval of them at one
> point.

She saw this as another instance of contradictions within herself.

For around 30 years, no one saw Baron's work, and she either didn't care, as
Brenson (1989) maintained, or actually preferred not to be in the marketplace. Both
through her words and through her actions, Baron expressed the common struggle
of the artist and trauma survivor—how much to reveal and how much to conceal.
Winnicott (1963/1965) wrote, "In the artist of all kinds I think one can detect an
inherent dilemma, that belongs to the co-existence of two trends, the urgent need to
communicate and the still more urgent need not to be found" (p. 185). It could be

said that all of us struggle with this theme in our life and have to arrive at a comfortable balance with regard to our private and our public self, but artists and trauma survivors are faced with a more extreme version of this universal conflict. The artist who shows her work exposes her internal private visions to the world for viewing and for judgment, while the trauma survivor struggles to keep the knowledge of horrors lived through from both her own consciousness and the eyes of others who may not understand or who may condemn. For Baron, both an artist and a trauma survivor, the importance of communicating her message outweighed her inclination to hide. Her "message" was what gave her work meaning and helped her come to terms with her suffering: "Through these mixed-media constructions, Baron sought to compose what she called 'the message': an imagery of human hope and suffering that was privately meaningful and publicly significant" (Schaffner, 2001, p. 1).

For other survivor-artists the motivation to reveal is less influenced by the need to convey a message to the world, and more by other factors. Some of these include the need to find and create witnesses to what has been endured alone; to find meaning through narrative where chaos and senselessness prevailed; to regain a sense of wholeness to counter the fragmentation of trauma; and to fulfill the responsibility cast on one by fate—of being witness to historical tragedies as they unfold. To speak the unspeakable, to overcome injunctions against speaking; to turn a passive state of helplessness into an active one of mastery—these are some of the reasons that survivor-artists rise to the challenge. The fulfillment of these goals counteracts the destructive effects of trauma and enables the survivor-artist to move along the long and arduous road to recovery.

Sometimes the imperative to tell the trauma story is complicated by a number of factors, such as the fallacy of memory, the sense that one is not in possession of all of the facts, or to the pain of directly facing what has happened. In those cases, writers will sometimes choose the novel over the memoir as a literary genre. Such is the case with Aharon Appelfeld, the Israeli writer, who survived as a young child on his own, and Philippe Grimbert, the French psychoanalyst and novelist whose parents were survivors. Both experienced greater freedom with a form of literature sometimes referred to as "autofiction." Both of these writers struggled with memory—its treacherous yet powerful hold on the psyche, and its reverberations across time and generations. Appelfeld (1994) wrote that he found, at first, that memory needed to be suppressed, but then it burst forth and took over his writing. It was not until he created a fictional character that represented him that he was freed from compulsive memory and felt more as an artist in charge of his story. Perhaps the artist identity provided him with the courage to face his despair. He wrote, "I believed, and I still do believe, that only art has the power of redeeming suffering from the abyss" (p. xv).

Grimbert's bestselling novel based on his own life is titled *Memory* (2004). Its original title, *Secret*, actually better revealed the theme of the book, which is the destructive influence of wartime secrets and how they are transmitted from generation to generation, resulting in a state of confusion, a sense of both knowing and not knowing what is real or imagined. Another child survivor with a similar history, who also chose to use the novel form to tell his wartime story, is Louis Begley, whose writing will be discussed in chapter 10.

Regardless of the medium, the form, or the style of self-expression, the survivor-artists described earlier have all found meaning and relief in the process of making art. For instance, comparing the expansive frescoes of Kołodziej and the small, contained box structures of Baron, we note dramatic differences in artistic sensibility, yet we know that for each of them, their particular artistic style is perfectly suited to what they want to express. That said, I wish to take up another assumption about what constitutes the "art of trauma."

One of the widespread post-Holocaust assumptions held by Laub, Caruth, and other Holocaust scholars is that trauma cannot be represented because it creates a wound or hole in the ego into which are inserted literal memories of trauma (Leys, 2000). However, Laub and Podell (1995) did make an exception for a specific kind of art which they called "the art of trauma." They believed that art that is unaestheticized, dialogic, and indirect can come close to representing the emptiness at the core of trauma, while still offering the survivor the possibility of restoration:

> In creating a holding, witnessing "other" that confirms the reality of the traumatic event, the artist can provide a structure or presence that counteracts the loss of the internal other, and thus can bestow form on chaos. Through such form the artist can "know" trauma. (p. 993)

Kołodziej's denial that his work is to be called "art" is consistent with Laub and Podell's criteria of being unaestheticized, although personally I find his work quite beautiful and striking. On the other hand, while it is clearly metaphoric and symbolic, it is realistically rendered and representational by design. Hence it doesn't seem to meet all of their criteria for legitimacy as the art of trauma. As far as I'm concerned, Kołodziej's work is unquestionably the art of trauma, regardless of how direct or representational it might be. As such, it highlights the problem with a rigid and restrictive definition of what is truly expressive of trauma. To talk about essential elements in the art of trauma is to take what is a subjective experience and to frame it in a supposedly objective way. For me, the art of trauma is the art that is produced by someone who has been traumatized and whose intention it is to communicate this traumatic experience; it is reflective of their individual experience, in combination with their particular style of expression, whether it meets someone else's criteria or not. Kołodziej's representational renditions are filled with personal and universal symbolism and metaphor that communicate the horror of his experience, and he is the judge of whether or not it is restorative or restitutive.

Vedran Smailović

I will end this section with a contemporary example of art in the context of genocide. In contrast to the delayed mourning we see in the life of Marian Kołodziej, and more similar to the powerful impulse we noted in Primo Levi to express what

123

he was feeling, Vedran Smailović, a survivor of the recent genocide in Bosnia, reminded us that there are dramatic individual differences in the ways that survivors coped with catastrophic trauma.

In 1992, during the bloody war in Bosnia, Smailović sparked the imagination of people all over the world with his unique and courageous act. After a mortar attack killed 22 people—men, women, and children who had lined up for bread in a square in Sarajevo—he was so distraught that he didn't sleep all night. The next morning, he dressed in his tuxedo, took his cello and a chair, walked down to the bombed-out square, sat down, and began to play his cello. He played at great risk to himself, as sniper fire and mortar attacks continued all around him.

Stuart Pizer (1998) wrote,

> [T]he cellist of Sarajevo, with the metaphoric strength and potential of his music, rendered his daily repetition of lament in the plaza for himself, and for all who could hear, and for all who could not hear. His act of despair was his act of hope, sending his message out to the surrounding hills in the strains of his music. (p. 135)

Smailović had been a serious musician who had played in the Sarajevo String Quartet, the Sarajevo Opera, the Sarajevo Philharmonic Orchestra, and other famous venues in the country where he was born. At the site of the massacre, he performed Albinoni's *Adagio in G Minor*, a hauntingly beautiful piece of music full of pathos and grief. His brave act inspired others; songs have been written in his honor, and books have used his image in their story. He became known the world over as the "Cellist of Sarajevo" and was recognized as a symbol of artistic resistance to the insanity of war. But he did not welcome the fame that his artistic protest had brought him. Shortly after the end of the Bosnian war, he left to live in Northern Ireland and retreated into relative obscurity. There, he continues to play and compose music. When interviewed in 2008, he expressed great resentment about the mythology that has developed around his action, and he felt misrepresented and exploited. In fact, he was so angry that he considered threatening to stage another protest and burn his famous cello in the same spot where he played Albinoni's *Adagio* 15 years prior. He was particularly bitter that a novelist had used his story without consent and that this has made it difficult for him to keep a low profile. Sharrock (2008) reported Smailović's words:

> I am not hiding here, but for 10 years I have not wanted to go out. I don't want to be involved any more as a peacemaker or a public person. I did what I did, and that was that, mission accomplished. I have a right to my privacy. I will do the occasional event for charity, on a voluntary basis, but I don't want to go public again, and now because of this book I am forced to. (Sharrock, 2008)

Smailović also wanted to set the record straight about the facts. Numerous references to the story on the Internet and in literature (Pizer, 1998) said that he had played on the spot where the massacre took place for 22 days to commemorate each of the lives that were lost in the massacre. When in actuality, he said,

> I didn't play for 22 days, I played all my life in Sarajevo and for the two years of the siege each and every day . . . They keep saying I played at four in the afternoon, but the explosion was at 10 in the morning and I am not stupid, I wasn't looking to get shot by snipers so I varied my routine . . . I never stopped playing music throughout the siege. My weapon was my cello. But if I do not get justice now I will burn it back in Sarajevo. (Sharrock, 2008)

In his rage, Smailović told Sharrock (2008) that he felt his name and identity were stolen. At another point, railing against the novelist Steven Galloway, who wrote *The Cellist of Sarajevo*, Smailović exclaimed, "I am not interested in his bloody fiction, I am interested in reality."

Vedran Smailović's act of courage, in the face of traumatic circumstances, poignantly illustrated how trauma evades verbalization; where words fail, art can articulate grief and loss for the artist as well as for those who come in contact with his art. As an artist, he could not stand by helplessly while his city was under attack and his neighbors and friends were being murdered. He needed to take some action, and the one he chose was made possible by his musical talent and his vast performing experience. I personally find the mournful sound of the cello to capture the emotions of lament and grief more effectively than just about any other instrument. By playing his cello amid the destruction of war, Smailović found a creative way to express his sorrow and his anger about the tragedy that had befallen his people and his country. As he himself said, his cello was his weapon. His was an anti-war statement and a memorial to those who had been killed; it was a creative act that stood in direct opposition to the destruction around him. His exquisite rendering of classical music was also a reminder of the potential for beauty in the world during a time of horror.

I find it especially interesting that Smailović had such a strong negative reaction to the distortion of the truth of what had happened as portrayed in the media, even though it concerns relatively small details about the events. When in the interview he exclaims, "I am not interested in his bloody fiction, I am interested in reality," I can relate to his frustration. Personally, I have always had difficulty with the liberties that people take with memoir for the sake of a better story. It is my conviction that an artist's integrity rests on the authenticity of his creation and that when writing autobiography, there is a responsibility to honesty and accuracy, even if the narrative truth is subjective, as it inevitably is.

The strength of Smailović's personality was evident not only in his actions at the time of the massacre, but also in his intense response to what he felt was a misrepresentation of his protest. He threatened to destroy his famous cello on the very spot where he had once triumphed. This passionate response to what he felt was unjust was in keeping with his emotionality. This is a man who has the capacity to assert his will—a characteristic that Otto Rank (1932/1989) associated with the artistic personality.

It is my contention that Smailović was in a dissociated state while he performed, and perhaps even before he sat down to play his instrument. When he described his state of mind on the morning after the explosion to Joan Baez, the folk-singer activist who visited him in Sarajevo, he said,

> I didn't sleep all night, next morning I just take my tuxedo, take my cello, walk down the street; I don't know where I'm going and what I'm doing, I just go down, I find myself on this spot and I start to play. (RAZOR & TIE, 2009)

His description of the event was reminiscent of a somnambulistic or hypnotic state. As I have indicated in earlier chapters, my theory of creativity is that when deeply engaged in the creative process, the artist enters a space somewhere between the internal and external world—a transitional space, where dissociation takes over. Smailović surrendered to the music; his passion was galvanized and his terror was held in abeyance. It is likely that dissociation actually made it possible for him to function as well as he did in this highly dangerous situation. Whatever rational concerns he may have had for his safety must have been set aside and did not inhibit his actions.

Ornstein (2013) pointed out that with mass tragedies, such as the Holocaust, mourning is often delayed because of an absence of culturally sanctioned mourning rituals. Memorial art, which communicates affects that facilitate the emergence of similar feelings in the listener, is able to create a memorial space that facilitates mourning. In the case of the cellist of Sarajevo, however, I believe that his constant presence in the city during the crisis, and his daily playing at various sites, functioned as a ritual for himself and for those around him, and hence mourning did not have to be delayed. What he was able to do was to create a memorial space in the rubble of a destroyed city at the time of the trauma. This remarkable man, with his act of mourning and protest, bore witness to the tragedy of Sarajevo. He not only memorialized the deaths he had witnessed, but he also called the attention of the world to the tragedy happening in Bosnia.

Art as the "Living Third"

The theme of witnessing weaves through the life and art of the artists in these pages. It is expressed either directly or implicitly in their words, and it concerns both aspects of witnessing—being witnessed and bearing witness. In the field of psychoanalysis, it is the role of the analyst as witness that has been most empha-sized. Samuel Gerson (2009) wrote about the essential function of the analyst as witness to Holocaust trauma. According to him, it is the active and attuned affec-tive responsiveness of the witnessing other that is essential to the enlivening of the survivor of massive psychic trauma. Gerson referred to this phenomenon as "the live third" function and contrasted it with "the dead third," which he con-ceptualized as the loss and absence of another—whether person, relationship, or institution. The "live third" ostensibly serves the elemental function of solidify-ing an individual's sense of personal continuity and meaning. The witness, as the "live third," counters the sense of deadness that Gerson seems to believe is the inevitable consequence of massive trauma.

Although I agree with Gerson about the importance of being witnessed, I have difficulty with his conceptualization of the person who is being witnessed. Like Laub and his associates, Gerson apparently believes in a "generic" survivor of genocide who is affected by traumatic events in essentially the same way, regard-less of personal experience or individual psychology. For instance, Gerson writes that the inevitable consequence of catastrophic trauma is the enduring presence of absence within the psyche of the survivor: "For survivors of the Holocaust and their children, truth often resides in the reality of the absence, or put another way, absence itself may becomes the abiding presence" (2009, p. 1346). While this may be true for some survivor families, it is also true that many children of survivors grow up not with absence, but rather with the presence of daily accounts of a lost world, constant links between past and present, too many stories and too much affect (Hirsch, 1996). A child of survivors born after the war, Hirsch has written about how she grew up with "a strange sense of plentitude rather than a feeling of absence" (p. 664).

For Gerson, like for Laub and his associates (Laub, 2005; Laub & Auerhahn, 1989), the essence of trauma is the survivor's realization that the world-at-large was unresponsive to his suffering and unconcerned about his fate, and that his consequent loss of faith in a protective world led to his sense of living in the presence of a "dead third." The expectation that the world-at-large should be interested in our individual well-being seems a bit idealistic to me. What about the rescuers? Most of us survivors owe our life to at least one person who, dur-ing those desperate times, cared enough to risk his own life to save another. Even if we don't take account of these acts of selflessness, the leap from an aware-ness that the "world" doesn't care to the conclusion that the good internal object has been lost or annihilated as a result is an assumption that I personally see no evidence for.

My difficulty is with totalizing statements that do not recognize the richness and diversity of individuals who have encountered similar tragic circumstances. Such conceptualizations do not account for different states within the individual, and by implication, different self–other configurations, which may shift from moment to moment and over time. Thus, while it may be so that many survivors live with an acute sense of absence, existing within the memory, reverberations, and echoes of loss, it is also true that those same survivors live with other internal realities and emotions. Human beings exist in different self-states—vibrant and engaged, depressed and despairing, dissociated and numb—and all of these states have their moments in the life of a survivor as they do in the lives of people who have not faced catastrophic events. In reducing the trauma response to just one self-state, Gerson inadvertently violates the complexity of the human response to traumatic circumstances. The question remains, Can one really be a witness to another if one has preconceived ideas about what is going on in his psyche? Can a witness who is wedded to a theoretical viewpoint approach the survivor with an attitude of openness and curiosity that makes it possible for that individual to feel known and understood, or does witnessing unwittingly become another opportunity for the confirmation of a theory?

The theme of living with trauma and transcending it, at the same time, is well-illustrated in the lives of the five artists whom we have encountered in this chapter. Their life force has been expressed in creative endeavors, as well as in the way they have chosen to live their lives. Deep within these individuals, the spark of creativity remained, as is the case for most survivors whom I have known, both personally and professionally. Creativity is synonymous with vitality and it is the antithesis of deadness; it fosters enlivenment and engagement in life and, at the same time, makes space for the expression of grieving and mourning.

We have encountered the idea of the *third* in different parts of this book, defined here as a potential space where art can take place. Art allows for reflection and meaning-making, and art serves a containing and witnessing function, as we have seen. Extending Gerson's concept of the "live third" as embodied in the concerned witness, I propose that art be conceptualized as a "living third." The term "*living* third" conveys the ongoing, enduring nature of creativity. Art as the "living third" serves the crucial function of witnessing. A painter I worked with many years ago referred to the canvas as witness to his trauma. Whether it is the canvas, the viewer, or the artist who functions as witness, a holding, witnessing presence is created that can validate the reality of the traumatic event and provide form to a chaotic experience. In addition to its witnessing function, art as the "living third" provides an opportunity for the survivor to face death in the safe context of life. Even when the theme of the work of art is death-related, as it often is, it must be remembered that the process of creation is intrinsically a life affirming one.

Notes

Parts of this chapter appeared in *Psychoanalytic Dialogues 23* (2013), 362–376.

1. It is noteworthy that Kuriloff (2010) also writes about this fantasy of Ornstein and sees it as an effective way of coping with Auschwitz, but she calls it reverie rather than dissociation, which she defines as a pathological phenomenon.

2. I am grateful to Sue Shapiro for alerting me to the life and work of Marian Kołodziej

3. For additional images, please visit: www.thelabyrinthdocumentary.com.

4. There are no titles to the Kołodziej drawings; these designations describe the specific images that are part of larger murals. Also, there are no dates listed for specific drawings. They were done between 1993 and 2009.

5. Both Albrecht Durer and Hans Memling were 15th-century artists working in the Northern Renaissance tradition. Durer's subjects included the Apocalypse, war, and suffering. Memling specialized in religious subjects.

6. This section is partially taken from an interview conducted by Mark Baron, the artist's son, in 1981.

6

CONVERSATIONS WITH ARTISTS

In their powerful book on war trauma and psychosis, *History Beyond Trauma* (2004), Davoine and Gaudillière made the important point that unspeakable catastrophe of war is handed down from one generation to the next; it comes to be relived in the present and haunts the individual. Their subtitle for the book is *Whereof one cannot speak, thereof one cannot stay silent*, a paraphrase of the words of Ludwig Wittgenstein that originally appeared in his philosophical treatise *Tractatus* (1918/1999). In the text, Davoine and Gaudillière further extended the phrase to "Whereof one cannot speak, thereof one cannot be silent and cannot help showing what cannot be said" (p. 79). To their important psychoanalytic idea that trauma that eludes verbalization is inevitably expressed in symptoms and behavior and passed on through the generations, I would add that through artistic expression, trauma can find a voice.

In this chapter, which features interviews with two artists, we see how the unspoken horrors of war and other social catastrophes handed down from the previous generation are revealed, transformed, and communicated through the arts. Both of the artists are dealing with intergenerational transmission of trauma in their work. Born shortly after the Second World War, both women, as young children, were exposed to family members who had been traumatized by war-related experiences, but who did not directly address their own suffering. Unconsciously, these survivors communicated their pain to their children in confusing and mystifying ways that led these bright and talented youngsters to struggle to make sense of the discrepancies and strange messages they were receiving from their loved ones. Ultimately, the struggle to understand and to reveal what had been unacknowledged turned into a preoccupation that found creative expression in adulthood.

It needs to be recognized, however, that even in circumstances where parents are determined to be authentic and eschew mystification, the second generation inevitably "inherits" memories that are not their own and are compelled to mourn what has not been lost firsthand. Marianne Hirsch (1996), writing about memory and mourning in second-generation survivors of Holocaust-related trauma, coined the term *postmemory* to describe the powerful form of memory "inherited" from parental losses. These "memories" are secondary memories of children of survivors who have a need to know, to remember, to replace, and to repair what their parents have lost:

> Postmemory characterizes the experience of those who grow up domi-nated by narratives that preceded their birth, whose own belated stories are displaced by the stories of the previous generation, shaped by trau-matic events that can be neither fully understood nor re-created. (Hirsch, 1996, p. 662)

The children of survivors are compelled to rebuild and to mourn the lost world of their parents. Such memories are not mediated through recollection but rather through imagination and creation. Hirsch maintained that much of contemporary European and American philosophy, literature, and art are influenced by Holo-caust postmemory. In chapter 4 we noted the work of Shimon Attie (1994), who attempted to create an aesthetic that would convey the mixture of "ambivalence and desire, mourning and recollection, presence and absence that characterize postmemory" (Hirsch, 1996, p. 659). The interviews that follow illustrate the struggle of second-generation survivors of mass tragedies to come to terms with their haunted history.

An Interview With Ofra Bloch—Filmmaker

It was the 10th anniversary conference of the International Association for Rela-tional Psychoanalysis and Psychotherapy (IARPP) in New York City in March of 2012. I attended a screening of the film entitled *Vivienne's Songbook*, a docu-mentary about transgenerational trauma, directed and produced by Ofra Bloch, a psychoanalyst and filmmaker. The write-up that drew me and a roomful of psy-choanalysts described the film this way:

> *Vivienne's Songbook* is an intimate and affecting portrait of the rela-tionship between a mother and her talented artist daughter that at once revolves around and also transcends the Holocaust experience. As she explores her mother's traumatic past, Vivienne gradually reveals the true legacy of her mother's Holocaust experience, hidden deep beneath the layers of paint that make Vivienne's paintings both beautiful and haunting. *Vivienne's Songbook* is a study of transgenerational trauma and the ways in which it defines Vivienne's symbiotic relationship with her mother. (Bloch, 2012)

The room was packed and the audience mesmerized as the film story unfolded. I reached for a tissue as my eyes welled up with tears again and again. When the film was over, I approached Bloch and asked where I could buy this film, and she told me that it is not commercially available but she would send me a copy. Later,

I asked if I could interview her and she graciously accepted. The interview took place in her home on the Upper West Side in New York in 2012.

There are several levels of loss, as well as several levels of creative mastery associated with this project. The artist who is the subject of the film, Vivienne, is a South African woman who grew up under Apartheid and left as a young woman before its end to study abroad. Her profound sense of loss due to immigration and displacement parallels her mother's losses of home and family a generation earlier. Ofra Bloch, the filmmaker, is an Israeli woman who grew up in the shadow of the Holocaust in Israel and immigrated to the United States with her husband, who is also an artist with a history of Holocaust-related trauma. On still another level in this mix, there is my personal history of Holocaust trauma that undoubtedly colors my own perspective on this creative project. Presumably, we are all engaged in the process of using some form of artistic expression as a means of integrating and working through our experiences of Holocaust-related loss.

Segments of the Interview and Commentary

"The past isn't dead. It isn't even past." This quote by William Faulkner prominently appears at the bottom of every e-mail that I received from Bloch during the course of our correspondence. The quotation boldly announces Ofra Bloch's philosophy of life and heralds the theme of her film. Curious about Bloch's interest in intergenerational transmission of Holocaust trauma I ask,[1]

SR   What is your interest in the intergenerational transmission of trauma? Do you have a personal relationship to the Holocaust?

OB   I have to go back to my background when you ask me why I became interested in transgenerational transmission. I was born in 1950 in Jerusalem. My mother was born in Israel; my father was born in Canada. It was the aftermath of World War II, and it felt to me as if everybody had numbers on their arms, and that everybody was whispering. A major person in my life, at the time, was my uncle Binyamin, to whom I dedicated the film. (I also dedicated it to my analyst.) Binyamin was a Holocaust survivor from Poland who lost his wife and two children, was in a concentration camp, came to Israel, and married my great aunt. My mother, already in her 20s when Binyamin arrived in Israel, became Binyamin's lost child, the source of love for him. Then I was born, and it was like God's gift on earth for him. I could do nothing wrong. I was his whole life. I was adored without judgment, with all his heart always. Now, they lived in Tel Aviv and I was in Jerusalem. We used to go there, and I would be sent there for vacations in August. He would tell me concentration camp jokes, about his time in the Lager, as he called it. It sounded like such a fun place.

SR   As in *Life Is Beautiful*![2]

OB   Yes, *Life Is Beautiful*. So, of course I wondered why my parents hadn't gone there. Like there was something wrong with them that they were not sent to this amazing place where Binyamin used to trick the *obersturmfuhrer* all the time and make fun of him. After a few years, my mother revealed to me that it was not a fun place. Then it is 1961, and there was the Eichmann trial. Eichmann was caught, and was being tried in the building across from my home. My mother got tickets to the courthouse. There was no TV in Israel, and the trial was broadcast on the radio all the time. I was 11 years old, and was glued to the radio. I started reading after that, and I have not stopped until today. It is as if I felt that I had to be reading about the Holocaust all the time. So, this is the background of my interest. My friends were all second generation. Everybody was second generation. The country, the State of Israel, is a state that suffers from severe PTSD as a country. That explains the aggression and everything else that is going on there. My best friends were people whose parents had been in the camps, were then in Cyprus because they were sent there by the British, and eventually they came to Israel. There was always a cloud of whispers, as if it's unspeakable, unspeakable.

SR So you could relate tremendously to this.

OB Yes. Then I married David. He watches *The World at War*[3] every day. The kids, my sons, joke that you can always find David watching something about Germans. It is part of my identity at this point. So there's an opportunity to work on my own issues here, not just theirs; understanding Vivienne helped me better understand myself; the guilt that my parents were not sent there, the guilt that my mother lost her mother at a young age . . . the guilt.

SR Yes, and needing to know.

OB And needing to know.

SR What made you decide to do a film in place of a traditional case presentation?

OB Well, that is a very personal story. You see, I have an unbelievable fear of public speaking, unbelievably paralyzing. I had just gone back to school. I was not an analyst when I did this work, and I was not even a social worker. I was in my first year of social work, and totally manic about the excitement of going back to school, I signed up to do two programs at the same time: going to Columbia for social work school, and to NYU for international trauma studies, which was a one-year program. I don't know how they accepted me because everybody there was experienced. They spoke about a final project. I said, "Oh my God, I have to present a patient?" I was walking home and I thought maybe I could make a movie instead. I was really going to focus just on Vivienne's art. But, when I interviewed her, it evolved and ended up being so many other things, especially their mother–daughter relationship.

SR Did you know ahead of time what you were going to ask or did it unfold as you were engaged in the process?

OB With Vivienne, I did not use a script. I did not know what was going to happen. I was totally open, and things happened.

SR I'm wondering if analytic training has influenced your work as a filmmaker; as you see it, is there a relationship between the two disciplines?

OB The same feeling I had when I was in a session with my first patient, is this same feeling I had when I was filming. Even more so when I was editing, which I feel is really an analyst's job. When filming, first of all, you're a witness, and this is the role of the camera filming the interview, catching the feeling, capturing the response. Then the editing is the process of making sense of all of it and giving it interpretation and bringing yourself into the equation. The analyst's subjectivity enters: the way you interpret, what you witness, how you create a story line—this is analysis, this is what we do. The creativity in both professions is very, very similar, as is the happiness you feel when you make sense of it.

SR I imagine that you must have communicated that enthusiasm, which is very important.

OB Yes, because I think it helps your engagement with the patient or with a subject in the film. I did not know Vivienne well before I embarked on it. What surprised me the most was really that both she and her mother opened up to me like that; there was no preparation, they just opened up. I also feel I served as a buffer between them. There was a *third* character in that film, and it was I. I was the facilitator for them, a buffer; they really needed that.

SR What was most meaningful about the experience? What was most surprising and unexpected for you in this project? Did you discover things about yourself in the process of filming?

OB You find out things about yourself in the process, because you are an artist, a writer. I did not realize I was in the film, and I started crying when I realized that. I really considered cutting out my questions, covering up my presence. It was shocking to realize that I was so much in it. It was like my subjectivity entered in my choices. . . . I didn't see myself as a filmmaker, I did not feel like an artist doing it, I did not realize it was art I was creating; I am still in awe that I was doing that.

SR When you were working on the film, did you imagine a viewer? How conscious were you of a potential audience to see and evaluate your work?

OB It's so amazing to me that people are interested; I had no audience in mind whatsoever. I never thought it would be shown. I did not think much about it after it was finished. It was just the doing of it. The doing was the most exciting experience for me. I never thought about an audience, and I think that freed me to do the work. Because I think this can be an obstacle in creativity all the time. When I work with people, patients who are trying to write stories, or trying to make movies, they are so occupied with the prizes, with the Academy Awards, that it stops them really from doing this; it paralyzes them. So, I am very thankful, actually, that I did not have anybody in mind; I was just doing it.

I ask Bloch about her next project.

OB Let me tell you about the second film. The second film is actually about David [her husband]. He is an artist, and his art is an expression of trying to make sense of his childhood experiences during World War II. David is a survivor even though he objects to the title. He spent two years in a Russian Gulag. He started to paint late in life. It was really after I insisted that we go to Poland. He did not want to go. I think that the visit opened the door to reconnecting to what, and where, he came from, and to trying to work on his experiences. He is such a visual person. He is not the type to go for analysis, ever. But he uses art as his own self-analysis. He started making art about 10 years ago. The pieces are very, very difficult pieces. They are not pieces that you would hang at home, because they are very difficult. I said to myself, "There is a story there, and I have not done anything with it." I did not know what to do, nor how. Then after encouragement from several friends, I made a decision to make a film, to do a studio tour basically, to tell the story to people other than myself, because of course, I know the story. I wanted it to be fresh. So I invited a friend of mine and her husband, a friend I had trained with, actually. They had not seen the art, and also they are younger people from a different generation, and their lives have had nothing to do with the Holocaust. I invited them, and they were wonderful and cooperated. David conducted a studio tour with them, and that is basically the film, as he describes his associations about his experiences related to each painting. In addition, he uses a lot of poetry in his work. He's crazy about poetry; he speaks a lot of languages and can read poetry in different languages. He can still recite by heart Polish and Russian poetry. So he incorporates a lot of poetry in his paintings, and also uses Yiddish phrases in an attempt to revive the Yiddish language. So, we enter a world of poetry, and painted imagery, and his memories. You'll be interested in the name—it's called *Black Milk*. That is a metaphor from a poem by Paul Celan called the *Death Fugue*. It is a very powerful poem. Celan was a survivor. His parents perished, and he later committed suicide. So the metaphor Black Milk does not need an explanation. He drank in the morning, he drank at night. This is the past shaping the present.

SR   The present shaping the past, too

OB   That is absolutely true.

Some months following this interview, I had an opportunity to see Bloch's second film. In its theme and in its style, it was quite similar to the first. In both, art is the means to reconnect and to mourn the past. Like Vivienne, David remembers his childhood experiences as he shows his artwork and tells the witnesses about the relationship between the art objects he has created and his memories. As he interprets each work and expresses the powerful emotions connected with it, he revisits his traumatic moments from a position of strength in the presence of interested others. In the invitation to the screening of the film Bloch wrote,

Black Milk depicts the unfolding consciousness of this man for whom the Holocaust related experience remained largely buried for much of his life, only to burst forth, almost without warning, as he began to express with increasing intensity through the simple act of creation—what had remained hidden for so long.

Film as an art form is particularly well suited to the expression of emotion and the exploration of the dynamic dimension in human experience (Daniel Stern, 2010). It is a form of vitality with a powerful ability to evoke, not only through words, but through images and through sounds—a combination of the senses. In both of her films, Bloch enhances the narrative with vivid imagery and haunting melodies to convey the themes of memory, loss, and longing. Her films are works of art that resonate at different levels of consciousness through the integration of the emotions and the intellect.

Bloch dedicated her first film to Uncle Binyamin, the uncle who turned his tragic experiences into concentration camp jokes. I presume that in some deep, unformulated place, Bloch knew that Uncle Binyamin was suffering, but she could not make sense of what she intuited because of the mystification surrounding her uncle's story. I presume that the discrepancy of the Holocaust world according to Uncle Binyamin, and the reality of what she was learning about the Holocaust, fueled her preoccupation with this period of history and its effect. With the creation of these two amazing and affecting films, Bloch has been able to accomplish what she could not do for Uncle Binyamin—she provided an artistic space in which the painful past could be encountered, examined, integrated through the creation of a coherent narrative, and mourned. Undoubtedly, Bloch herself was enriched by the act of creation and, through this process, discovered a new identity—that of filmmaker.

An Interview With Susan Erony—Visual Artist

Susan Erony is an artist whom I interviewed at her home and studio in Gloucester, Massachusetts, in 2012, with the sound of seagulls and the smell of seawater permeating the air. Her works, as well as those of her husband, a talented photographer, cover the walls of the large loft-like space that they inhabit and work in.

Her artwork is primarily mixed-media, combining photo montage, collage, and assemblage with painting, rendered in styles that range from realistic to expressionist to abstract forms, and varying in size and in presentation—some individual works, others involving a series dedicated to multiple explorations of a single subject. Social history and the human condition are common themes in Erony's art. Through her artwork, she provides a social commentary and attempts to answer questions about how history, science, and politics inform individual identity and social culture. Her subject matter tends to be dark and includes genocide, the Holocaust, the methods and consequences of war and torture, and ethnic cleansing—social tragedies all over the world. She gives a voice to the silenced, exposes the hidden, and memorializes what is in danger of being forgotten.

After leaving a career as a psychotherapist, Erony traveled to Europe to study and research her Eastern European roots. This research resulted in a series of works that are a penetrating discourse on mass killing. In a 1995 artist statement, Erony wrote about her interest in the Holocaust:

> Since 1989, in an effort to come to terms with a history that defies any attempt to derive meaning from it, I have been making art about the Holocaust, the European Jewish culture that was destroyed by it, and the biblical roots of western civilization. I do so in an attempt at artistic research. The work is the way I deal with questions I cannot avoid and answers I cannot find. I cannot let such themes alone, not only because I am Jewish and mourn my tribe, but also because my Jewishness ingrains in me a reverence for memory and a mandate to preserve and distribute it. This is true even though I grew up in the United States and am not a child of Holocaust survivors.
>
> I decided to go to Poland and Austria, hoping to resolve my conflict by visiting sites of historical events. I have extended my research visits to Germany, the Czech Republic, Russia, Latvia, and Lithuania. I photographed concentration camps, Jewish cemeteries and German steel plants. I did a first cycle of work over a period of three and one-half years, creating mixed-media pieces using the photographs themselves as part of the imagery. I had initially thought I would photograph Auschwitz and come home and paint it. Instead, I came home and had waking nightmares, and used the photographs and the art I made with them as an exorcism.
>
> I grew up in a house where no one talked about the Holocaust. It was not considered relevant to my family. My father had witnessed the murders of four of his siblings in Russian pogroms. He was jailed three times for his Zionist activities, the first time when he was fourteen. He barely escaped from his home, the Ukraine, in the 1920's, finally coming illegally into the United States in the 1930's. But he told just a few set stories about his life, about the pigeons he raised, and the snowfall in winter. My mother's family, of whom I know almost nothing, also came from the Pale of Settlement, that area in Czarist Russia where Jews were allowed to live.
>
> My current belief is that the Holocaust and the pogroms in my father's life are what have defined me as a Jew. On a personal level, my artistic research fills in the holes of my family history. I paint and preserve other people's memories and history as substitutes for my own. I try to understand myself, an American Jew born in 1949, and to make sense of my family.[4]

Interview

SR   Did you say that you thought there is a direct connection between being traumatized and being creative?[5]

SE   No, no. Actually, I'm not sure. Jay [her husband] and I were talking about it last night. He asked me what you were focusing on, and I said that I thought that it had to do with trauma and creativity and the relationship. So we started to talk about it. Do we really think there is a relationship? And you know, in my head, intellectually, I'd want to say no. Probably because it brings me back to stereotypical thinking about the creative process coming out of pain and the idea that you have to struggle and suffer to be an artist. Actually, though, I think it's true. I think that the people who do the most interesting work are often quite troubled, and I do not mean that they went through huge historical trauma or, you know, necessarily horrendous sexual abuse, I'm not saying that. But I do think that to achieve depth in creative work, a struggle is part of the process, that there is a wrestling with what one is doing and that maybe if you are too peaceful and happy, it does not feel worth doing. Artists serve as voices for the unconscious of society. One of the values of an artist is to give society a way to look at itself—whether they are doing it consciously or not—to say to society this is what your values are.

SR   I have a sense about you from the things that I read about you and your work, that there is a struggle to understand, to grasp in some way, to make sense of things, and that art for you captures that. Would you say that this is accurate?

SE   I'd say that is very accurate. I stopped making art because I couldn't understand what my art would do in the world. I just did not feel like it had value. I had to understand what art itself brought to humanity in order to allow myself to do it again. I still struggle with understanding that. I mean, when I am in my studio, if I am in the process of making art, the questions all go away, if I am really in the process. It is the only thing that stops them. If I'm not deeply in the process, I have the same questions that every artist friend I know has, like what's the point? How can I spend my life making stupid little marks on canvas or whatever I happen to do? Who needs another still-life? Who needs another depressing painting? You know, there is so much stuff in the world, why should I be adding to it?

SR   It is interesting that when you are engaged in the process, those questions don't come to you. So how do you understand that?

SE   I'm not sure that I do. I know that I stopped making art when I was 20 and then I started again. I was still doing hand work, I was a jeweler, and I was in art school, which I graduated from. But I was mostly doing research on World War II and writing about Albert Spear.

SR   When did you first identify yourself as an artist? When did you say, "I'm an artist," or feel like an artist?

SE   I don't think I have thought about it, but from the moment I could pick up a pencil, I was drawing. So I just always did stuff. My mother had been an artist. She was one of the first two women to go to Boston University School of Art (which was not called that back then). She ended up becoming an art teacher for a very short period of time because World War II broke out, and she lost her job in a Catholic school, I think. She started to work in civil service jobs and never really went back to making art, though she always did needle work and knitting and things like that. I really think that her creativity was frustrated. She was very supportive when I was young of my making art. I don't remember if she took me to the Museum of Fine Arts in Boston, but I was always there. My father was somewhat appalled by the whole thing, which is interesting, because he was the parent that I really identified with. Anyway, he was a refugee from the Ukraine. I think he just wanted me to do something safe and practical. He wanted me to be a teacher or a secretary.

SR   So he was not encouraging?

SE   Not at all, not at all. I don't know how he would have felt later. He died when I was 25, and he was 70. He was 10 years older than my mother. The place he and I really connected was in talking about history. Once I started to deal with history, in my work especially, the Holocaust and Jewish stuff, I think he might have been able to understand it better.

SR   So it was such an interesting integration of the interests of both parents—your art and your history. Your mother was thrilled by your developing the art, and your father was interested in the history part of it, and you did both.

SE   Thank you, Sophia. That really is interesting. I never had realized that. Seriously, thank you.

SR   So, tell me more about your interest in genocide and the Holocaust, which I guess your father was also interested in?

SE   He must have been. We did talk about World War II all the time, not the Holocaust, but the war and the Depression and the WPA[6] and FDR, which is a period I'm just nuts about and have lectured and written about. I always thought that my father was interested in genocide, even though he did not go through the Holocaust; he grew up with pogroms in the Ukraine. He saw four of his brothers murdered, and he saw his baby brother murdered in his mother's arms, while he was hidden in the closet. I did not think of it then as traumatized, but it was very extreme. He was almost, not catatonic in the sense of immobility, but he was *so* withdrawn and *so* anxious and *so* kind of obsessive and stressed and worried. I was not really very nice to him in some ways, though I adored him. I used to say to him, "it's like you're always waiting for the next pogrom," and he was. Of course, *I* still do, too. But I never could figure him out. I used to badger him with questions, and he would never tell me anything except for these three stories that I always think of.

SR   The stories are of the pogroms?

SE   No, he did not tell me that. His sisters told me that and his brother. There were 11 children, two mothers. Most of them made it to Mexico. A couple made it to the United States. My grandparents were able to come into the United States, but it was because of Dutch Schultz, a Jewish gangster. The family, who moved to Mexico, seemed to really make good lives for themselves and be quite happy and successful, part of a real community. My father and two brothers went to New York. My father was the last one to come. He did not get into this country. He went to Mexico. He hitchhiked and walked from Mexico, coming into the United States illegally. One of his older brothers in New York was Dutch Schultz's lawyer and was engaged to his sister. They never did get married, but they stayed friends. Dutch Schultz got my father false papers. Really, he was never legitimate—though he later became a citizen. Also, Dutch Schultz was able to get my grandparents in; my grandfather had been rejected at Ellis Island.

SR   His sisters told you about the pogroms and about the loss of the siblings, and there were four brothers who were murdered? So you knew on some level that he was traumatized.

SE   I knew something was up, and then I found out more details. I think my mother probably told me that he had escaped from pogroms.

SR   When you tried to ask him about it?

SE   He wouldn't talk to me.

SR   So do you think there is a relationship between his reaction and your interest in genocide?

SE   I know there is. I worked in the civil rights movement when I was in high school. As part of our training, we were shown some films about racism and in this case anti-Semitism. *Night and Fog*[7] was the first thing I really knew about the Holocaust. When I saw it, I thought, oh *geez*, no wonder my father is the way he is. I was able to use that history to explain my father to myself.

SR   How did he feel about that particular direction that your interest took?

SE   I don't know if I talked to him about *Night and Fog*, but mostly, I think he was afraid. I was working in Roxbury which was a primarily African-American part of Boston, and I was teaching and tutoring for a couple of years. He was just so scared and so worried about me. I think that overrode anything else for him.

SR   It sounds like your own trauma really came from the transmission of your father's experiences.

SE   I think most of it came from that. I also did have some sexual abuse when I was a child by an uncle that I pretty much remember, when I was 3. There is so much sexual abuse of children around, but so many times you think, oh my God, I never would have thought, my uncle! It was my mother's uncle; he was my great uncle. He used to baby-sit for me with his girlfriends. I always felt a sort of revulsion around him.

SR   So was this always within your consciousness?

SE   No. It wasn't until my late 20s that I had flashbacks, and it's kind of what took me back to making art again—because around the time I was having flashbacks, I just was desperate. It seemed like nothing helped. I don't know if I went to therapy then, actually. You know, Sophia, I don't even remember. All I remember is one day having this compulsion to draw pictures of a female figure, like myself, who was in the situation that I was in with my uncle, and it was the only thing that gave me any peace. It sort of knocked me over. It did not make everything go away, but it really did help drawing those figures.

SR They were adult figures?

SE Yeah, I drew them as an adult. Then, I also drew some as a baby or a very young child. But I started out just drawing this as an adult. I had been very promiscuous.

SR Around that time?

SE And before, from the time I was about 18. Then I had an open marriage in my last marriage, so that didn't help. But I really felt there was a connection. I stopped being so promiscuous. I also got very depressed for a number of years.

SR Around the time you were making these connections?

SE Yes

SR So art was a way of becoming more aware of what was happening? Yet it didn't affect your mood in a positive direction?

SE Not very much, no, but it did help with flashbacks. It must have given me a little sense of control and being able to externalize.

SR Do you know what triggered the memory?

SE I kind of had a collapse. I had been working very, very intensely as a group therapist. I worked so much and took it so seriously. I really burned myself out, and I collapsed. I think it was, just from what I have read, a kind of typical burnout. So my defenses were down, and it was after that. I don't remember any specific incident happening, other than that it was a huge life change for me to just walk away from what I thought was going to be my career.

SR It was around that time with the defenses down that you had flashbacks, and you turned to drawing; so the drawing was like the beginning of a working through process?

SE Yes. I think also that doing the drawings made the memories more concrete because I had given them form.

SR Some people have talked about having a kind of internal object relationship with the art, so I am just wondering if those forms became almost like objects to you, where the artwork took on a certain reality. I don't know if I am making that clear.

SE Well, I think so, because I felt so badly for the woman in the drawings. I felt huge sadness. I think I was able to feel compassion.

SR I am very interested in the concept of witnessing, and in that process it seems to me that you became a witness.

SE I was able to be a witness to my own pain, my own self by putting it outside, by putting myself outside of myself. I went back to making art at 34, and once I did I decided that I had to do work dealing with the Holocaust—it was what I could do with my pain and sadness. That is really still what my art is about. I just don't know what else to do with how I feel about the world. I have done other things like being a psychotherapist or working in the civil rights movement or being a Big Sister, whatever. None of it has given me the relief that art has. When I have not been involved with art in my life, I have not been in a good place—except, I should say, when I was first a group therapist because I had a "young therapist saving the world complex," very prevalent in the early 1970s when I was initially trained.

SR   You trained primarily as a group therapist?

SE   Yes, at first. Then, I went back when I was in my 30s to get my master's degree and I was going to go on for a PhD in psychology. That is when I started to make art again. There were these little winter intersession short courses we had to take, and I took one on guided imagery. It was not the sort of thing that was really me, but I had a dear friend for whom it is. And I thought, maybe I should try this, maybe I should learn about it. Going through guided imagery processes, I started to draw again because I had images come into my head that I had to draw. That is when I figured out, "Oh, when I draw, I feel better." If I draw more, I feel better, better. Then I thought, maybe I should try painting again even though I probably have no skill at all. I started to paint and had more skill than I had stopped with, I thought. It was really surprising. I heard that this is not uncommon, that somehow your hands learn even though you are not making art.

SR   You can grow without the actual practice, but there is something happening internally, some kind of growth process. What happens in guided imagery, I believe, is that you go into a kind of altered state in which certain visual images come to mind more readily. Do you find that when you are engaged in the creative process that you enter an altered state of some kind?

SE   I have, but not lately. I have to be making art more regularly for that to happen. But when I have been, then yes. Everything else is just gone. I have had moments where it is almost as if I have lost consciousness, one in particular. That was unfortunately the only one that was *that* intense. I did a portrait of my grandfather, and I was painting his eyes, and three hours went by. I did not know where they went.

SR   Yes, that is exactly the state I am talking about.

SE   Oh! It was wonderful. That was my mother's father who lived with us. He died when I was about 9 or 10, and his wife, my grandmother, died the next year, probably 8 and 9 or 9 and 10. He was wonderful. He is the saint of the family, of my mother's family. He was a wonderful doctor. Who knows what downsides he had? But what I knew of him was just this adoring grandfather who was funny, and kind, and just great, and whom my father adored, and I think probably kept my father going.

SR   So when you were engaged in that, you felt so transported that you lost consciousness? It was a feeling that was pleasurable, it sounds like you wish you had it more?

SE   Extremely; it was a peak moment.

SR So that sense of being in a kind of altered state, is not always experienced when you paint; it happens only under certain circumstances. Do you have some sense of what allows that to happen and under what circumstances?

SE I think part of it is a sense of mastery. I think a lot when I work. I am not someone who goes out and sketches, I wish I were. I wish I could be more casual about some of my work, but I am not casual about anything—certainly not my artwork. I take it really seriously. I think the rare moments when I feel like I have control, and know what I am doing, are when that can happen. I've had lots of other times when it's been incredibly pleasurable, when I have forgotten about the rest of the world and feel safe. Making art makes me feels safe. It's the one thing I can count on to make me feel safe. But I have to be able to turn my head off enough to just go with the process and to trust myself enough that I won't make a total mess for that to happen. There are some kinds of work I do intentionally that is very repetitive, obsessive work, like covering the surface of a piece with pencil marks.

SR I want to go back to a couple of things that you've said. What makes you feel safe about making art?

SE I have thought about this, which is why I am answering quickly. I think it has to do again with a sense of control. I think that one of the magics of making art for me is the sense that *this* I can control. I can control almost nothing out in the world, but there is a sense that on my canvas, on the piece of art I am making, unless it is a commission, it is mine, it is my universe. I can do whatever I want on that. That feels safe. I think it is also a meditative thing, because when I am doing very repetitive kinds of work, it really has some of the same benefits for me I think as meditation. I love doing it.

SR So can we shift gears a little bit? I have noticed there are lots of eyes that are looking at me, and I'd like to know what that means to you. [I refer here to the numerous art works around the room that prominently features eyes.]

SE Those eyes are . . . they are my eyes, but they are Jay's work. All of the photographic eyes, those are Jay's. However, I have also done a lot of work with eyes like that. In fact, now I am using my own eyes that Jay photographed in my own work. I have painted a lot of eyes and taken eyes from paintings and used them

SR What is the significance of these eyes?

SE The eyes to me—I mean it is the cliché about the windows to the soul. But I also think—you were talking about witnessing before. I think it is so much about witnessing for me. There is a piece I am working on now that really is about that in terms of seeing the injustice in the world, and the importance of acknowledging it.

As I look at some of the art around me, I notice that many of the pieces feature a heavy layering of paint piled into rounded shapes that she refers to as "a mound." I ask about a piece that she calls "Unseen Eyes, Unspeaking Lips," and she tells me about it.

SE   It really started out as a different piece; it started as a repair for the *Tower of Babel* in the Bible. So, with the Tower of Babel, we lose the ability to understand each other. I have done a lot of pieces on Towers of Babel. I have an obsession with mounds. Or towers like the Tower of Babel, but it is really a mound; it is not really a tower.

SR   What is a mound? How would you describe a mound?

SE   Like a hill; a small mountain.

SR   Do you know what it means to you?

SE   I have no idea. The first work I did on the Holocaust was based on the image of the train tracks going through the gate of Birkenau. If you take a train track or any kind of path, and make it go into the distance and it gets smaller, it instantly creates depth and a sense of drama. It is a very compelling image to see the train tracks. You see it a lot. *Shoah*[8] starts with it. I think it is a combination of the train tracks and the arches leading up to these mounds. The only thing I can figure out about them is that I did one where I built a haystack to remember my father's brothers who were unsuccessfully hidden. This is the one piece that I did about my father.

SR   My own association is that it looks almost like a mound of bodies.

SE   It is a burial mound.

SR   Yes. This has a feeling of bodies being sort of on top of one another.

SE   So is it the images of Auschwitz? I don't know.

SR   Well, it sounds like there are different connections to it; arches, train tracks, and maybe my own association of bodies and mounds. I did want to talk about one painting in particular that was mentioned in your writing—it's about your father's raincoat.

SE   My father's coat, his winter coat.

SR   Can you tell me about that work, and what that meant to you and why the burying of it?

SE   Yes; there was a coat that my mother gave me after my father died. I used to wear men's overcoats. She gave me two of my father's overcoats, one of which I still have and still wear, and it is my favorite piece of clothing. The other one, I wore until it deteriorated. It was torn so badly that even I couldn't wear it anymore. I could not give it away, you know. It was in such bad shape, maybe I could have cut it up, but I just could not get rid of it. I didn't know what to do with it. I had it for a couple of years. I made a bed with it for my beloved ex-dog to sleep on. I finally figured, okay, I have to do a piece with this. I finally have to do a piece about my father, and this will give me a way to do it. I kind of thought I would have to at some point. Like the Holocaust, I had no idea how. So, I cut the coat up, and I did what I seem to do over and over again, which was to build a mound with the pieces. Then, I did a background like a sky with the lining, which was sort of silky gold material, satin/gold material. Just as I was working on it, I was thinking about my father's brothers and how I needed to give them a good burial and maybe my father, too. So I thought how my father and his two older brothers had been kind of destined to go to Palestine and be part of the creation of the State of Israel. Anyway, they had all set out in life with these grand dreams. My grandfather was apparently a very, very devoted Zionist. All three of them ended up in New York in the garment business, which none of them liked. My father hated it. I wanted to talk about his lost dreams. That is what the piece ended up being about. I also had been doing a lot of reading about the Gulag and Stalin's horrific policies, and I thought, you know, my family lost their home due to this revolution that was supposed to save mankind, and what a horrible disappointment that ended up being, and there were so many lost dreams and lost hopes. That is what the piece ended up being about. It was called *My Father's Coat* [see Figure 6.1].

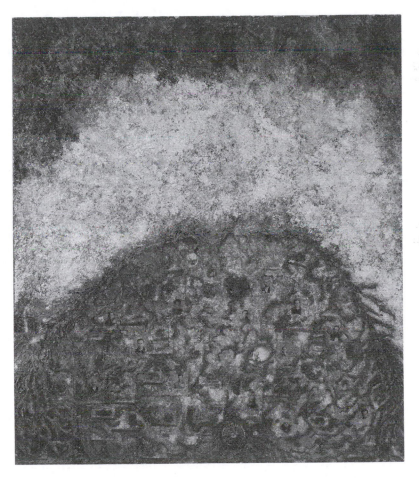

Figure 6.1 Susan Erony, *My Father's Coat* (2001). Acrylic, charcoal, pencil, burnt paper, seaweed, mushrooms, photographs, lead on canvas; 5 × 6 feet. The original is in color. Collection Cape Ann Museum. Photo credit: Cape Ann Museum.

It is now owned by the Cape Ann Museum, which is down the street from here. It is very close.

SR I guess it serves multiple functions. It's a garment, and he was in the garment business, so it represents that piece, and the burial, and your connection with him—you wore this coat until it was in tatters, right? And you also say it represented his brothers as well?

SE Well, the mound of his coat ended up being his life. Three of his brothers were murdered in a haystack. The painting symbolically is like the shape of the haystack where they were hidden.

SR So in terms of the pieces that have been most meaningful for you? You have pieces that you would consider your favorites?

SE They change except for one. *My Father's Coat* is really important to me. One reason I agreed to the museum here having it—which is a wonderful museum I should say, it's really great—is that one of the things I wanted to do with that coat was make my father safe. It's one of the reasons I buried his coat. I mean, I did it very lovingly, though it seems grim because it is buried in burnt paper, but it was an act of love on my part. What could be farther from the perilous life in the Ukraine my father led than the permanent collection of the Cape Ann Museum in Gloucester, Massachusetts? I thought, *whoa,* he is really safe now. It was so important to me. The piece was the last I did in a series, the wrap up of 12 years of work overtly on genocide. Even though the history of the Soviet Gulag, it was not, it still is not considered genocide, because it was political, so it is politicide. But what is the difference, you know?

SR There's something so touching and moving about the way this piece integrates so many aspects that are meaningful to you.

SE It felt like that when I did it. It was very satisfying. That is one of my favorites. But the only piece I've ever cared about owning and keeping—I don't want to keep my work, I want it out when I finish it. I am not attached to it—except for this [points to a large painting of a man's face on the wall]. That's from 1993, and it's a portrait of a Chilean disappeared. I was doing work on this history then, too. This was the first one I did in a small series. It was the easiest piece I ever did, another one of those moments where I almost lost consciousness. It was not quite like my grandfather's eyes, but it was close. My work takes me forever, but that piece, I think I did the drawing in an afternoon. It's not totally what I would like it to be, but there was something about it that said everything I had to say at that time [see Figure 6.2].

SR It looks like a photograph. Is this charcoal?

SE That's charcoal on a painted ground. Meaning, I did the background first. In this case, it is layers and layers of translucent acrylic paint. I wanted to make it look like parchment.

SR [I read] April 10, 1974, was that the date that he disappeared?

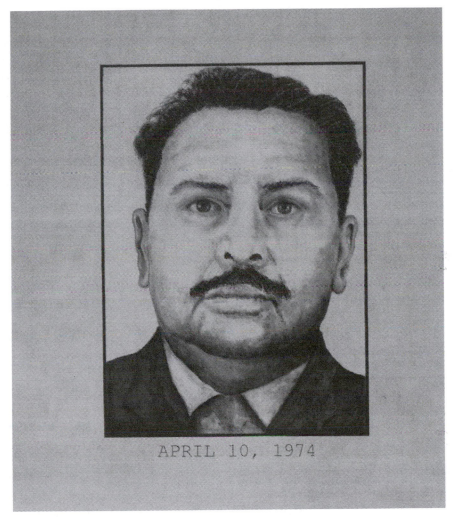

APRIL 10, 1974

Figure 6.2 Susan Erony, *Chilean Disappeared April 10, 1974* (1993). Acrylic and charcoal on Canvas, 54 × 64 inches. Private Collection. Photo Credit: Jay Jaroslav.

SE   It's not the day he disappeared. I'm not sure that I like what I did there. I was dealing with the idea of people's identities being completely torn away from them. In the case of the Holocaust, the Nazis had such a reign on the record keeping, it is one of the reasons the Holocaust is such a good case study; there is so much information by the perpetrators. But, in disappearing people, the policy was to just make them go away as if they had never lived. That was so horrifying. Not that this didn't happen in the Holocaust, that people didn't

147

know what happened to their loved ones, it happened so much. But this, the government set up to get around an Amnesty International campaign to protest jailed political prisoners. No rhyme or reasons. A friend of mine had gone to Chile in 1989 right before I went to Auschwitz actually, and I had been thinking about doing something on the Disappeared in Latin America, partly because of the questions about the American role. I just felt I had a responsibility as an American citizen to look at it. So, coincidentally, this person I knew was going down to Chile. He had been there when Allende was murdered. He's American, and he escaped by the skin of his teeth because he was on the left. He brought back from this 1989 trip, posters and books that had been assembled by the Catholic Church of everyone they could find to document who had disappeared. They were doing this as a service. So, I had them for five years, these pictures, and I never could figure out what to do with them, and I cut all of the photographs out, and I just shuffled them around. I mean there were hundreds of them. Then, I married Jay in 1993, and we were talking about where to go with these. Unfortunately, Jay had spent time in Latin America for his work and was very troubled by what had gone on there. We were talking about the arbitrariness, the way the people had disappeared and how it was almost as if . . . it came to seem that I should cut away their identifying information from the photographs, all of it, the dates, everything, which I'm not at peace with, but I did it to experience what I was sort of researching. So I put the period of the disappearances, just cut pieces of paper for the months, the days, and the years and put them in hats, and we picked. So it's an arbitrary date.

SR   Is there something about his eyes or his expression that spoke to you more than the others?

SE   Absolutely; it just looked familiar, and iconic of a kind of mix of people who were in South America in terms of Spanish and indigenous heritage. You know, I thought he looked innocent and kind. Of course, the photographs were photographs the families had. They were not photographs taken by the perpetrators. So, this was not a photograph where he was afraid.

SR   He looks afraid.

SE   Yes, he does look very afraid, probably because of my knowledge about him when I painted it. It is my fear of what happened to him, what people do to each other.

SR   There's one painting I want you to tell me about—your self-portrait.

SE   Oh, my self-portrait; amazingly that's also in the collection of the Cape Ann Museum, God knows why! It's so unlike the work they have, but there it is. I had to do a piece for a book that was being published in Berlin—a self-portrait. I did a portrait with half of my face alive and half as a skull [see Figure 6.3].[9] It is like a dance of death. So, that's what that piece is. It was pretty interesting to do, facing my mortality—in not a very deep way, I don't think.

SR   Why do you say not deep?

SE   I'm not sure I let myself go very deep. I did it in 2000, I think. It must have been around then. It was 10 years ago, so I was 52 or 53. At that point, I was

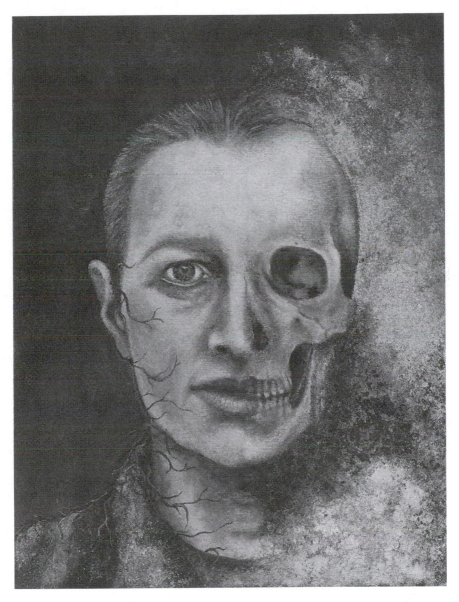

Figure 6.3 Susan Erony, *Self-Portrait* (2000). Oil on canvas, 24 × 18 inches. Collection Cape Ann Museum. Photo credit: Cape Ann Museum. The original in color can be seen at www.SusanErony.com.

doing so many skulls . . . and I love skulls. Aesthetically, I do. So, they almost were not ghoulish to me by then. It's like punk kids who have skull earrings. It's probably another one of those feeling a sense of control moments. But, also, I think there is real beauty. I have always liked bones visually. In the late 19th century, every library had a human skeleton to contemplate. Of course, artists study them in our training; they are very beautiful. It also is a way of not thinking about what they really mean.

SR This painting seems to come from a cognitive place within you, as if you don't have an emotional connection with it. Am I wrong?

SE No; I don't feel one. I really don't. It almost felt like an exercise that I should do for the book. It really was very intellectual. It is not a piece I would have come up with on my own. The whole issue of the self-portrait, I can't imagine doing a self-portrait. I used to fight with an artist friend of mine who tried to get me to do a self-portrait. The whole idea just made me cringe.

SR Is this the first and only self-portrait that you have done?

SE Except for drawing assignments in college—yes.

SR How do you feel about it?

SE I think it is accurate. I think it is a successful self-portrait of who I really am. I just think it is me. It feels right to me. I also, I mean this whole thing about these vines which I have used . . .

SR Tell me about the vines.

SE The vines are nature taking everything back again to itself. No matter what we do as human beings, nature is going to do what nature does, and every-thing will go back to nature—except for plastic and Styrofoam, unfortu-nately, maybe in a million years—but anything organic.

SR So this really feels like you.

SE I could not imagine doing a more accurate self-portrait of the way I feel and the things I think about and who I am.

SR Are you aware of an internal presence when you're working? A kind of wit-ness to what you are doing? Do you have an internal dialogue with an imagi-nary other? If so, is the other a neutral observer or an affirming presence or a critical one?

SE I feel as if I have an internal dialogue with myself that almost never stops. It's certainly there when I am working, unless I am in that flow kind of period, and it's definitely a critic.

SR Does that critic block you sometimes?

SE Definitely.

SR How do you deal with the blocking?

SE These days I don't work. I never had trouble getting to work before 10 years ago. Ten years ago, I had to start working full-time at a day job. I was also doing a lot of caretaking. Since then, I've had times when I just procrastinate, like I never used to. It is like I lost my discipline, or the kind of discipline I used to have. It feels very much like fear, and the critical voice. I mean, it is almost physical the fear I feel about making art. It has always been there. It only goes away when I am working basically full-time as an artist. It mostly comes out with oil paint. I know this might sound really silly, but I am really afraid of oil paint. I know, when I'm working as an artist, I have culture shock when I stop. That's why I have never been able to have a job that was not totally contained within a specific time period, that I did not take home with me, that I did not think about, and make art. I could not do both because making art is such a different way of being in the world for me. It's like my skin dissolves. I mean, that's generally a problem for me anyway.

SR Is it like a problem with boundaries?

SE I think I keep up my boundaries because I am afraid to let them down.

SR Because making art is so consuming and you struggle against being consumed by it?

SE Right, and not being able to transition back to regular life. Jay was the first person I've had in my life, the first man I've had in my life who really understands that. I mean, oddly, you know, accepts that in me, more than anyone else I have known as a love partner. But it helps, yet in a way maybe it doesn't give me something to fight against. I grew up in a house where everyone argued all the time. So maybe the lack of that about my art is part of the problem. But, yeah, I think I'm afraid of what's in there. I'm afraid my work will be as dark as it has been. When I'm making art, I just think about inhumanity constantly. One of the reasons I'm painting still lifes now is to counter some of that. And I love doing them. It doesn't feel like a bad thing to do at all. Even though I'm afraid of oil paint, it's what—it's sort of what I aspire back to. The still lifes are a way for me to get back to using oil. They are beautiful. I feel like I need to do them. I mean, still lifes are beautiful.

SR I'm very interested in your struggle with art—being compelled to it, and yet afraid that it would consume you somehow. So, would you say you have an ambivalent relationship with art?

SE No, I wouldn't. The only way I know who I am is by being an artist. Nothing else feels authentic, even though there are other things I care about and like doing, like writing about our history, curatorial work, teaching. I don't feel like any of those things. I only feel like an artist. It's the only way I can make sense to myself. So, it's not ambivalent. Because I don't feel like I have a choice. But my ability to do the work at this point does feel ambivalent. What I'm really afraid about now is—I'm afraid of the art world. The art world is such a market now. It's such anathema to who I am, and how I feel about art. It's almost sacrilegious. I'm terrible at dealing with my art work as a product; it's painful.

SR It is always open to evaluation, I guess.

SE It's not just that, but it becomes decoration. You know—art is sacred.

SR It feels like there's no real meaning to it.

SE Right; absolutely, it becomes decoration, an investment. I don't even think there is anything bad with decorative art. I really don't. There's a lot of it I love and love looking at. But it's not what I'm about.

Commentary

At this point in her life, Erony has a strong sense of who she is and what her history is about. It took years of research and exploration into her past to create a coherent narrative about her life in the context of her family's history. For many years, she found herself drawn to subjects that were in some ways related to her father's trauma—genocide, politicide, ethnic cleansing, the Chilean disappeared, and other instances of oppression and inhumanity. Her preoccupation with mounds and with the Tower of Babel appear to be fitting symbols of what her father endured but could not face or communicate. The unacknowledged and unmourned traumas in his life were given expression in her artwork. The art is an example of *postmemory* aesthetics (Hirsch, 1996), the second-generation memory of collective traumatic events such as the pogroms of Eastern Europe, the Chilean Disappeared, and the Holocaust. Through her imaginative recreation, Erony calls attention to and helps us remember these disenfranchised groups; she commemorates and mourns their experience and in so doing facilitates mourning and remembrance in her viewers.

Before I met Erony, I had some idea of her family history and her interest in the art of trauma, but I had no inkling that she was a victim of child sexual abuse. It was especially enlightening to learn about how the creative process facilitated the retrieval of her memories and helped her cope with what she remembered. In her late 20s, she began to have flashbacks, which she said, took her back to making art:

> All I remember is one day having this compulsion to draw pictures of a female figure, like myself, who was in the situation that I was in with my uncle, and it was the only thing that gave me any peace . . . doing the drawings made the memories more concrete because I had given them form . . . I felt so badly for the woman in the drawings. I felt huge sadness. I think I was able to feel compassion . . . I was able to be a witness to my own pain, my own self by putting it outside, by putting myself outside of myself.

She talked about the fact that art always makes her feel safe in that it is the only area of her life where she has a sense of mastery and where she truly feels in control:

> I can control almost nothing out in the world, but there is a sense of on my canvas, on the piece of art I am making, unless it is a commission, it is mine, it is my universe. I can do whatever I want on that. That feels safe. I think it is also a meditative thing because when I am doing very repetitive kinds of work, it really has some of the same benefits for me I think as meditation which I love doing.

Both spontaneously and in response to my questions, Erony made a number of references to the aspect of the creative process that I have referred to as a dissociative phenomenon, a trance-like experience integral to making art (see chapter 3). At one point, she told me that in graduate school, she took a class in guided imagery and that as a result of her experience with this technique, she started to draw again because of the images coming into her head. She welcomes this altered state and said that for it to happen, she has to be making art on a regular basis and "turn my head off enough to just go with the process and to trust myself enough." At those times, she was so immersed in the process that all questions about the value of what she was doing seemed to disappear. She described the experience this way:

> Everything else is just gone. I have had moments where it is almost as if I have lost consciousness . . . I did a portrait of my grandfather, and I was painting his eyes, and three hours went by, I did not know where they went.

Erony made a point of letting me know that this state of flow is not always present for her. That she has to feel safe as a prerequisite and has to be exclusively engaged in the process of making art. One of the things that interfere is a dialogue with an internal critic that has a blocking effect on her work. Yet at the same time she has a fear of being consumed, "like my skin dissolves," and of "not being able to transition back to regular life." Another concern is the darkness of her art: "When I'm making art, I just think about inhumanity constantly. One of the reasons I'm painting still lifes now is to counter some of that."

Erony's struggle with her art is reminiscent of Otto Rank's (1932/1989) analysis of the artist's fight with art. He wrote, "The inhibitions of which artists complain, both during creation and its intervals, are the ego's necessary protections against being swallowed up by creativity" (p. 386). Rank's understanding of the psychology of the artist is that he/she has an unusually strong tendency to become deeply absorbed and is inclined to flee from life into creation, an area where he/she can exercise total control. However, Rank believes that the same dynamic gets played out in the area of creation with the result that strong boundaries must be erected by the artist to protect the self from total surrender to the work. Ways of self-protecting include becoming involved in more than one project at a time or setting aside the work because of an inability or an unwillingness to complete it. Rank also observes that another way in which the artist protects the self against complete exhaustion in the creative process is by the diversion of artistic creation from a formative into a cognitive scientific process.

This seems to be the case with Erony's rendition of her haunting, unsettling self-portrait. This highly realistic piece of artwork in oil, acrylic, and burnt paper features her face split into two halves; one an attractive woman with an earnest expression, the other a skull representing death and decay. "It's like a dance of death," she says, adding, "It was pretty interesting to do, facing my mortality in not a very deep way." She presented the piece as an intellectual exercise devoid of emotionality, and yet the effect of this work on the viewer is chilling. Similarly, she told me that she loves skulls and finds bones aesthetically beautiful, yet at the same time she seems to recognize her own defensive process when she spontaneously acknowledged that thinking of skulls as beautiful is "also a way of not thinking about what they really mean."

The split in the self-image is reminiscent of Rank's (1941/1958) concept of the "double" or the doppelganger, the projected split-off part of the self—a common phenomenon found in folklore and literature. According to Rank, the artist takes the traditional folktale and lifts it from its superstitious entanglements into a human struggle for immortality. The double is the reminder of the individual's mortality and in its most primitive form represents both the living and the dead person (p. 71). Egon Schiele is another artist who used the doppelganger in a number of double self-portraits. One in particular, titled *Death and Man*, where he fuses his face with a skeleton-like figure of death standing behind him, is reminiscent of Erony's juxtaposition (Kandel, 2012; Knafo, 1991a).

In much of her artwork, Erony has dealt with the theme of death, most of it focused on the past and on memory, but in her self-portrait, she moved beyond the present into the future by projecting the self forward into a time when her flesh will be gone. Even in the "live" version of the face, there are symbols that foreshadow death in the form of vines: "The vines are nature taking everything back again to itself." Paradoxically, in the expression of her mortality, Erony reaches toward immortality through her art. Erony's artwork has also given life to her father who died when she was only 25. His story, which he could never tell her, found its way into her art. Through the process of creation, she was able to maintain her deep connection with her father, give him a voice, memorialize his life and his losses, and make sense of her own trauma history.

Both of the artists whom I interviewed in this chapter had been deeply influenced by the mystifications of the previous generation who, unable to face their own trauma, transmitted it to their loved ones without conscious intention. Apparently, as young children, Ofra Bloch and Susan Erony were intensely curious about what they sensed but could not grasp. Initially I did not approach these interviews with this common theme in mind; it emerged as the interviews evolved. But even more striking was the sudden realization, as I was completing this chapter, that this theme, which I found so compelling, actually mirrored my own childhood experience of growing up in the shadow of the Holocaust and living with the unacknowledged known during my years in hiding and beyond (Richman, 2012). The irony is that this dark legacy that was handed down to the three of us actually inspired us in adulthood to create affecting, emotionally charged, and meaningful art, and thus bring to light what had been hidden in the shadows.

Notes

1. This interview has been edited for clarity, length, and content. For a description and analysis of the film, see the review in *Psychoanalytic Perspectives* by Oltarsh-McCarthy (2007).

2. I refer to the 1997 Italian film directed by and starring Roberto Benigni as an Italian Jew imprisoned in a concentration camp with his young son. In this tragic comedy genre, Benigni turns the experience into a game to shield his son from the horrors around him. Part of the film came from Benigni's own family history; before his birth, Roberto's father had survived three years in the Bergen-Belsen concentration camp.

3. *The World at War* is a 26-episode British television documentary series chronicling the events of the Second World War.

4. Erony's artist's statement from 1995–2000.

5. This interview has been edited for clarity and length.

6. WPA stands for the Works Progress Administration, a relief measure established in 1935 to provide work for the unemployed. FDR are the initials commonly used to refer to Franklin Delano Roosevelt, the President of the United States between 1933 and 1945.

7. *Night and Fog* is a 1955 documentary film about the Nazi concentration camps; it is one of the first films about the horrors of the Holocaust.

8. *Shoah* is a 9½ hour documentary film about the Holocaust by Claude Lanzmann, who interviews survivors, witnesses, and ex-Nazis.

9. To see this painting in color go to the artist's website: www.SusanErony.com.

7

MUSIC AND THE GREAT WOUND

Spyros D. Orfanos

Two generations before the Trojan War, Orpheus was born at the sacred foot of Mount Olympus to Calliope, the wise Muse of epic poetry with the beautiful voice. He travelled to foreign lands at a young age and when he returned he had a lyre, a gift from his father, the god Apollo. He became the most celebrated musician, poet, and prophet of ancient Greece, enchanting wild beasts and trees alike. According to Aeschylus and Euripides, his lyrical powers were such that he was capable even of charming the stones.

Orpheus loved Eurydice, who was a girl born to wood nymphs. He was loved by her above every mortal creature. While nature was preparing their harmonious union, a small serpent bit the nymph and she died and descended to the Underworld. For Orpheus, it was the end of the world he knew.

Orpheus wandered far and wide and reached the Underworld with nothing but his lyre as his only weapon. His songs were so soothing to the souls in the Underworld that the god Hades finally yielded and agreed to allow Orpheus to return to the light with his beloved. There was, however, one condition: that Eurydice should not see Orpheus' face, only his back, on their return to the light. Just before the pair reached the upper world of the living, Orpheus turned to look upon the shadow that was following him. Immediately, Eurydice changed back into what she had been: unrecognizable and invisible.

Orpheus was inconsolable at this second loss of his beloved. He turned harsh toward life and could not endure paying homage to the gods. Over time, his hair whitened and he returned to his homeland Thrace, and no one ever heard him grieve again over death. Except after he was ripped to shreds by frenzied women for never loving again, his severed head would lament and sing wildly about grief. His singing filled the valleys and oceans with mournful sounds that had never been heard before or since. No one on Mount Olympus ever forgot Orpheus or his hymns. The spirit of the prophet-musician ran in the blood of the Greeks and other seafaring peoples everywhere who longed for Eros and feared Thanatos.

The myth of Orpheus and Eurydice is a very old Greek story about Eros and Thanatos and endures for many reasons. Here it is adapted by this writer and with some help from the British classicist Nigel Spivey (2005). One of the first operas ever created, Monteverdi's *L'Orfeo*, composed in 1607, still has the honor of being regularly performed and speaks to the relevance of artists dealing with the subject of death. The poet Rainer Maria Rilke wrote a lyrically intense cycle of 55 sonnets in 1922 titled *Sonnets of Orpheus* as a "grave marker" to the memory of his daughter's dead playmate. In 1947, the choreographer George Balanchine collaborated with the composer Igor Stravinsky to create the ballet *Orpheus*. The playwright Tennessee Williams used the legend to address the trauma of racism in his 1957 play *Orpheus Descending*. And in 1959, the French filmmaker Marcel Camus created *Orfeu Negro* with Antonio Carlos Jobim's sizzling samba soundtrack following the doomed lovers through Rio de Janeiro. As recently as 2010, Vermont-based Anaïs Mitchell composed *Hadestown,* a folk opera based on the myth. Clearly, a theme for these creators and countless others is the use of art to make some kind of sense out of tragic and traumatic loss. Over the millennia countless artists have been inspired by the myth, no doubt because it places art and trauma at the center of its story. It has been part of our cultural heritage, perhaps not only for its narrative motifs but also because it deals with what it means to be human and our inability to master nature and death.

The Greeks were not likely to have invented the Orpheus and Eurydice myth, but they were likely the first to think about it. Their thinking was poetic. The central problem, or indeed privilege, with much if not all of Greek mythology is its multiplicity and heterogeneity. For the Greeks, the mythical ability of Orpheus to descend into Hades expresses symbolic faith in the power of art.

Music is positioned properly with Eros and Thanatos; they interpenetrate. The ancients referred to music as *mousike*.[1] Their thinking about *mousike* was also poetic. Plato says, "Just as we have exercise for the body, so for the soul we have music (*mousike*)" (Badiou, 2012, p. 302). But the soul, as Orpheus knows, suffers, and music expresses this suffering well.

While this and other myths may easily represent romantic and nostalgic Freudian ideas (Trilling, 2000; Wilson, 1932), the current essay takes a more contemporary, relational psychoanalytic approach. I am interested in the dynamic nonlinear relations among events. This approach values an aesthetic that is based on complex multiplicities and contexts. It does not necessarily privilege inner or outer psychological worlds. It resists the myth of the sick artist or the idea that all those wounded are pathological. It resists causal connections (i.e., between the fantasy of castration and artistic power). Weakness does not preclude strength nor strength weakness. The relational aesthetic is polyphonic and polydialectic.

A Very Short and Selective History of Music and Psychoanalysis

Freud had an unremarkable relationship to music.[2] Given the gregarious Vienna of his day, a city that loved its music in all forms, its world-famous opera, its excellent theater, its composers, writers, poets, actors and actresses, it is of interest that Freud admitted music meant little to him. "I am no great connoisseur of music," he once remarked to a patient (Wortis, 1954).[3] During an earlier period, he wrote, ". . . with music, I am almost incapable of obtaining any pleasure. Some rationalistic, or perhaps analytic, turn of mind in me rebels against being moved by a thing without knowing why I am thus affected and what it is that affects me (Freud, 1914/1953, p. 211).

If we sidestep psychoanalytic mischief and reject the idea that there may have been extremely strong motives for Freud to reject this important part of his culture, motives as we see below that might be associated with his early relationship to his mother, we are left with the hypothesis that Freud's artistic interests (1908/1958) were predisposed to literature, sculpture, and to a lesser extent paintings. The unconscious mind for Freud was a fertile place for visual representation of any kind (Bergstein, 2010). Auditory representation in mental life was undervalued.

The early Freudian world, however, was open to areas of study not especially valued by the father of psychoanalysis. Thus, the Wednesday Society did spend considerable time investigating the psychology of great musicians in the process of composing music. One of the founding members of the Wednesday Society, Max Graf, was a musicologist, who presented material about "the psychological processes of Beethoven and Richard Wagner in writing music" (Graf, 1942). As the first to apply Freud's clinical findings and theoretical formulations to musical creativity, Graf noted in 1911 that Wagner produced innovative musical pieces (opera styles) involving new conceptual forms in relation to life's vicissitudes, rather than on the basis of psychopathology. Wagner was understood to be expressing in highly artistic ways his personalized needs and conflicts and in so doing transforming the very medium of opera.

Psychoanalyst and violinist Richard Sterba (1965), also a member of the Wednesday Society, reviewed the state of music and psychoanalysis up to the 1940s and noted that, despite the significance of musical activity for society and culture, relatively little had appeared on the subject in the psychoanalytic literature, compared with studies of other forms of artistic expression. Basically, music was understood to be a regressive experience during the period of classical psychoanalysis; it had to do with early development, ego boundaries, and narcissistic pleasures. Composers wrote music when they had advanced ego abilities and were trying to safeguard against massive threatening regression. In short, sublimation was the explanation for creativity.

With the appearance of Ernst Kris's 1952 classic, *Psychoanalytic Explorations in Art,* ego psychology replaced id psychology as the preferred explanation for creativity. Kris coined the alluring conceptual phrase "regression in the service of the ego." Soon after, the ideas behind the phrase were critiqued by Ernst Schachtel (1959/1984) in his brilliant treatise *Metamorphosis.* Schachtel introduced the importance of affect as a primary motivational condition and thus opened the way for creativity to be accounted for by curiosity, environmental stimulation, exploratory activity, and competence.

By the middle of the 20th century, music as a topic for psychoanalysts had lost its elevated status. Heinz Kohut was the exception. Prior to developing self psychology, Kohut (1957) addressed music but did so in a fashion typical for his day. That is, he focused on explanations that favored sublimation and ego mastery. Lachmann (2001) points out, however, that Kohut hinted at three novel ideas having to do with music and psychoanalysis. First, Kohut encouraged analysts to listen to the sounds of the patient's voice and the music that lies behind the voice. Second, he highlighted the central role of repetition and rhythm in musical composition, something he also did with the clinical encounter. Lastly, he compared music to "play," thereby moving away from the discharge-reduction model. The influence of these three tantalizing ideas on the study of music and psychoanalysis took time to be realized. For this writer, an additional important idea heralded by Kohut was that "the extraverbal nature of music lends itself particularly well by offering a subtle transition to preverbal modes of psychological functioning" (1957, p. 407). Kohut clearly was leaning in the direction of music as a pre-verbal mode of experience.

There was another interesting exception in the study of psychoanalysis and music during the mid-20th century. In 1953, Theodore Reik published an astonishingly revealing and entertaining memoir for a psychoanalyst of that era about his experiences in life and music. He attempts to answer the question, "What does it mean when some tune follows you, occurs to you again and again so that it becomes a haunting melody?" Reik takes us through a 28-year personal journey and reveals his block at writing a book-length study of the composer Mahler. His self-analysis points to a misguided reverence underpinned by unconscious grandiosity and a fear of death.

Pinchas Noy (1968) hypothesized a "primary empathy" in relation to how music affects a listener's emotions. A person's response to the recognition of the close similarity of visceral and auditory contours is based on pre-verbal, pre-wired sensitivity to another's emotions. Interestingly, there is support for this hypothesis in contemporary neuroscience (Rose, 2004). Compatible with the above are Lachmann's (2001) observations about music and infant research. First, both music and infant research focus on rhythms. This explains how powerful connections are forged on the one hand between infant and caregiver and on the other hand among composer, performer, and listener. Second, he notes the interactive nature of the participants and their co-constructed regulation of satisfaction and frustration. In a compelling analysis of the composer and conductor Leonard Bernstein's ideas about surface and depth music aesthetics, Lachmann demonstrates the relevance of empirically informed psychoanalysis to music. Interestingly, Nagel (2013) also turns to Leonard Bernstein as a model for examining the value and uses of music and psychoanalytic knowledge. She analyses Bernstein's *West Side Story* score for the intersection of musical theory and theories of the mind. Nagel finds ambiguity, conflict, and the opportunity for "working through" Bernstein's intrapsychic world by way of the music.

Following the recent clinical turn to affective attunement, Gilbert Rose (2004) has emphasized affect regulation and trauma. He writes about the healing powers of music and its role in clinical cases of traumatic stress. He concludes that music elicits pre-verbal internalizations that embody and encode affective memories, which contribute to affect regulation. In addition, he believes that the affective interplay with music may itself become internalized as a non-verbal affect-regulating presence. In some ways, the work of Rose is cutting-edge in that it employs neuroscience and affective attunement, but ultimately, his theoretical speculations are too grand and his clinical evidence too thin.

Oswald (1997) favors a theory of music derived from the work of Winnicott, who did not articulate a theory of music but whose formulations on transitional objects and phenomena are quite applicable to music. Winnicott included the infant's use of noises, sounds, and words within his earliest thoughts about transitional phenomena. Extending Winnicott's ideas, we can view music as a transitional object, not unlike a pillow, a blanket, or a toy. Music can be a way of maintaining a sense of security for the baby when she or he is separated from the mother—tunes, fragments of songs, rhymes, and media noises may be taken along by a child in his or her quest for independence, to be repeated while playing alone, during moments of solitude, or while falling asleep (Winnicott, 1953). Thus, while music can become an object, it is also linked to meaning-making of the self. Children may also rearrange the sound and rhythm they have heard—a kind of primitive interest in composing new pieces or decomposing the old ones.

As children grow older, certain aspects of music often continue to be mental links or reminders of earlier experiences that have been associated with feelings or states of security, closeness, pleasure, and intimacy. One can observe this introspectively when familiar songs and musical pieces evoke strong memories and emotions of childhood situations. The process may be similar to that of mourning for someone who has been lost forever. The history of music offers numerous examples of the transitional linking properties of musical themes particularly around loss and mourning (Pollock, 1978).

Recently, Stein (2012) has conceptually outlined psychoanalysis and music as connected by three common concerns: the study of meaning, the nature of expression of affects, and the forms of communication. He writes that the fundamental nexus of music and psychoanalysis is the interpretation of meaning from sound. This is a conceptual approach to understanding the psychological meaning of music and has an affinity with numerous previous authors. It has been the meaning of the music that most psychoanalysts have been after rather than its unconscious structure. In a different and inspired metapsychological approach, Slavin (2012) seeks to locate the birth of existential anxiety in a complex set of gains and losses when humans initially moved away from their connectedness with nature. Using a sophisticated evolutionary lens, Slavin finds art, particularly music, to be a complementary form of communication. As we evolve it permits us to maintain an ongoing creative tension with that new, far more dis-embodied abstract/linguistic dimension of our being. Sacred art, music, and rituals expressed in the prehistoric caves about 40,000 years ago created a "transitional" or "potential space," in line with Winnicottian ideas. Thus, the deep structures of musical form

160

became connected to the universal aspects of the human condition and our sense of self in the world.

In a more experience-near approach, Lachmann (2012) creatively takes up the matter of music's emotional engagement and how it can bypass meaning or language. He argues that in order to strike an emotional chord, music must meet, surpass, but especially violate expectations. This idea was originally proposed by the music critic Leonard B. Meyer (1956), who pointed out that emotions in response to music depend on violations of expectations, or in other words, on novelty in music. Meyer hypothesized that listeners need a basic implicit or explicit knowledge about the patterns of the music they listen to. Expectations can only be violated when there is a preconceived notion of what to expect from a piece. Focusing exclusively on the mind, Lachmann finds validation for this idea in the empirical work of Beebe and Lachmann (2002), which proposes that infants have a built-in motivation to detect patterns and contingent relations and generate procedural expectancies of the occurrence of events.[4] Although there are many variations of expectations, core expectations are of living in a predictable world as well as expectations of an emotionally responsive caretaker. Lachmann writes that

> violations of these expectations through traumatic childhood experiences, evocative music, or misguided or pleasantly surprising therapeutic interactions can transform positive affect into fear, or can transform fear and anxiety into a positive, calming or even intimate affective experience. (2012, p. 9).

Clearly, the chills, awe, and tears we experience when listening to music can be the result of our expectations as influenced by a conductor or a composer. Correspondingly, humans, both child and adult, depend on pattern recognition of emotions and interactions. They react to the manipulations and/or violations of expectations by significant others.

In summary, the movement in music and psychoanalysis over the past 100 years has been from id psychology to ego psychology to pluralistic explorations that avoid reductionism and the pathologizing of art and artists (Nass, 1989). Affect regulation and nonverbal interactions now dominate speculations about music. Large theoretical speculations now use an interdisciplinary approach.

"Song of Songs"

A great hero of the Greeks enters the ancient Herodion Atticus amphitheater at the southern slope of the Acropolis on the evening of the 29th of September in 2007. Aides guide him slowly and carefully across the large semi-circle area between the front of the stage and the first row of seats. He is tentative in his steps but confident of purpose. The audience of 5,000 gives him a standing ovation for once again coming to the aid of the Greeks with his music. He is raising funds to aid the victims of the devastating summer fires in the historic Peloponnesus region. As he struggles to guide his tall, failing, 83-year-old body onto the front row marble seat, he acknowledges the Hellenes by raising his right hand over his unruly white mane of hair and smiles as if to say, "Together, we will triumph over tragedy." The Athenians applaud wildly as they have done hundreds, maybe thousands, of times before. Mikis Theodorakis is leading the Greeks once again in mourning and celebration. He is linking Apollo and Dionysius.

This night and the next one are dedicated to dealing with tragedy with song, an old Greek custom, but maybe even a universal one. The songs are all by Theodorakis. For over seven decades he has composed songs about tragedy and trauma—songs for the concert stage, songs for seashore taverns and village squares, songs for the victims of oppression and torture. He creates songs about bread and wine, and about love and death. He weds his deep melodies to Nobel Prize–winning poetry and has every intellectual and waiter singing the same songs. He weds art and politics.

The Athenian taxi drivers still gossip about the cause of the catastrophic fires—arsonists motivated by real estate greed, or is it the Bush administration trying to undermine the Greek olive industry? Even Theodorakis has his suspicions. Weeks earlier he asked that I translate into English his statement about the crisis. While I struggled and failed to do justice to the rhythm, tone, and melody of his written words, his daughter, Margarita, was busy producing two historic concerts at the most sacred, most architecturally breathtaking of outdoor concert sites: the Odeon of Herodion Atticus. Margarita Theodorakis produced a fundraiser that proved even the ancient stones sing her father's songs. She assembled all the great vocalists in Greece: lyrical voices, jazz voices, rock voices, rural voices, and blues voices. And with her father's blessings, she invited one young woman from America, Lina Orfanos.

The audience knows Theodorakis is in poor health. Years of torture, detention, solitary confinement, and exile for "crimes against the state" have taken their toll on his body. The audience understands that this night might be the last time they see him. He is their greatest creator. He is also a political hero. He may have an international reputation as a composer of popular and symphonic music, but Theodorakis is a Greek in temperament, intellect, and ambition. He violated artistic expectations when he set off the cultural revolution in Greece in 1960 with a song cycle about a mother's lament for her murdered son. His brave opposition to the brutal military junta of 1967–1974 is legendary. His activism continues to inspire social and political progressives in a nation that is currently under a devastating economic depression. Early in this century, the Greek government nominated him for the Nobel Peace Prize for his peace efforts with Turkey and his advocacy of human rights.

The performers are all dressed in black. The audience is in short sleeves and summer dresses, the politicians in suits. Herodion holds 5,000 people, seated on marble rows. It is now three hours into the concert, and my wife, Sophia, and I are reaching new heights of anxiety. Much earlier in the evening, we bid Lina good luck backstage, as she joined the ranks of the greatest Greek vocalists. She has never performed in front of such a large audience, and while she has a natural stage presence, sophisticated training, and a voice that Theodorakis himself has called beautiful and suited for his lyrical songs, Sophia and I worry. True to our psychologies, her mother worries that Lina will have stage fright; I worry that she will not hit all the notes dead center. But we both know, too, that this is her destiny, to be on this stage, on this night, with this particular song: "Song of Songs." We know she will rise to the occasion. That is what Lina does. She is our hero. Lina's expressive gifts are more cunning than her brain tumor. She is a survivor of 12 years. The tumor, reduced by surgery, now lies dormant in her skull. Lina knows trauma.[5]

The master of ceremonies is about to introduce Lina. I have a frightening thought: What if he says she is from the United States? Will the audience disapprove because of their outrage over the Iraq war? Will they take out their frustrations on Lina? Will they boo her? Will she become flustered? Will she stay on stage? The master of ceremonies announces that Lina Orfanos is a third-generation Greek from New York City on her father's side and that her mother is a Polish Jew. The audience bursts into applause as if acknowledging their own immigrant relatives in New York City.

The lights dim and we see Lina's silhouette as she walks onto the large stage with the 11-piece orchestra composed of classical and folk musicians. Along with her music she is carrying a white handkerchief belonging to the elderly Bonika Kassoutou Nahmias, one of the few Greek Jews who survived Auschwitz. The long, mournful introduction, a line of sheer beauty, heralds a song that was introduced in 1965 as part of a cycle of songs titled *Mauthausen Cantata*. The song cycle is a requiem for Holocaust victims and raised the consciousness of all Greeks. Its sublime melodic lines, extended harmonies and rhythms, forced listeners to ask, "What happened to our Jews?" With original text and quotes from the Old Testament, "Song of Songs" is part of a poem cycle about the Mauthausen concentration camp, the Greek Jews and political prisoners it housed and murdered.

> *How lovely is my love*
> *in her everyday dress*
> *with a little comb in her hair.*
> *No one knew how lovely she was.*
>
> *Girls of Auschwitz,*
> *girls of Dachau.*
> *Did you see my love?*
>
> *We saw her on a long journey;*
> *She wasn't wearing her everyday dress*
> *or the little comb in her hair.*

How lovely is my love
caressed by her mother,
and her brother's kisses.
Nobody knew how lovely she was.

Girls of Mauthausen,
girls of Belsen.
Did you see my love?

We saw her in the frozen square
with a number on her white hand
and a yellow star on her heart.[6]

The song is a true love story about two prisoners. The interpenetration of melody and word make it an extraordinary representation of Eros and Thanatos. Iakovos Kambanellis, the poet and the father of contemporary Greek theater, was interned at the Nazi concentration camp of Mauthausen in Austria. Not adhering to Theodor Adorno's famous dictum that it would be barbaric to write lyrical poetry after Auschwitz, Kambanellis wrote his poems in 1964 and in the following year presented them to Theodorakis. The composer worked on them and created songs that have entered the pantheon of acclaimed song cycles.[7] The *Mauthausen* Cantata has been sung in Greek, Hebrew, German, and English. It has been performed all over the world and was featured at the 50th anniversary of the liberation of the Mauthausen concentration camp.

With a huge screen behind the orchestra showing photographic images of the Holocaust, Lina enters the song. Sophia and I clutch hands. After her first words, the audience applauds in recognition. Lina is emotionally expressive but unsentimental. Having taken up a suggestion from me and then approved by Theodorakis himself, she sings in both Greek and Hebrew. She knows what she is singing about, and she knows that, in part, she is addressing her mother, who was a hidden child during the Nazi terrors in Europe; her father, who wept when he first heard this deep song and still does; and Theodorakis himself, who once explained that "Pop music helps us forget. Greek music helps us remember" (Orfanos, 1997). The audience wildly applauds young Lina twice more as her voice reveals despair and depth. Theodorakis is also applauding. His face reveals admiration, gratitude, and surprise.[8]

By Way of Music and Meaning

This essay includes a real-world event in order to underscore the immense complexity of grasping what relations exist among musical creativity, performance, and meaning. Words and music, the personal and the political, remembering and forgetting, trauma and recovery, and villains and heroes are all dialectical components of the concert presented that night on the Acropolis. My effort here is to think about music in the broadest sense, including the social and historical surrounds (Jameson, 2009), and the various subjectivities, at least to give an illustration of such. In this essay, I am not particularly interested in "art for art's sake": *l'art pour l'art.*

We know that music has the capacity to mesmerize, excite, soothe, and heal. It communicates emotions, aesthetics, history, and even philosophy. Yet "music" is an inadequate word to encompass all the forms of culture that can be ascribed to it. Music is not a singular phenomenon with a fully knowable relationship to human biology, mind, and behavior. Rather, it exists as *musics*—diverse, multiple, and unknowable within a single unitary framework of scales and notations. We are in all likelihood speaking about a multiplicity of activities and experiences. In addition, we are likely speaking about both activity and aesthetics. Music is a small word, yet what it signifies is large.

It is uncertain what music "really" is, but one of the things on which we probably do agree, at least some of the time, is that music sounds the way moods feel. An additional principle that many might agree upon is that music is performance art. According to Cook (1998), the meaning of music lies more in what it does than in what it represents. But both representation and action are at play, and this is one of music's unique qualities as a form of art. While the Herodion concert represents much from the past, it also is, in its transactions among the players both on and off the stage, clearly a performance activity. It is not simply representing a reality outside of music; the performance itself also *constructs* a reality of tragedy and trauma. With "Song of Songs," Theodorakis captures something deep about how the Holocaust felt, and in turn changed the culture of Greece.[9] By assigning music to the material, he intensifies the words so that the Holocaust can be conceived—by performing "Song of Songs" Theodorakis and his interpreters further the understanding of the listener, in vivo. Musical performance constructs reality, in addition to representing it.

While the sights and scents on the evening of September 29, 2007, were profound, it was the music in the amphitheater, at least for this listener, which underscored the experience. The feeling was of being in a sonorous envelope. While Lina's song was plaintive and heralded mourning, I felt pleasure being surrounded by the sounds of "Song of Songs." The pleasure was in her vocal pragmatics and in the details of the musical structure of the song. This was art. Simultaneously, I felt anxiety about the other space I was in—a space that had elements of entrapment. That is, the personal context of Lina's physical trauma and the historical trauma represented by the song were horrifying to me. Still, this, too, was art. The intermingling of pleasure and horror—what the music critic David Schwarz (1997) refers to as the "crossing of the sonorous envelope"—is what gives music dynamic force. This is a subjective register that I believe is another of the unique attainments of music.

It is true that my experience was enhanced by the Holocaust photographs projected onto the huge screen behind the orchestra. The images stimulated my optical unconscious—murder, prejudice, swastikas, trains, emaciated bodies—as these images unfolded in my vision. But it was the sonorous envelope that actually made for my experience of awe. The music created a space for me that crossed the threshold between my clearly bounded body with its own rhythms and my archaic psyche with its memories and hopes. My experience shifted from linear time into something quite different—an unpredictable ebb and flow that was strangely synchronized with past, present, and future. It is too reductive to call this an "oceanic" feeling, as Freud might put it. I was in a different self-state. I was mentally alert. Music critics might say, I had "shivers down my spine," and "goose bumps."

Evidence of extended relational processes can be discovered at the Herodion. For instance, the theme of creativity and trauma was everywhere. One can easily identify a number of traumas: the Holocaust; the national tragedy of the fires in the Peloponnese; the internment and beatings suffered by the composer at the hands of the World War II fascists; the internment of the poet at Mauthausen; Lina's life-threatening brain tumor; and her mother's survival of the Holocaust as a hidden child. And then there is the experience of this narrator, who as a very young boy listened to countless retellings of his own mother's frightening stories about rescuing Greek Jews. Thinking hard about the overlap, the levels within levels of what went on that night at the Herodion, leaves me feeling overwhelmed. Yet somewhere in the creative experience there is the important matter of musical art as a way to transcend individual and collective trauma, as a way to heal that which cannot be healed.

Creativity as a Memorializing Aesthetic

Creativity is intimately involved in everyday experiences, in the construction and expression of personal and political values. Memorializing art has been with us since the time of the ancient Egyptians, who delighted in architectural commemorations of bulls and goats. We have come to know it from art as diverse as the Vietnam War Memorial in Washington, D.C., to the ongoing AIDS Memorial Quilt that began as a community arts project in 1987. The passion that memorializing involves can be found in this century in the intense and angry debates over a memorial at Ground Zero for the victims of the September 11 attacks. Mikis Theodorakis harnessed the passion of mourning for the deep damage done to his country and joined it to his unique compositional gifts, thereby creating memorializing art of the first order.

Theodorakis's "Song of Songs" was created as the composer was looking to move beyond his astonishingly popular "folk" music of the early 1960s. His popularity in Greece surpassed that of the Beatles in the Anglophone world. The artistic merits of his songs were being debated in all major Athenian intellectual circles because Theodorakis had dared to bridge the gap between high art and low art (mass culture). He did this by wedding sophisticated poetry to the *bouzouki*, a folk instrument of the lower classes. He wedded the music of the concert halls to music of workers and the poor. Like many creators, he was moving to increasingly complex structures in his work. He would not rest on his laurels and formulaically repeat compositions for the marketplace. His musical gifts coupled with social and political engagement made for a restless and revolutionary spirit. He was the model of the engaged artist.

Greece lost close to 87% of its Jews during the Holocaust, and as a man of the Left, Theodorakis knew that the only organized Greek group that officially and proactively worked to save them from the Nazis was the Communist Party. His historical consciousness was such that he immediately took up the opportunity when presented with the poems by his fellow Leftist Kambanellis. He had already laid the groundwork for songs based on poetry and memory, but the Holocaust required different colors and instruments.[10] For five years he had caught the ears of the Greeks like few other composers of his generation. His public was alert to every new work he recorded and every concert he gave as if they thirsted for an art that would transform their cultural identity. The early 1960s were dark days for Greece, largely due to the vacuum in political leadership and the legacies of World War II and the Civil War that raged after it. Theodorakis's publically stated cultural aim was"music for the masses." His project became prominent in daily life as if feeding the self-esteem of the entire nation. People waited with great anticipation for his new compositions. They paid emotional and intellectual attention. The public was an active recipient. The dynamic poetics of the times were unprecedented. It was a golden age of culture.

Meanwhile, Theodorakis used an unknown, 18-year-old female named Maria Farantouri, who was in possession of a powerful coloratura voice. A victim of polio at the age of 2, Farantouri seemed to be more than a simple middleperson between the composer and the audience. As she became legendary over the next four decades, in part for singing the Mauthausen songs, Farantouri, with her beautiful voice and a serious limp, came to symbolize the nation.[11]

Why did Theodorakis decide to set the Kambanellis poems in the first place? "I did this with much pleasure," he explains,

> Firstly because I liked the poetry of the texts, and secondly because I was myself locked up during the Nazi occupation in Italian and German prisons, but mainly because this composition gives us the chance to remind the younger generation of history, that history must never be forgotten . . . the *Mauthausen Cantata* is addressed to all those who suffered under Fascism and fought against it. We must keep the Nazi crimes continually in our minds, because that is the only guarantee and the only way to assure that they are not repeated. And we can see every day that the ghost of Fascism is far from being laid to rest. It seldom shows its real face, but Fascist cultures and mentalities exist all over the world. For us, who had to live through this time of horror, the most important task is to protect our children against this peril.[12]

His aim was to oppose historical amnesia.

We live in ironic political times, and in 2003 Theodorakis was alarmingly accused of anti-Semitism. Kambanellis was also accused. Like many other members of the European Left, both men perceive successive Israeli governments as resorting to excessive military force for security. Both are passionate human-rights activists even in their old age and feel strongly that the policy of some Israeli leaders, particularly of the Right, is the oppression of Palestinians and opposition to a two-state solution. But it is Theodorakis, with the more public persona and his stronger ties to the Israeli Left, who has been given the greater media attention.

At a press conference for the launching of a book based on his own poetry, Theodorakis began to berate the then-Sharon government and the State of Israel. In the presence of Greek government officials, he said, "The Jews are at the root of evil." This statement was then taken out of context and circulated through the world. It became an extraordinary source of embarrassment for him and his supporters. Some leaders of the Greek Jewish community tossed it off as the words of an old man.[13] When I had the opportunity to confront him about this,[14] he explained in a matter-of-fact tone that his views about the Israeli people are well-known, as are his feelings about racism and other forms of hatred. He claimed not to confuse the struggles of a people with the aggression of their government. "True," he stated, "I did make a poor choice of words and there are segments of Greek society that fan the flames of hatred against the Israelites, but what I said was about Sharon's oppressive tactics—that's what we were speaking about." Theodorakis believes it was his duty to raise consciousness about the Holocaust. When he tried to mediate between Alon and Arafat in 1972, he also felt it was his duty. Given Mikis Theodorakis's committed pacifism, his feelings about Israeli military aggression can be understood in context. Yet his words may have unintentionally fanned old stereotypes.

There is reason to believe that the past, the present, and the future are created as mutually interacting modes of time and experience. By extension, an individual not only has a history, but he or she is history by virtue of memorial activity. The past of an individual can be put to different uses: it can be forgotten, sentimentalized, idealized, fetishized, or memorialized. Governments have frequently found ways of appropriating their countries' pasts and, at dangerous times, politicizing the memorial activity. The memorial activities of many of the Greek governments of the 20th century, for one, point to such political uses of the past. Holst-Warhaft (1992) has argued that mourning, and by implication memorial activity, has often challenged the social and political order. She traces this trend back to the Greece of the sixth century bce.

The past has been put to use by Theodorakis, also, albeit in quite a different way than repressive Greek governments. Many, if not most, of his great works, such as *Symphony No. 1* (1948–1953), *Epitaphios* (1960), *Mauthausen* (1965), and *Symphony No. 7* (1982), to name only a few, can be conceptualized as memorial art. These musical works stimulate memories and link them to trauma and tragedy. By using ordinary scenes from daily life, they stay close to lived experience. But the ordinary scenes do not just act to recast the past as we remember it; they are reinserted into the present. They evoke the killings and execution of close friends in the context of the German occupation and the Greek Civil War (*Symphony No. 1*), a mother's lament for her son killed by police in a tobacco workers' strike in 1936 (*Epitaphios*), a number tattoo on the arm of a girl imprisoned by the Nazi death machine (*Mauthausen*), and the courage and dignity of Athena, the female partisan, before and during her execution (*Symphony No. 7*). This memorial music creates a "potential space" in which the listener has an opportunity—perhaps even a responsibility—to create his or her own response. In my view, this potentiality generates a certain freedom for the listener. He or she is not told what to think and how to react. Theodorakis creates a climate for the lifting of the all too frequent denial and confusion surrounding such tragic historical events. He stimulates memories that governments often seek to repress, and in the process he memorializes the tragic events and the people involved in such events.

Theodorakis creates an intimate dialogue between himself and the listener. Composer and audience collaborate to create a memorializing dialogue by way of relational mourning (Harris, 2004). This dialogue affirms the powerful feelings of loss and death. It does not dissociate feelings from thinking, affects from words. It has the effect of holding the feelings of loss in a ritualized and social manner. The music Theodorakis composes serves to intensify the meaning of the words—having the effect, on a collective level, of lifting suppression and healing trauma. It also helps healing on an individual level, not unlike a therapeutic intervention. He does not compose music that is distant, abstract, and inaccessible; for Theodorakis, relationships of the past are to be memorialized, celebrated, and accepted as human glory and tragedy. This generates a freedom for himself and for those who appreciate and participate in his music. Under such conditions, memorializing music is creativity at its most caring and compassionate.

A Starry Night in 2007

Backstage after the Herodion concert, Lina received congratulations from many, including the composer. She was pleased with her performance. She had felt anxious when she first walked onto the stage, but then just dissociated. "I heard everything, the music was clear and I knew what I was doing, but I didn't know. I think I was on automatic!" she exclaimed. She remembered only that she looked directly at the composer before and after the song. When the great Maria Farantouri approached Lina, Sophia and I wondered what would be said. We knew that the moment was pregnant with intergenerational meaning. Farantouri kissed Lina on both cheeks and congratulated her, saying, "You have the tragic element. In the low ranges," and pointed her finger to the earth. Then she pointed upward to the starry night sky and added, "And in the high ranges."

Days of 2010

In the summer days of 2010 Lina is on tour singing Theodorakis in different parts of Greece. She once again performs "Song of Songs." She is in even better voice and sings as if the song belongs to her and her alone. "It is my song," she declares. Theodorakis recognizes this and enthusiastically says, "You are getting better and better." He looks deeply into her eyes and adds, "Singing the Mauthausen songs in Greek and Hebrew is magnificent. The Greeks have difficulty understanding the Hebrew, but it expands their listening. " His artistic and activist visions are perceptible in Lina's personality and performance. The composer is deeply content. The performer feels deeply recognized.

At her final summer performance, this time at the 85th birthday celebration for Mikis Theodorakis on July 29, the master of ceremonies introduces Lina to the 4,000 celebrants at the Lycabettus Hill outdoor theater as a "child of the Holocaust."[15] They applaud respectfully. As Lina starts to sing, "How lovely is my love in her everyday dress . . ." an invisible trembling wave, observes Margarita Theodorakis, moves from the stage across the theater and settles there amid the listeners. The lament, the performer, and the audience are linked, and a symbolic gravestone is placed on the unknown graves of the murdered.

At the end of the concert, Theodorakis responds to a standing ovation and moves toward the stage to sing an encore song that is practically a national anthem: "On the secret seashore." Before the song, he warmly thanks all at Lycabettus. And then he says prophetically, as if anticipating the economic and political nightmare and consequent despair that is about to befall Greece, "I want to remind you of something I once said—that a Greek needs to feel that he cannot retreat further. He moves back and back and when he touches the wall, then the Greek becomes either a traitor or a hero. Pay attention, because that moment will arrive for you, the younger generation. Choose!"

A few weeks later, Lina now back in the United States receives the following e-mail letter from Theodorakis.[16]

My dear Lina,

I thank you very much for your participation at Lycabettus and your thrilling interpretation of Mauthausen.

Reading the "in-depth" interview you gave (9 August 2010) I love and respect you even more, along with your amazing parents and especially your "witness" mother.

As you understand, the tragedy at the death camps is the most traumatic and torturous experience of my life. It goes beyond human comprehension and becomes a constant nightmare that has entered my blood, and is present every moment . . . And ever since fills me with ambivalences and fear for humankind. Because those who did these things were humans and also educated, nursed on Mozart, Beethoven and Wagner! Therefore, the Beast-Chaos is, it seems, stronger than the Harmony-Goodness-Love inside every human, ready to knock us down at every moment.

That which saved me was and is Music, that sublime gift to humans who can still be considered humans. Because most especially today, slide possibly without wishing towards Chaos.

You, like me, have two strong claims to hold you Upright, True and Strong in this distressing situation that surrounds us. Music and the Great Wound . . . So you have learned my secret: All my notes are nothing but blood which drips from my incurable wound. (Because do not forget that besides the Great Beast of the Nazis we had our own Beasts; Our own jails, torture chambers and death camps). So listening to you yesterday, my music abruptly became heartache . . .

It was all those innocent children that were led by women-beasts into the gas chambers and then they returned peacefully and well to their country, they had children, grandchildren, and drive around in Mercedes and now with money as a weapon they are in with the Bankers of Europe and of America like locusts on our land. It was not enough the 1,000,000 victims their grandfathers left behind, now they wish for the rest of our blood and to transform us into human shadows. The only things that are missing are the barbed wires, the numbers on our arms and the "yellow star on the heart" . . .

Lina, I love you and I thank you and I wish you now that you know the Divine Gift of Eros, to find happiness with the chosen one of your heart that Nicaraguan in New Jersey, while embracing Music and Song.

Kisses to your parents,

Yours,
Mikis Theodorakis

Coda

"I find my heroes were I seek them," claims the celebrated Chilean poet Pablo Neruda (1983). Certainly, the psychoanalytic study of creativity, courage, adversity, and idealization proves this sort of projection time and time again. But contemporary analytic views (Grand, 2010; Orfanos, 2013) also hold that the hero, mythical or real, is an antidote to human tragedy and suffering. For Greeks, the activist and gifted composer Theodorakis and the passionate witnessing poet Kambanellis are modern artistic heroes because they imagined real lovers and wedded them to a vast psychological, cultural, and historical territory. Moreover, they created a ritual space (Slochower, 2004) for others to confront the sorrow and the pity of losses and gulags. They changed the culture through memorializing acts. The tortured Mikis Theodorakis, the imprisoned Iakovos Kambanellis, the soloists Maria Farantouri and Lina Orfanos, both with their compromised bodies, all combined to declare the deep humanity of tragedy and trauma. Their audience, also wounded by history, responded. To paraphrase and update Plato, this is an interpenetration of subjectivities that resists comprehensive rational analysis by anyone.

Meaningful *mousike* is a relational act of vitality. It leads to deeper personal awareness, influences public events, and battles historical amnesia. It cannot, however, block bullets or ethnic cleansing. It cannot rescue from the obscenities of hunger and unemployment. It cannot put neo-Nazis on trial. But it can help the experience of suffering and it can bear witness both for the individual and the collective. In the final analysis, and there is no real final analysis, the music and wounds of Mikis Theodorakis, his fellow artists, and his listeners inspire creative acts of freedom. They give voice to Eros in the face of Thanatos. Their art offers the prospect of a certain courageous resolution however contrary to the contemporary times.

Notes

1. For the Greeks, *mousike* was a large set of practices, a term more broad than "music" that covered all the arts associated with the Muses, including singing and dancing as well as music in its narrow sense. Greece was and continues to be a "musical" culture. Inspiration is not required to observe the etymological links among the words "music," "mousike," and "Muses." The *Oxford English Dictionary* notes that there may even be a link to the Indo-European base for the noun "mind."
2. Portions of this section and the three next sections that follow are substantive revisions of a previously published paper (Orfanos, 2010).
3. The American psychiatrist Wortis (1954) saw Freud in Vienna for a short didactic analysis in 1934 and was struck by Freud's unfamiliarity with composers.
4. In an intriguing empirical study of 272 premature infants and their parents (Loewy, Steward, Dassler, Telsey, & Homel (2013), researchers concluded that parent-preferred lullabies, sung live, slowed the heartbeats of infants and calmed their breathing. Live music and singing seemed to aid sleep and promoted states of quiet alertness in the premature babies. Moreover, there was a decrease in perceived parental stress during the ongoing traumatic experiences of premature infant care. The results of this study offer partial scientific validation for music as a healing art—a phenomenon identified as early as ancient times.
5. See chapter 1 for a detailed account of Lina's trauma.
6. Translation by Gail Holst-Warhaft. Holst-Warhaft is a poet, translator, and leading Theodorakis scholar. During the years of the Greek military junta (1967–1974) she performed in the orchestra of Mikis Theodorakis. She has written highly insightful musical criticism on Theodorakis' popular and classical compositions (Holst-Warhaft, 1980/2014).
7. "Song of Songs" is the first aria in the cycle of the *Mauthausen Cantata*. It is based in part on erotic passages from the Old Testament's "Song of Songs." The second and third songs of the *Mauthausen Cantata* tell of hard labor and escape. The final song, "If the War Ends," is a fantasy of the lovers' union.
8. To see and hear the actual performance go to: www.youtube.com/watch?v= AqfxfJRohMI.
9. Think of the song "Strange Fruit," a dirge-like, protest cry for civil rights. It was originally sung in 1939 by Billie Holiday and astonished, if not shocked, American listeners. Now multiply that by 100 to better understand the enormity of the psychological and cultural impact of "Song of Songs" on Greek listeners.

10. M. Theodorakis, personal communication, January 13, 1995.
11. The French often refer to Maria Farantouri as the Goddess Hera for her strength, purity, and vigilance. The British say her voice is a gift from the Gods of Olympus.
12. M. Theodorakis, personal communication, January 11, 1995.
13. J. Ventura, personal communication, December 7, 2004.
14. M. Theodorakis, personal communication, December 6, 2004.
15. To see and hear this Lycabettus performance, go to www.youtube.com/watch?v=E-E55xupBrQ.
16. Translation from the Greek by Spyros D. Orfanos. This e-mail letter is in many ways vintage Theodorakis. He wears his heart on his sleeve. Like his music, his thinking and writing frequently link the personal, the communal, the historical, the political, and the moral. For his contributions to Greece, Theodorakis was inducted into the prestigious Academy of Athens on December 3, 2013 (Holst-Warhaft & Orfanos, 2013).

8

WHEN THE ANALYST WRITES
A MEMOIR

Psychoanalysts and Self-Disclosure

The issue of self-revelation has been a complicated one for psychoanalysts and psychotherapists who traditionally have shown great ambivalence about disclosing aspects of their personal life. Freud's (1912) characterization of the psychoanalyst as a "blank screen" set the stage for generations of analysts who upheld anonymity and neutrality as an ideal, despite the fact that Freud himself did not practice what he preached.[1] He was hardly a blank screen to his daughter Anna when he set out to analyze her in 1918 and his penchant for drawing on his personal experiences and those of family members were evident from his writings (Boulanger, 2007).

A number of prominent analysts (Bettelheim, 1979; Mahler, 1988; Rado, 1977; Reik, 1949; Sterba, 1982) who barely escaped from Europe during the Second World War found refuge in England and America and published memoirs that chronicled the details of their escapes and adjustment to their adopted countries (Kuriloff, 2010). Some like Jacobson (1949) and Kohut (1979) either minimized or denied their personal experiences as escapees, and its impact on their theoretical formulations. Jacobson for example underplayed the effect of her own imprisonment in a concentration camp as a source for her paper on the psychological effects of imprisonment (Kuriloff, 2010). Kohut hid his Jewish identity as well as other aspects of his life that did not fit in with the image he attempted to project to the world. Thus he never revealed that his groundbreaking case study, "The Two Analyses of Mr. Z," was pure autobiography (Strozier, 2001).

Some of Freud's contemporaries, like Jung (1961/1989) and Ferenczi (1932/1988), also used their own lives as psychological subject matter, as did psychoanalysts who came later (Guntrip, 1975; Miller, 1988; Milner, 1950; among others). Whether or not they acknowledged that case material was based on them, psychoanalysts have used their own lives as psychological subject matter for years; regardless, self-revelation on the part of the analyst, remained one of the great psychoanalytic taboos until fairly recently in the history of psychoanalysis.

With changing theoretical models of psychoanalysis, a veritable transformation has taken place in our field with regard to the concept of self-disclosure.

Contemporary psychoanalysts, particularly those with a relational orientation, have questioned traditional assumptions about the importance of anonymity, pointing out that not only is its desirability questionable, but in fact it is an impossible myth, because, whether we are aware of it or not, we constantly reveal ourselves to our patients—in our dress, in our office décor, in our interpretations, and in the subtle shifts of state in our consulting room. With the information revolution, striving for anonymity has become even more of a challenge. Progressively more patients come to us after having looked us up on Google, where they have discovered things about us that we have not always been able to control. Furthermore, as we recognize and acknowledge the importance of interaction and enactment in psychoanalysis, we realize that self-disclosure on the part of the analyst can be a useful aspect of analytic technique and that it can enhance rather than interfere with the process.

With the relational turn in psychoanalysis there has been a greater recognition of the potential benefits of selective, judicious self-disclosure. Increasingly, professionals are willing to become more open about their lives. A few of us have even written our memoirs.

Some of the contemporary psychoanalysts whose autobiographical narratives I have read include Fern Cohen (2007), Magda Denes (1997), Sue Erikson Bloland (2005), Viktor Frankl (1967, 1984, 1997), Esther Menaker (1989), Louis Micheels (1989), David Newman (2006, 2011), Anna Ornstein (2004), Henri Parens (2004), and Allen Wheelis (1999). In each case, the story was a testament to what had been endured and to the life lessons learned from it. For most of us, writing provides an opportunity to expose hypocrisy, redress wrongs, set the record straight, and share what we have learned with others. Additionally, for those of us who are Holocaust survivors, it serves another important function, namely, a chance to fulfill a responsibility to those who were murdered and cannot speak for themselves. We are their witness, our voice speaks for them, and we memorialize them so that they are not wiped off the face of this earth without a trace left behind.

Our theoretical orientations, our clinical choices, our view of what is curative are all no doubt influenced by our personal history as well as by our training and experience. In a kind of parallel process, there has been a transformation in my personal life with regard to my attitude about self-disclosure. My work over the past four decades has been influenced by the change in the professional zeitgeist, as well as by internal psychological changes that can only make sense if understood in the context of my life. So let me begin at the beginning.

Personal History

Hiding has been my salvation and my burden since the earliest of days of my life. Born into the Holocaust, a Jewish child marked for death, I spent the first four years of my life hidden in plain sight. Within a few months of the Nazi invasion of the Soviet-occupied part of Poland where we lived, my father was imprisoned in a concentration camp. Shortly after, my mother obtained false identity papers and we went into hiding as Polish Christians in a small village near Lwów, the city where I was born.

About a year later, my father escaped from the camp and was reunited with us through the help of some gentile friends. My mother hid him in the attic, where he remained for about a year and a half until we were liberated by the Russian army. As a toddler, I was warned to stay away from the attic and told that there was a dangerous wolf living there. My earliest memory was of the attic door opening and a man emerging. Once he had revealed himself to me, I was expected to keep my father's presence a secret from the rest of the world, including people whom I saw every day, like the landlady of the house where we lived. By the age of 3 I was well schooled in deception. Disclosure would have meant certain death for the three of us.

Miraculously, my father was never discovered, and our identity never exposed. We three survived as a family, a very rare occurrence in those dark days. After the war, as refugees we searched for a place to call home. The multiple traumas of facing death, losing loved ones, and migration and displacement were lived through, but not processed. For many years after the war, we focused on creating a new life. My parents disclosed little. They didn't want to dwell in the past; there was a challenging present to adjust to—a new language to learn, work to be found, a different culture to negotiate, and so forth. They shared their stories with other survivors, but not with the world outside, and not with me. They wanted to shield me from what we had lived through. Their assumption was that because I was so young during the war years, I would not remember what had happened, and if I did not remember, then, they reasoned, I would not be affected by it. I followed their injunction, and acted as if my life began at the age of 5 when we immigrated to Paris. I did have my memories, however, fragmented images from the past, but since I was unable to put them in a context, I kept them to myself. If I did talk about my history to outsiders, which I did rarely, it was usually in a robot-like voice, as if I was describing someone else's life. For me, dissociation came in the form of numbness, not forgetting.

My family's silence about the Holocaust was reflected in the society at large. Survivors did not want to tell, and people did not want to know. In those days, mental health professionals were also reluctant to open these wounds. When I entered analysis in my 20s, my analyst, who was classically trained, was interested in my childhood, but not especially in the part about the Holocaust. As a result, he missed important opportunities to make connections between some of my life choices and symptoms, and what I had lived through as a child.

This analyst, whom I shall call Dr. Bunsen, was a good example of the classical model that exhorts anonymity, abstinence, and neutrality in psychoanalytic work. Dr. Bunsen, like so many classical analysts of his time, had the illusion that he was a blank screen to his patients. In fact, I knew a great deal about Dr. Bunsen from my observations, and I certainly came to know that he was hardly neutral.

My initial work with Dr. Bunsen coincided with the beginning of my career in psychology. I was working as a college counselor and seeing clients for brief psychotherapy. At that point, I had limited supervision and no training in psychotherapy. My personal therapy became my guide on technique, and Dr. Bunsen was my role model. Fortunately, I could never be as aloof and distant as he was, but like him, I refrained from revealing anything personal. I answered questions with questions and tried to control my emotion and be as impassive as I could.

Remaining hidden was a natural state for me. I had chosen a profession that was well suited to my temperament and my early learning. Psychoanalysts are the keepers of secrets, and I had learned my lessons well. Yet at the same time, there was the opposite impulse that I struggled with throughout my life. There was a desire to come out of hiding, a wish to be less inhibited and more spontaneous. My childhood ordeal had made me excessively cautious.

As I began analytic training in the early 1970s, the paradigm in our field was beginning to shift. The authoritarian approach to treatment gradually gave way to a more collaborative one. The conceptual basis for the notion of analytic anonymity was challenged by those who pointed out that self-disclosure is inevitable. The analyst reveals herself by the clothes she wears, the office she works in, the interpretations she makes, and even in subtle movements in response to her patient's associations. Patients pick up disclosures of our emotional state, state shifts, and affective reactions, whether or not we or they are conscious of these.

My thinking about technical considerations, such as disclosure and neutrality, was influenced by my teachers and supervisors, but even more by a personal experience with my analyst, Dr. Bunsen. In my sixth year of analysis, I met a young man who would eventually become my husband. We were an odd couple; we came from very different worlds and we were at different stages in our lives. I was a professional in my second year of analytic training, he was more than 10 years my junior and a waiter at his family's Greek coffee shop. Many in our circle of family and friends were skeptical about this unconventional relationship, but the most vocal critic turned out to be Dr. Bunsen. It is ironic that this traditional analyst, who rigidly held to the analytic frame, would unabashedly take such a biased position. Apparently his idea of neutrality was detachment and anonymity rather than absence of value judgments. His authoritarian posture, however, was consistent with his attitude that "the analyst knows best."

After more than 40 years in a healing, loving relationship with the young waiter who eventually became a prominent and respected psychoanalyst, I can say with confidence that Dr. Bunsen did not know best. And even if his dire predictions had come to pass, it was not his place to tell me how to live my life.

In time I was able to make a better choice of analyst, someone who was not invested in my making one decision or another. He was neutral in that respect, but never detached. I had known him in various roles and I appreciated his openness. He had given the subject of therapist disclosure a great deal of thought; in fact, he had written about it.

Another event that profoundly influenced my thinking on the subject of therapist disclosure was my pregnancy. In 1980, my private life entered the consulting room in a big way. A pregnant analyst can't hide from her patients; the intrusion into the analytic space can't be ignored. At the time, there was relatively little written on the subject of the analyst's pregnancy, so I was left on my own to grapple with the effects of this turn of events. I learned from that experience that patients' reactions varied considerably, and that the event brought our relationship (transferential and real) to center stage. I also realized that the event brought many conflicts to the surface and, with them, an increased potential for therapeutic growth. It highlighted the absurdity of the notion that when the analyst's anonymity is compromised, the development of the transference is so disturbed that the work suffers as a result. I suppose it set the precedent for my future attitude toward self-disclosure.

Yet, at this point in my life, I was never truly comfortable with the act of self-revelation, either as an analyst or as a person. Like so many other survivors who had been in hiding during the war, the tendency to remain hidden continued. Gradually, as the curtain of silence over the Holocaust lifted and books and films about the Holocaust appeared, we began to emerge. By the 1980s and 1990s there was a proliferation of Holocaust-related material. Because of the dwindling population of survivors there was a sense of urgency about recording our stories before the disappearance of the last living witnesses. Archives were established to interview survivors. My father had published a memoir in the mid 1970s (Richman, 1975; see chapter 1), and by the early 1980s my mother had given her testimony to the Yale Archives for Holocaust Testimony. By 1990, I was invited to give my story as well. For so many years I had denied the traumatic impact of the war on my life; now finally I was beginning to identify myself as a survivor and a hidden child.

The next step was to accept my role of witness and to add to the growing literature on the Holocaust that could be passed on to future generations. Although many Holocaust memoirs have been written, few deal with the long-term effects of the Holocaust trauma. As a psychoanalyst who is intimately familiar with suffering, I felt that I could speak authoritatively on the reverberations of trauma throughout the lifespan and thereby make a contribution to other trauma survivors struggling to integrate their experience, as well as to the mental health professionals dedicated to helping them.

Still, there was another reason to write a memoir. For me, writing the memoir was part of a long journey out of the Holocaust. It was the culmination of the lifelong struggle to come out of hiding and come to terms with who I am. Writing continued the process of healing that psychoanalysis had begun. Through writing I was able to integrate the fragmented pieces of my past into a coherent narrative. I experienced a powerful drive to express myself. The process took over; it seemed to have a life of its own. I had a full-time private practice, so there was little time for writing, but nothing could stop the flow.

Of course, once written, the book did not have to be published, or it could have been published under an assumed name, as a colleague had done. But I no longer wished to hide. I was prepared to take responsibility for my observations and conclusions, even if it meant exposing myself to the scrutiny of patients, colleagues, and strangers. Shortly before the publication of my book, my concerns about self-exposure occasionally made their appearance in the middle of the night. But in the light of day, they were banished by a powerful force within me. I had made the commitment to tell my story to the world, and I wanted it to be as honest and clear as I could make it. With regard to its impact on my practice, I was aware that I was embarking on a journey that had no clear maps. The road was not likely to be smooth, but the trip promised to be interesting.

Biographic Self-Disclosure

There is little in the psychoanalytic literature that is directly relevant to the subject of this chapter—the revelation of a substantial aspect of the analyst's personal biography in the form of a memoir. Few analysts have written their autobiographies, and none have systematically studied the impact of this type of disclosure on the analytic process. The disclosure of information about the personal life of the analyst is a relatively rare phenomenon, with some minor exceptions. Those include a slowly growing body of literature on the role of the therapist's major life crises on the treatment, such as the analyst's pregnancy (Barbanel, 1980; Fenster, Phillips & Rapoport (1994); Gerson, 1994) and severe illness (Abend, 1982; Dewald, 1982; Morrison, 1997; Pizer, 1997; Singer, 1971). In these cases, as in the situation with the memoir, the intrusion into the analysis is prompted by the needs of the analyst and involves a disruption in the frame. Professionals who have written about the act of sharing personal details of their lives with patients have all expressed a deep concern about the impact of such revelations, and described a rigorous process of self-scrutiny with regard to their motivations prior to the introduction of the material (Crastnopol, 1997; Morrison, 1997; Singer, 1971).

Notwithstanding the similarities, there are significant differences between the type of biographical self-disclosure discussed here and that which has been written about previously. The literature on crises in the life of the analyst relates to a current situation that threatens the continuity of the analysis and hence must be addressed. In contrast, the memoir deals with events that have taken place in the past and do not have direct relevance for the treatment. Furthermore, the biographical information revealed is of a different order. When one bares one's soul in a memoir, one is sharing countless, intimate, personal details that reveal one's character, basic values, and philosophy of life. This is bound to be much more complicated than the revelation of limited facts about oneself.

There is no word that adequately describes the type of self-disclosure that is the subject of this chapter. *Self-disclosure* is a broad term that describes a variety of self-revelatory behavior on the part of the analyst. Some recent papers have attempted to define terms. In an effort to bring clarity to the concept, Pizer (1997) articulated a framework for thinking about various analytic disclosures in different clinical contexts. She wrote about her personal bout with cancer and the disclosure of the illness to her patients. In her paper "When the Analyst Is Ill: Dimensions of Self-Disclosure," she differentiated between three overlapping yet distinguishable dimensions of disclosure: "inescapable" ones, such as the therapist's pregnancy;

"inadvertent" disclosures (the spontaneous and unreflective enactments of an analyst's subjectivity); and "deliberate" disclosures (the conscious choice of the analyst to share something that is deemed relevant in the context of the work).

The kind of disclosure that I am writing about does not fit neatly into any of the categories described above. All of these categories refer to the selective sharing of the analyst's experience, conscious or otherwise, in the context of the treatment situation. The disclosure of personal information addressed here does not arise out of the transference-countertransference matrix. It begins as a purposeful action incidental to the therapy process and only becomes relevant when it enters the consulting room, whether directly when brought up by the patient or the analyst, or indirectly when it is known but not spoken about.

Once the memoir is introduced into a session, it is no longer simply a biographic form of disclosure. Decisions on how to handle the fact of the memoir are complex and specific to the case and the clinical moment when the issue arises. The way it is introduced defines whether disclosure is deliberate, inadvertent, or inescapable. When it becomes the subject of an analytic hour, it opens the way to countertransference disclosure, as defined by Ehrenberg (1995). As such it becomes an integral part of the analytic process and can be used to advance it.

In general, my decision to introduce the memoir was based on my best clinical judgment of the impact of this revelation, whether it would advance or inhibit the work with a particular individual at a particular point in time. When patients discovered the memoir on their own, my goal was to turn this development to analytic advantage, to use the knowledge in the service of potential growth. Ultimately, for me, the major question is whether the event of the memoir inhibits or facilitates the therapeutic process in a specific analysis. Will it open or close analytic inquiry?

I don't disclose easily. I am aware of the responsibility inherent in its impact and consequences. My personality style is somewhat reserved and restrained. A psychiatrist patient of mine had once described me as "non-intrusive to a fault." It is with great caution that I introduce the memoir into sessions. At this point,[2] about three years after the publication of my memoir, about half of my patients are aware of it. Of those, some know because I chose to tell them, some because they discovered it on their own. The choice of who to tell, why, and when is always an important process, but perhaps not always a conscious one for me.

Several brief vignettes will illustrate ways in which the subject of the memoir entered the consulting room. It should be noted that this chapter is offered as a preliminary overview of initial clinical moments rather than as an in-depth, detailed analysis of clinical material. Some cases are more developed than others, but the intention is to present the full range of reactions that I observed during the first three years after the memoir was published. Six months before my memoir was scheduled to be published, Mr. A, a friend of a former patient, called me for an appointment. He was a journalist who had written a book, and as his book was going to press, he was experiencing panic attacks. In our first session I learned that this book, which was not his first, was more personally revealing than anything he had written before. "What have I done?" he exclaimed. He was terrified about the impact of his disclosures. Did he accurately represent the people he wrote about? Many were his friends, and some were his family members. He had not disguised his subjects. Would they feel exposed? Betrayed? I listened nervously but also with special interest. Should I reveal that I was in the same boat? Should I tell him that I too had written a very self-revealing book? Should I confess that in my worst moments I could relate to the anxiety that he was describing? I decided that a first session was too early to say anything. The second session passed, the third session, several months passed. Before each session, I wondered if my silence about the memoir would ultimately be experienced as betrayal once he discovered the book. We lived in the same small, suburban community, and he was bound to come across it. As my publication date drew near, I knew that I would need to let him know about it. In the meantime, we had established a solid relationship, and the focus of our work had gone beyond his presenting concerns.

Just before my book appeared in bookstores, I told Mr. A about it. I asked how he felt. He had trouble responding. He bought the book, but didn't read it. I asked him about that. He said he was too busy, it was on his list. Eventually, three months later, he read it. How did he feel about it? I asked. It made him feel his own sense of weakness. He compared himself to me and felt diminished by the comparison. He saw me as courageous and himself as cowardly. I took risks in my life, while he agonized over every small decision. I seemed to be doing so well after such a difficult life, how could he complain about his relatively small concerns?

These reactions alerted me to Mr. A's tendency to compare himself to others and to feel that he did not measure up. Issues of envy and competition were thus brought to light early in the treatment and were subsequently explored in the years that followed his initial encounter with my memoir.

Mr. A's response to my memoir also touched on a deep concern of mine, namely that the magnitude of my traumatic history would dwarf the experiences of my patients and hence make it more difficult for them to discuss their own troubles. From time to time, similar comments have been made by others. It has been a relief to note that such reactions tend to be fleeting and patients return to their preoccupations before long. Nevertheless, if my experience brings perspective into the mix and discourages kvetching, I don't consider it a bad thing.

Mr. and Mrs. B learned about the book in a couple's session, when I decided to answer Mr. B's questions about my background. The issue of answering questions, particularly personal ones, is directly related to one's attitude about disclosure. Over the years, I have come to realize that when the patient asks a question, and my response is silence or another question, such as "why do you ask?" some patients feel humiliated and stop asking questions. When that happens, an important avenue for exploration is lost. So in general, I have come to respond directly and then explore associations.

One of the questions that I encounter from time to time relates to my foreign accent. It is slight, and most people don't recognize it, but occasionally someone will ask me where I am from. So when Mr. B asked, I answered. One question led to another, and before long Mr. and Mrs. B learned that I had written a memoir.

The following session, Mr. B brought in my memoir and asked if he could read me a section that he felt was particularly meaningful for him. First he read the epigraph, a poem that captures in metaphor the experience of trauma followed by repression followed by healing. He said he was considering a different ending to the poem and read a line that he had written. He then proceeded to read a short paragraph from the preface. He read my words back to me:

> I was numbed emotionally to the events of my childhood. I did not hide my Holocaust history; I simply treated it as irrelevant. The price of forced forgetting is that individual parts remain secluded and unavailable to experience life fully. Sometimes those unacknowledged aspect of experience are reenacted in behavior that has lost its essential connection to its source and therefore appears strange. One can't mourn what one doesn't acknowledge, and one can't heal if one does not mourn. (Richman, 2002, p. xiv)

Mr. B felt a bond with me as a result of our shared experience. He was not a Holocaust survivor, but he too had been robbed of a childhood by traumatic circumstances, and like me, he had minimized the impact of those early years on his current life. He was just recently beginning the long process of mourning in his individual analysis with the colleague who had referred him to me for couple's therapy. Mrs. B was pleased that her husband could relate to me. Previous couple's therapy had been unsuccessful, partly because Mr. B had felt that the therapist took his wife's side and didn't understand him. Mrs. B hoped that her husband's sense of connection with me would ultimately prove helpful in our work together.

When patients come across the memoir without my awareness, some of the most complicated reactions follow. For instance, Mrs. C learned about my book from a friend when I did a reading at a local bookstore, shortly after it came out. It had been advertised in the local paper, and her friend was planning to attend the reading. I had no idea that Mrs. C had read my book until a year later when she revealed it. Mrs. C had lost her father in childhood. Her mother had remarried and moved the children far from the extended family. These losses were compounded by a physical problem that made her feel different and isolated from others. She longed to feel connected. She presented as somewhat distant and dissociated.

Since I wrote the memoir, I have listened especially carefully, with my third ear, for any references to the book. With Mrs. C, I never suspected that she had read the book until one day she announced that she had had a dream about being in a public toilet. My ears perked up. I had written about my recurrent nightmare of public toilets and its relationship to the secrets I had to keep as a child. The following session she mentioned that there were many secrets in her family. On her way out, with her hand on the door knob, she said, "We have to talk about secrets next time." If she wasn't going to bring up the memoir, I was prepared to ask her about it. Happily, the following session, she confessed.

She had read the book a year ago. Why had she kept this a secret? She thought she wasn't supposed to know about it because I didn't volunteer the information. She was concerned about violating the boundaries of our relationship, and she could not risk losing me. In her family of origin, when tragedies happened, they were not talked about even among family members. Numerous secrets contributed to the prevailing sense of shame and isolation. Under the guise of protecting her mother, she kept her at a distance by keeping herself hidden. What became clearer was her concern about not getting too close to me while at the same time longing for more connection. Although I didn't know that she had read the book, I had noticed that our work had become deeper and that she had formed a stronger bond with me over the past year. Maybe the secret between us was the condition for greater intimacy. She knew my secrets as I knew hers; at the same time, she had power over me because she knew something about me that I didn't know that she knew.

This case illustrates another interesting phenomenon. I can never be sure whether a patient has come across the book. The internet has made it easy for patients to learn certain facts about us from outside sources. They can Google us without our knowledge or consent, and deprive us of the opportunity to explore what meaning the information has for them. The risk of inadvertent self-disclosure is ever present. If the knowledge is not directly brought into the session, it can become "the elephant in the room." The twist for me is that the memoir has the potential to become another secret. Do I reveal it, or do I keep it private? My childhood dilemma is reenacted again.

Knowing and Being Known: A Central Conflict

The struggle with the issue of how much to reveal and how much to conceal is universal. The conflict between the desire to know and be known on the one hand, and the wish to hide and not to know, on the other, has been identified as a central conflict in life (Aron, 1996). The ambivalence about protecting a secret self and at the same time wanting to communicate and to be found was captured by Winnicott (1963) when he wrote, "It is a sophisticated game of hide-and-seek in which it is a joy to be hidden but disaster not to be found" (p. 186).

The therapeutic enterprise brings this ambivalence directly into focus. Terms like resistance, repression, dissociation, and authenticity all reflect our attempt to deal with the conflict about knowing ourselves and being known by others. We wish to hide in order to protect ourselves, and at the same time we wish to be known. We hide from others, and we hide from ourselves. After reading my memoir, one of my patients said, "What I found most meaningful in your book is the theme of hiding. We all do that, and that's why we go to therapy, so we can come out of hiding."

As analysts, however, we tend to subscribe to a double standard. We want our patients to come out of hiding, but we ourselves as a rule prefer to remain hidden.

Many analysts are anxious about being seen as imperfect by their patients. As Jonathan Slavin (2002) points out, when we work with patients, some part of us feels that we need to appear as whole and unblemished. In that context, our theories about self-disclosure provide us with a convenient rationale to hide. Patients want to see us as wise and in charge of our lives, and we are happy not to contradict their image of us, even when we know it arises out of their idealization. Aspects of ourselves that we are ashamed of tend not to appear in the consulting room.

With the relational turn in psychoanalysis some of these attitudes are beginning to change, and the ripple effects are felt in the profession as a whole. Even some of the more traditional analysts are recognizing both the inevitability and potential benefits of selective, judicious self-disclosure. Today, most analysts are willing to chart a course between unconstrained self-disclosure and classical anonymity (Meissner, 2002). When it comes to the revelation of intimate details about an analyst's life in memoir form, however, we enter uncharted waters. Memoir writing as a literary form is gradually gaining momentum and there is a growing recognition that our understanding of human behavior begins with our self-understanding.

> Perhaps the best kept secret in the life of a psychoanalyst is that the patient of longest duration, the patient he at times loves and hates the most, the patient who is often the most central and preoccupying, the patient who often provides both his most triumphant successes and his most disheartening and bitter failures—is himself. (Mitchell, 1993, p. xiii)

In recent years, there has been a resurgence of interest in self-analysis as a process that both parallels and shapes the analytic inquiry into the patient's inner world (Barron, 1993). At the same time there has been another evolution taking place in our field, one toward more candid self-exposure (Renik, 1999). Increased appreciation of self-analysis combined with a greater willingness to share our reflective process with others has led to a new and distinctive genre of psychoanalytic literature. In the last few years, in response to a heightened interest in autobiographical narratives, several edited books have appeared in which psychoanalysts are interviewed or write about the details of their private and professional lives (Bornstein, 2004; Gerson, 2001; Goodman & Meyers, (2012); Kuchuck, (2014); Raymond & Rosbrow-Reich, 1997; Rudnytsky, 2000). It is understood that who the analyst is as a person impacts on his or her world view, theories, personal style of working. Many of the readers of these books are analysands. One wonders what impact such information will have on their analyses. Can analysts share their personal insights in a way that will promote the analytic process?

Some contemporary relational analysts emphasize the importance of the patient's awareness of the analyst's subjectivity. Aron (1991) believes that the exploration of the patient's experience of the analyst's subjectivity represents one of the most important yet underemphasized aspects of the analysis of transference. Similarly, Crastnopol (1997) maintains that the analyst as person plays a critical yet underacknowledged role in the patient's subjective experience of the treatment.

Unconscious perceptions, impressions, and fantasies about the analyst's private life are ever-present and markedly influence the therapeutic endeavor. Crastnopol warns that unless these are brought into the treatment and become the subject of mutual analytic scrutiny their effect will be haphazard. She believes that it is important to gauge how much is known about the analyst and to monitor what this knowledge means to the patient.

The recognition of the subjectivity of the other is an important developmental achievement, whether it concerns the child–parent or patient–analyst relationship (Aron, 1991; Benjamin, 1988; Hoffman, 1998). Patients seek to connect to their analysts, to know them and to probe beneath their professional facade in ways that are reminiscent of children's attempts to penetrate their parents' inner worlds. This desire to know, however, is not without ambivalence, for there is a fundamental conflict between the interest and emergence of the analyst as a subject, and its opposite, an interest in the submergence of the analyst's subjectivity. This conflict has its precursors in childhood when the child viewed the parent's private experiences (sexual and otherwise) as both aversive and magnetic (Hoffman, 1998).

Although Aron (1991) makes a strong case for the importance of establishing one's own subjectivity in the analytic situation, he also cautions that there are potential difficulties, such as the fact that patients may be deprived of the opportunity to uncover and find the analyst as a separate subject in their own way and at their own rate. His words of caution speak to my own concern about the possibility of the memoir becoming an intrusion into the analytic space.

Intrusion Into the Analytic Space

Some critics of self-disclosure by the analyst frame the issue as one of boundary violations (Gabbard & Lester, 1995). Although these critics acknowledge that some degree of disclosure is inevitable, they maintain that revealing personal information is rarely useful and constitutes a breach of analytic boundaries. In response to such critics I would point out that the nature of the analytic frame and the flexibility of boundaries are dependent on the theoretical orientation of the analyst. Further, the frame is negotiated by the patient's needs and the analyst's subjectivity. It is co-constructed. The precise nature of the frame and the so-called rules vary according to the interactive matrix defined by each analytic dyad (Greenberg, 1995). Self disclosure has different meanings and varying implications; some analysts are more comfortable with it than others and some patients welcome it while others are threatened by it. Furthermore, it remains to be determined whether it is true, as Gabbard and Lester (1995) claim, that revealing personal information is "rarely useful." That judgment should be based not on theory, but on clinical reports such as this one, which have been rare to this point.

It cannot be denied that in certain cases at least, self-disclosure on the part of the analyst is problematic. The fact that the memoir was born out of my own needs without consideration for the needs of individual patients is the most troublesome aspect of my enterprise. As a dedicated professional and responsible person, it is sometimes difficult for me to reconcile the fact that I have given priority to the fulfillment of my own need to express myself and that it has not been in the best interest of certain patients.

Mitchell (1997) pointed out that while for many patients the analyst's self-disclosure offers a unique and precious authenticity and honesty, for others who come from families in which their personal experience was crushed by the narcissistic needs of their parents, the analyst's disclosure may be experienced as a repetition of old patterns of exploitation.

This proved to be the case with Mr. D. We had been working together for a relatively short time, a few months on a once weekly basis, when Mr. D was confronted by the existence of my memoir. With some trepidation, he had decided to look me up on the internet. He was curious to know more about me and at the same time he was fearful of what he might discover. What if he learned something about me that would make him mistrust me? He was not a person who trusted easily. His mother had been a successful professional with a prominent career who had little time or energy for family. His father, a man who never lived up to his wife's expectations or his own grandiose fantasies, battled mental illness throughout his life. The father's illnesses, both real and imagined, took center stage at home. With every opportunity, the mother escaped into outside activities, leaving Mr. D alone with his self-absorbed father.

The most prominent theme in our work together had been Mr. D's constant disappointments in the authority figures in his life. From the very first session, Mr. D. had complained about the fact that professionals in whom he had put his trust were not behaving in trustworthy ways. He described one instance after another of incompetent physicians, insensitive and inadequate teachers, and disappointing friendships. Initial idealization was followed by disillusionment and rage. We had explored this theme as it related to his life outside of the consulting room. I found myself wondering when my turn would come. It came soon enough with his discovery of the memoir. In the transference, I became one more person who let him down.

Mr. D had no interest in reading my memoir, just its existence was enough to set off a rageful reaction. The session after he googled me, Mr. D confronted me: What a narcissistic endeavor it was to write a memoir! Wasn't it highly unusual for therapists to do such a thing? He needed me to be a solid predictable person, not someone who would engage in controversial behavior like his crazy father or someone who had a life outside of the consulting room like his abandoning mother. Even more to the point, the memoir was proof that I put my needs ahead of those of my patients—a familiar theme for him.

Yet even as he raged at me, Mr. D was able to recognize the opportunity that this crisis afforded us to gain more insight and to work through this recurrent pattern in his life. In the next few months we returned to the memoir again and again. Sometimes he raised the subject; at other times I did, when I heard veiled references to it. At those times he tended to become angry and said that just as he feared, I was making everything about me.

186

In the months that followed, it became evident that Mr. D used the memoir to create distance between us whenever he relaxed his defenses. He acknowledged that when he thought about telling me how badly he felt about something going on in his life, he would conjure up the thought of the memoir, feel exploited, and pull back from me. His longing for my empathic response was immediately followed by a reminder that I could not be trusted. He alternated between suspicion and optimism that we could work our way through the impasse and use it as "grist for the mill."

As this crisis between us was unfolding, he was exploring work possibilities outside of the state. Within five months an opportunity presented itself, an offer that he could not refuse, one that required relocation. Although he expressed regret that we would no longer be able to work together, we both recognized it as a way out of the impasse. My own feelings were mixed as well—a combination of disappointment and relief. I was disappointed to miss the opportunity to fully explore the consequences and ripple effects of biographic self-disclosure, but at the same time, I found myself somewhat relieved that I would not have to deal with the powerful negative transference that had developed.

It is likely that bad timing was an important factor in our failure to repair the rupture that ensued when Mr. D encountered my subjectivity. We were unable to use the reenactment to analytic advantage because at that early point in treatment our relationship was not yet solid enough to withstand the discordance between us, and Mr. D was not yet ready to experience me as a separate person.

While I agree with Mitchell (1997) that for some patients the analyst's self-disclosures are appreciated as a new way of relating and for others they are viewed as a repetition, my experience suggests that it is often more complicated than either of these alternatives suggests by itself. The same patient can have a positive and negative reaction at different times, as was the case with Mrs. E.

Mrs. E,[3] a trauma survivor who had been working with me for several years, learned of the memoir when I inadvertently brought it up in a session. She was talking about her decision to write the story of what happened to her and said that she found the writing experience immensely healing. I nodded, and said "I know." "Do you really know?" she asked. She must have picked up on a feeling of kinship, some special understanding between us. "Yes," I said, "I have found writing very healing personally." Then I told her about the memoir. By the next session, five days later, she had ordered it online, had it sent Federal Express, and had read it twice. She came in with many questions and great excitement in her voice. She could see so many similarities between us. For her, that was reassuring. She had always felt different, and her trauma had further created a chasm between herself and others. Initially with me, she had been somewhat reserved. My self-revelations seemed to free her and created a greater sense of trust. My self-disclosures encouraged her own. In truth, it also freed me to be more spontaneous with her.

What began as inadvertent self-disclosure on my part facilitated a powerful level of engagement that lasted for several years. Then, however, the darker side of self-disclosure emerged in our work together. The very same event that had fostered Mrs. E's trust in me became a focus of her mistrust when life circumstances changed. Two of her closest friends were diagnosed with life-threatening illnesses and her own health began to deteriorate. Her husband, who was always a strong paternal figure in her life, was suddenly emotionally unavailable as a result of a work-related crisis. She had lost her beloved father in her 20s and was especially vulnerable to abandonment.

As she was going through this difficult time, I was undergoing my own personal health crisis. After a severe allergic reaction during my summer break, I developed a series of systemic problems that lingered after my return from vacation. What later turned out to be a connective tissue disease, autoimmune in nature, was extremely difficult to diagnose and for over a year I suffered with numerous puzzling symptoms, most invisible, but some, like a slight limp could be seen by observant patients.

Mrs. E was one of the first to notice. She brought in a dream that revealed her concern. In the dream she found out that I was leaving my practice and would no longer be available in my New York office where I see her. When we analyzed the dream, she revealed that she had seen me having difficulty moving and had been noticing that I was not looking well. Apparently she had picked up the fact that something was wrong with my health without having consciously processed what it meant in terms of jeopardizing our relationship. I acknowledged that I was ill, but tried to reassure her that it was not life-threatening and that I had no current plans to limit my practice.

Shortly following this interchange, Mrs. E began to question my ability to help her. She returned to the subject of the memoir and for the first time framed it as a breach, an unconventional behavior that made me suspect as a therapist. She became worried that my interest in her responses to the memoir was self-serving, and that I was really interested in her so that I could write about her case. Also, she said that knowing so much about my life made it difficult for her to talk about certain things with me. This was the first time she expressed such inhibition—she attributed her reticence to knowledge gained from the memoir rather than from her observation of my current state of ill health. She consulted friends who supported her concern and suggested that she change therapists.

Mrs. E dropped out of therapy for several months. She returned when she felt ready to talk about the fears that had led her to leave and expressed a desire to understand what had transpired between us and why she had been so angry with me. In the interim, her health had dramatically improved as a result of a surgical procedure; one of her friends had died and the other seemed to be in remission. I, too, was in a different place medically speaking. I finally had a diagnosis and a sense of security that my medical condition would not interfere with my ability to continue working. I shared this information with her, including my diagnosis and prognosis, and she was relieved. We were then able to explore how her reaction had been influenced by her perception of my vulnerability and her anticipation of another potential abandonment.

The Vulnerable Analyst

Certain schools of psychoanalysis maintain that a degree of idealization of the analyst is an important factor in treatment particularly in the initial stages. Hoffman (1998) wrote that the ritual of psychoanalysis is designed to cultivate a certain aura and mystique that accompanies the role of analyst. In that role, the analyst is invested with superior knowledge, wisdom, and power. The fact that the patient knows so much less about the analyst than the analyst knows about him or her fosters regard and protects the analyst from being seen as flawed. If, as Hoffman maintains, it is the factor of relative anonymity that contributes to the analyst's power, then, I wondered, what impact will the memoir have on my credibility and my effectiveness?

Patients who read the memoir learn intimate details about my life, including my personal problems, the origin of those difficulties, and my struggles to deal with them. They become aware of my limitations and my blind spots. I wondered if my power would be diminished by the act of allowing myself to be scrutinized in this way. Further, would the fact that I have experienced trauma in my life make patients more apt to see me as damaged, weak, or in need of caretaking? Or would their perception of me as vulnerable make it more difficult for them to express aggression toward me?

It is likely that there has been a self-selective factor, so that patients who run the risk of experiencing me as exposed and vulnerable do not remain to work with me or make the decision to not read the memoir. Several patients have chosen not to read the memoir. I believe that their decision comes from their awareness that learning more about me could threaten our relationship. In these cases patients fear that knowledge of my subjectivity will interfere with their need to see me in a particular way. For instance, when Ms. F learned about the existence of the memoir and its subject matter (evident from the subtitle) she told me that she is pleased that I know trauma from the inside out, she's impressed with my courage to write about it, but she has no intention of reading the book, despite her curiosity about it. When we explored her decision, she told me that she doesn't want to think about the fact that I have a life outside the consulting room. She let me know that she fears that if she discovered my demons, she might no longer feel that I am the powerful, dependable mother that she needs me to be, a mother so different from her own.

In general, those patients who have chosen to remain with me and to read the memoir have expressed respect and positive regard. They appreciate the fact that I am not afraid to be known and that I allow myself to be emotionally vulnerable. My willingness to reveal my weakness is seen, paradoxically, as a sign of strength. Words most often used to describe me by those who have read the memoir are "resilient" and "courageous." Consistently, the feedback from readers is that the memoir inspires hope. Apparently, knowing that I have been able to overcome tragedy and emerge intact with a strong sense of self inspires others to believe that this is possible for them as well. Overall, knowledge of my life experiences seems to have increased rather than diminished my credibility.

Further, some patients and supervisees have sought me out because of the memoir. Those most drawn to my work are people who have suffered trauma in their own lives. Personal tragedy is followed by a pervasive sense of estrangement and isolation. This is eloquently described in an article by Stolorow (1999) when he writes about the loss of his wife and its impact on him. What lies at the heart of psychological trauma is a profound despair about having one's experience understood. I believe that when a traumatized individual meets another member of the same club, so to speak, the connection that is made often counteracts the isolation that is felt. Knowing that the analyst has suffered similar feelings can contribute to the hope that the analyst will truly understand. Of course, the identification with suffering is not exclusive to traumatized individuals. Insofar as patients come to treatment because of their psychic pain, it is reassuring to know that they are understood on a deep level by a therapist who is sensitive to suffering.

According to Singer (1977), there is hope in knowing that the analyst, as representative of the outside world, is also subject to common sorrows and anxieties. Revealing one's own humanity and fallibility communicates the fact that a fulfilling life is possible in spite of human frailty. Furthermore, when the analyst reveals her own process of self-reflection, she not only models the behavior that is being encouraged, but also communicates that we are united in our struggle to understand and come to terms with the human condition. Bollas (1987) has written that when the analysand discovers that the analyst is considering his own inner life, and that they share the same self-analytic function, he feels profoundly supported. "He knows us then not to be a distant interpretive presence, or simply a kind and empathic person, but someone who like himself struggles to know and may often find the struggle painful and unpleasant" (p. 255).

When the Relationship Takes Center Stage

My experience with the memoir has not borne out Freud's (1912) concerns. It has been my experience that, if the analyst self-discloses (always judiciously, paying careful attention to the patient and the circumstances), neither does the patient show more interest in talking about the analyst than about himself nor does the patient become insatiable and want to know more and more about the analyst. I have found that, as a general rule, while reactions to the memoir are intense, they tend to be the focus of attention for only a brief time. Within a couple of sessions, patients return to talking about whatever material has been preoccupying them. Awareness of the memoir seems to recede into the background. Part of the reason may be that despite the temporary break in the frame, I maintain my usual analytic stance and consistently attend to the patient's subjective experience. Of course, it may also be argued that it is my own defenses that do not allow for greater exploration of the full impact of my very intimate revelations. I am not comfortable with the position of being at the center of the treatment, and it is possible that both my patients and I collude to keep the evocative intimate details of my life out of the room. Such a possibility keeps me constantly alert to undertones and veiled references to the memoir. The latter has become part of the transference-countertransference matrix, and as such is ever-present even if it is only in the background.

I have noted that when transference-countertransference moves into the foreground, a sense of immediacy and excitement develops. No matter how tired or bored I may be feeling during a session, when the subject turns to the interactions in the room, there is a feeling of engagement and aliveness in both participants.

Once the memoir has entered the consulting room, there is the implicit acknowledgment that the patient has permission to verbalize her or his perceptions and reactions to my subjectivity. What may have existed as unformulated experience up until that time in the analysis is encouraged to enter consciousness. In this way, the memoir stimulates dialogue about transference, countertransference, and our relationship, and encourages a collaborative process of discovery. Although the asymmetry of the analytic relationship is maintained, since the patient's life is always the focus of our investigation, nevertheless, we are partners in the exploration. While I don't always "play my cards face up," I agree with Renik (1999) that it is important to make my views and values known so that patients will understand where I am coming from. In such an open atmosphere, I have found that patients are more likely to claim greater authority and accept joint responsibility in the analytic process.

What happens to the transference when patients are privy to so much of the analyst's "real" life, her innermost thoughts and feelings, her dreams and her fantasies? Traditionally, the objection against self-disclosure on the part of the analyst was based on a particular, projective view of transference in which the analyst's participation is minimal. In the classical theoretical framework, the patient's distorting perceptions of the analyst came from his past experiences as structured by his intrapsychic dynamisms. Therefore the reality of the analyst and his personality confused the picture and needed to be minimized. As a one-person psychology has given way to the two-person model, the issue of the contamination of transference is no longer a relevant one. In the two-person model, transference is interactional. It is regarded as the patient's attempt to arrive at a plausible understanding of the analytic relationship and is influenced by the analyst's behavior. The concern is less with the patient's distortions and more with the constriction in modes of understanding (Basescu, 1990).

Menaker (1990), my former teacher, has written about the impact of analyst self-disclosure on the transference. Menaker, whose first analyst was Anna Freud, is an American who trained in Vienna in the early days of psychoanalysis. In time, she became disillusioned with certain aspects of the classical model, particularly the notion of anonymity. She points out that because transference is an individual's way of relating to others, it occurs inevitably both in life and in the analytic situation. Analysts who maintain a stance of anonymity actually intensify and distort the transference by their lack of responsiveness. We are no doubt influenced in our attitudes by those whom we respect, and Menaker reveals that her second analyst, Willi Hoffer, readily shared biographical material with her. His lack of fear of self-disclosure (as she put it) reinforced her own inclination to share her life situation when she felt it to be relevant in her work with patients. Eventually, Menaker published a memoir (1989).

The authenticity of the analyst as a critical factor in therapeutic efficacy has been identified by a number of contemporary analysts (Frank, 1997; Menaker, 1990; Singer, 1977). Menaker expressed it eloquently when she wrote "when the 'other' is felt as authentic, the delineation of the self is thereby furthered: differences and similarities come into sharper relief and the self, as well as the capacity for mature relatedness, is enhanced" (p. 114).

Menaker maintains that the patient is most helped when the analyst is seen as a real person with strengths and weaknesses and with values that are similar or different from the patient's. When the analyst reveals something about her life, it can become an echo of the patient's own experience and thus serve to cement a bond between the patient and the analyst. Furthermore, the powerful bond does not preclude the development of transference.

Reactions to my memoir have validated the fact that transference prevails no matter what. Faced with the same stimulus—my life story—patients react in diverse ways depending on their past experience with significant others. There is plenty of room for projection in the material of the memoir; what patients choose to focus on, how they interpret the material, what is most meaningful to them, all become opportunities for the expression of transference. Of course, this should not surprise us, because we know that transference is a ubiquitous phenomenon, present to varying degrees in all relationships. Knowing the facts about someone's life does not eliminate transference distortions. Those of us who work with couples can vouch for the fact that intimate knowledge about a partner's life does not prevent transference from entering and affecting the relationship.

What the memoir has done is to encourage the emergence of transference material. When it is the subject of discussion, it puts the relationship, both in its real and transferential aspects, into the center. Once the memoir has entered the consulting room, it is clear that something has changed. Often the atmosphere is one of greater emotional intensity. Of course, given the reciprocal nature of the analytic process, it is likely that my own enthusiasm and interest is communicated to the patient. I feel freer, more spontaneous and connected, and the patient responds in kind. As Aron (1996) points out, the attitude of the analyst toward the disclosure determines in large part what impact it will have on the patient.

The shift in climate toward greater intimacy has been observed by others when they shared personal experiences with patients. Erwin Singer (1971), another of my teachers, noted that when he told his patients about the crisis in his life precipitated by his wife's serious illness, they responded with great empathy and appreciated the opportunity to be supportive and useful. Singer, a pioneer in the interpersonal movement in psychoanalysis, did not have the benefit of consulting an existing body of literature on the subject of self-disclosure. He struggled with the decision to reveal this personal information, worrying about its potential negative impact. To his surprise, he discovered that his self-exposure was actually therapeutic and stimulated emotional growth in all of his patients to varying degrees. He reported that in no single instance did his disclosures have any ill effects on the treatment.

Although I can't report the same unequivocally positive findings described by Singer, I can conclude that the experience to date has been remarkably productive. My willingness to be known by my patients seems to have encouraged a powerful level of engagement and openness, has facilitated collaboration, and enriched the work in almost every case.

It must be noted, however, that this is a work in progress and that it is still too early to know how transference-countertransference interactions will be impacted in the long run. Self-revelation on the part of the analyst is a complicated phenomenon with reverberations that are not always anticipated. When these revelations are as extensive and dramatic as they are in a memoir, it is especially difficult to gauge how patients will ultimately process this complex material. Consequently, it is important that we gather experiential data to evaluate the impact of biographic disclosure on the analytic process. This preliminary report is offered in that spirit.

Notes

An earlier version of this chapter appeared in *Contemporary Psychoanalysis 42* (2006), 367–392.

1. It has recently come to light that Anna Freud's analysis with her father was only one instance of analysis with relatives. In a historical study of psychoanalysis, Falzeder (2005/2006) found that border violations were common in the early years. Psychoanalysts slept with their patients, spouses and lovers analyzed each other, and parents often analyzed their own children. A substantial discrepancy existed between what appeared in the formal literature and what was known through informal exchanges and memoirs.
2. This refers to the original article published in 2006, on data collected three years after the publication of the memoir.
3. Mrs. E, also referred to as Marnie, is discussed in more detail in chapter 4.

9

JUNG'S MEMOIRS

Carl Gustav Jung's creative contributions have been appreciated by many over the years and continue to exert their influence to this day. Even if one is not inclined to agree with his theories, the man's honesty and courage in self-exploration and self-revelation is laudable. Personally, I find the autobiographical writing that he bequeathed to us to be a most valuable gift.

For much of his life, Jung kept detailed daily journals filled with self-observations, random thoughts, and dreams. He kept these notes in a series of black leather notebooks and in his late 30s, during a time of crisis in his life, he transferred the contents of these books into an ornate volume bound in red leather known as the *Red Book*. This book only became available to the public in 2009, 48 years after his death, and it helps explain some of the origins of Jung's theory of creativity.

At 81, Jung began yet another autobiographical project, *Memories, Dreams, Reflections*, an autobiographical account that began with his early years and featured details about his life and his ideas. It was first published the year of his death in 1961.

In examining Jung's life and some of his psychoanalytic ideas I hope to illustrate a number of the themes that are the subject of this book, namely, the complex relationship between the metapsychology and the subjective world of its creator; the healing potential of creative activities such as memoir writing, painting, and drawing; and the creation of elaborate philosophical and theoretical structures. By examining autobiographical information provided by Jung himself, one can follow Jung's process of working through as it is expressed in creative action.

Jung's Autobiography

In *Memories, Dreams, Reflections* (1961/1989) Jung gave us insight into his difficult childhood experiences, which shaped his life as well as his metapsychology. His biography is less about the events of his life and more about his understanding of the impact of these events on his psyche. It is an analysis of his inner life of dreams, visions, and spiritual experiences. He began writing the book in 1957, when he was over 80, dictating it to his biographer Aniela Jaffe and then taking over the writing as his enthusiasm for the project grew. What had originally been taken on with some ambivalence became a task with some urgency. Thus he wrote,

> It has become a necessity for me to write down my early memories. If I neglect to do so for a single day, unpleasant physical symptoms immediately follow. As soon as I set to work they vanish and my head feels perfectly clear. (p. vi)

The early memories reveal a difficult childhood with profound breaks in the mother–child relationship and an atmosphere of intense conflict between the parents. His father who was a Protestant minister at a local parish was the more reliable caretaker. During Jung's early months of life, his mother's emotional instability led to recurrent absences and, in his toddler years, a major separation when she was institutionalized for several months. These traumatic disruptions of the tie between himself and his mother resulted in an irreparable breach of trust.

Winnicott's review of the memoir (1964) gives us additional insight into both the pathology and the remarkable strength of this major figure in psychoanalysis. According to Winnicott, Jung suffered from childhood schizophrenia and through his own efforts ultimately managed to heal himself. His infancy was disturbed by maternal depression and his early years by the estrangement between his parents. Before the age of 4, he had a psychotic breakdown and the threat of its recurrence was a constant fact in his life. The defenses erected against the threat of disintegration took the form of a splitting of the personality—a divided self.

In his memoir, Jung reveals his secret world in childhood—a world of religious fantasy images and symbolic objects that he imbued with magical powers. Between the ages of 7 and 10 when he entered school, Jung wrote that he experienced a sense of division between the person he was internally and his social self. His sense of security shaken, he developed a set of symbolic games, which I will describe here because of their relevance to the theme of making art as a means of coping.

During his 10th year Jung carved and painted a little wooden figure, 2 inches in height, decorated with a frock coat—such as was typically worn by members of the clergy—a top hat and shiny black boots. He made a little bed for his wooden manikin inside of his pencil case and placed a stone by his side. The stone was smooth and painted with water colors into upper and lower halves. He then hid the pencil case with its contents in the attic. Periodically he returned to the manikin with a little piece of paper on which he had written a message in a secret language of his own invention. Once the little manikin was in his secret place, Jung reported that he felt safe and no longer at odds with himself. He wrote,

> In all difficult situations, whenever I had done something wrong or my feelings had been hurt, or when my father's irritability or my mother's invalidism oppressed me, I thought of my carefully bedded down and wrapped up manikin and his smooth, prettily colored stone. (p. 21)

This ritual became a powerful source of security in his early life, helping him to maintain his stability in the face of unendurable anxiety. Jung considered the secrecy involved around this ritual to be the essential factor of his boyhood. The little wooden figure with the stone was a first attempt to give shape to the secret.

An interpretation of the significance of this "game" has been offered by Stolorow and Atwood (1979). They view the danger of self-obliteration as the core issue around which Jung's early emotional life revolved. They conceptualized the manikin as a transitional self-object and the ritual as a striving to gain mastery over the omnipotence of objects and ensure the stability and integrity of Jung's self-representation.

The elements of the ritual are multiply determined by troubling experiences and his attempts to cope with them. As a young child, Jung was witness to numerous funerals and burials at which his pastor father officiated. In his autobiography he described the memory of a scene of men dressed in frock coats, top hats, and shiny black boots lowering a black box into a hole in the ground. These images filled him with terror and were the subject of the nightmares that haunted him throughout his life. The ritual of the manikin in the box incorporated this disturbing image as well as his power over it. Hiding the manikin in the box and hiding the box in the attic allowed him to turn what had passively been experienced into an active process of recovering what was buried.

Jung's own hidden self was a deep secret and the hidden pencil case with its manikin inside was an attempt to give his secret a tangible form according to Stolorow and Atwood (1979). The elaborate precautions were symbolic actions meant to conceal and hide, and constituted defensive attempts to ward off self-loss through merger with objects (p. 97). Thus the ritual was a symbol of a profound withdrawal from external object ties into a world of self-sufficiency and omnipotence (Stolorow & Atwood, 1979).

Jung suffered from a deep sense of isolation and loneliness. The conflict between the need to retreat into a world of secrecy and safety in order to prevent self-loss and the longing to reestablish connection and communication with others was a recurrent theme in his life. In adolescence he found a solution to the conflict by splitting his self-image into two separate personalities that he called Personality No. 1 and Personality No. 2. Personality No. 1 was the outer self known to others, the self for which social ties and external reality were of great significance. Personality No. 2 was a hidden self, unknown to others, belonging to another world, a world of cosmic feelings and images that helped him escape the painful interpersonal situations in which his No. 2 personality was involved. This two-fold self-image represented the two sides of his conflict—the struggle between the safety of his private world and his need for connection. By recognizing and honoring both personalities, he was able to be involved in relationships with others while remaining safely protected in his fantasy life.

In his review of Jung's memoir, Winnicott (1964) connects the two personalities to a False Self and a True Self. Personality Number 1, the False Self, appeared normal to the outside world, while Personality Number 2, the True

Self, was the one that felt more real and more compelling for Jung, yet had to be hidden from others.

Jung's *Red Book*

Measuring $18 \times 12.3 \times 2.4$ inches and weighing 9.6 pounds, the *Red Book*, a 404-page tome, is Jung's masterpiece. He wrote it by hand on folio-sized sheets of parchment then pasted these onto thick white pages reminiscent of medieval Gospel books. He did the Latin and German calligraphy himself and illustrated it with vivid, color-saturated miniatures and full-page paintings. Then he had it bound in a red leather cover embossed with gold leaf (Epstein, 2009a).

This amazing artistic and literary oeuvre provides an intimate look at the process of creativity born of trauma finding expression in an artistic product with the potential to heal its creator. What has come to light in recent years with the publication of the *Red Book* (2009) is that Jung used his own personal experience as a template for his understanding of creativity and the creative process. Through a technique he developed, he was able to reach deep within himself and come up with images and powerful associations that he later recorded in writing and in painting. This material ultimately became the basis of his theories.

I am less interested in Jung's ideas about the specific nature of creativity than about the process by which he developed these ideas. An in-depth look at how the *Red Book* was created will give the reader an understanding of the creative process as I conceptualize it. At one time a devoted disciple of Freud, Jung broke with his mentor when he was in his late 30s. A tense relationship between them had developed as a result of differences in their theoretical propensities, as well as their personal competition and sensitivities (Gedo, 1989) When the rupture took place, Jung felt abandoned by his colleagues and resigned from numerous professional organizations and commitments. Up to that point, his career had been flourishing and he seemed to have all the trappings of a good life—marriage and children, wealth and prestige. Then suddenly in 1913, after the break with Freud, he came to a critical juncture in his life.

His mental state has been described alternately as a psychotic episode, a creative illness, or a mid-life crisis as he himself referred to it. He identified it as a voluntary confrontation with the unconscious. However one chooses to see it, it was an extensive and intense spiritual journey into the depths of his soul. During this period beginning in 1914 and for the next 16 years, Jung took on the momentous task of recording the journey into his inner life in detail using his artistic and considerable intellectual powers to describe and illustrate his experiences. In his youth he had studied painting and calligraphy, and he brought his impressive talent to this task. At first he recorded his visions and thoughts into numerous small, black journals known as the *Black Books* and later elaborated and analyzed them as he transcribed the material into the *Red Book*. The visions and hallucinations recorded in elaborate Gothic script and vivid, intricately detailed paintings imbue the work with a bizarre, psychedelic-like quality. Referring to the process, Jung wrote that the powerfully intrusive images "burst forth from the unconscious and flooded me like an enigmatic stream and threatened to break me" (in Epstein, 2009a).

During this internally chaotic time in his life, somehow Jung managed to continue to work with patients and to spend time with his family. Corbett (2009) reported that "between appointments with patients, after dinner with his wife and children, whenever there was a spare hour or two, Jung sat in a book-lined office on the second floor of his home and actually induced hallucinations—what he called active imaginations" (p. 36–37). In his memoir, Jung (1961/1989) wrote that his family and his professional work helped to ground him at a time when he was working on fantasies:

> It was most essential for me to have a normal life in the real world as a counterpoise to that strange inner world. My family and my profession remained the base to which I could always return, assuring me that I was an actually existing, ordinary person. The unconscious contents could have driven me out of my wits. (p. 189).

The fact that Jung could compartmentalize this process to a specific time and place is evidence of his capacity to control it. He analyzed these visualizations and reworked his notes into narratives which he recorded in a series of notebooks and eventually transferred to the parchment pages of the *Red Book.*

He worked on this book on and off for about 16 years, long after his personal crisis had passed, but never managed to finish it, possibly reflecting his conflict about its publication. A few friends and colleagues had read it, but he and his heirs were reluctant to publish it. During his lifetime he reported that his adult children were concerned that his autobiographical revelations showed him in a negative light and urged him to stop writing. In spite of their pressure, he secretly continued. "When my children say: the biography belongs in the family, I simply have to leave that aside . . . The demon and the creative force have absolutely and recklessly gotten their way in me" (Bair, 2003, p. 597). Clearly the need to express himself was so powerful that he would not be stopped.

In 1959, two years before his death, Jung wrote an epilogue for the book that broke off mid-sentence. In it he acknowledged that it might appear as madness to the superficial observer and confessed that it would have likely developed into madness "had I not been able to absorb the overpowering force of the original experiences" (in Epstein, 2009a).

Jung's coping process in childhood, as described in his autobiography, and in midlife as evident from the *Red Book,* appears quite similar. Thus when he was in a state of crisis and threatened with the danger of self-dissolution, Jung turned to artistic endeavors as a means of self-healing. He used his intellect, his fertile imagination, and his artistic talent to create a world in which he could encounter and work through the disparate aspects of his self. The struggle between his longing for connection and his terror of it because of the threat to self-integrity found expression in his play, his drawing, and his writing.

The theme of the secret self is a prominent one in his autobiography, but it is also expressed in the fate of the *Red Book,* which was hidden away in a locked cupboard like the manikin in the box hidden in the attic. The meanings and functions of secrets from an object-relations point of view appeared in the writings of Khan (1978) and Winnicott (1971/1990). Secrets in the object-relations model are understood as the creation of a potential space that is essential to the development of the self (Skolnick & Davies, 1992). Secrets allow for parts of the self to absent themselves both from the internal world and from the traumatizing aspects of one's external environment. It is as though a vulnerable part of the self is placed in suspended animation, tucked away for safekeeping with the hope that eventually the person will be able to emerge from it and be found and thus become a whole person (Khan, 1978, in Skolnick & Davies, 1992).

In severe psychopathology, according to Winnicott, the hiding of the secret self is a defense against the threat of annihilation of the core self by intrusion. In ordinary human development one can see a benign version of this phenomenon of the splitting of the personality. The conflict between the need to hide and the need to communicate is a universal one, and it is particularly prominent in the artist (Winnicott, 1963/1965).

From this perspective, Jung's secrets played a life-affirming role in the preservation of his vulnerable self. His secrets were created adaptively to protect his troubled self from further trauma. The question of whether or not to ultimately share these secrets seemed to preoccupy Jung to the end of his life. It is interesting that on the one hand he wrote such honest and self-revealing material meant to be seen and read, but on the other hand, the autobiography was not published until shortly after his death, and the *Red Book* was not available to be seen until 48 years after his death. Presumably he felt considerable conflict about whether or not to reveal his life story.

The universal struggle between the desire to be known and the impulse to hide is further complicated by the fact that Jung was a prominent mental health professional whose standing in the community could be threatened by revelations of serious personal pathology. Jung's tremendous ambivalence about his private versus public self is understandable in the light of the societal pressures on him. At the time that he was writing, the injunction against self-disclosure was the prevailing philosophy. Although Freud himself violated his own dictum against self-disclosure, the pressures against self-revelation in the profession were strong.

Psychoanalysts have always used their personal experiences to understand human behavior. The subjective world of the theorist inevitably is translated into his view of human nature (Stolorow & Atwood, 1979, p. 17). Traditionally, psychoanalysts have grappled with how much to reveal about the genesis of their theoretical positions. Some theorists like Kohut have resolved the dilemma by disguising their own stories as case material (Strozier, 2001). Others like Freud and his daughter Anna have used snippets of their experiences to illustrate various phenomena; still others like Jung, Rank, and Ferenczi have courageously been open about their work with patients as well as their own troubled lives. Our understanding is enriched by their willingness to reveal the depth of their internal struggle. Knowing about their pathology has not led us to question their credibility, in fact quite the contrary.

From Self-Analysis to Universals: Jung's Contributions

Jung's theoretical constructions were largely a product of his self analysis. He believed that dreaming or meditating allows us to connect with our personal unconscious, drawing us closer to ours true selves. His premise was that one can create a bridge between the conscious ego and the unconscious through visualization and personification (the creation of images meant to symbolize certain themes of significance to the individual and collective psyche). The fantasy images that are created by these processes allow one to know different aspects of self and of one's feelings.

Much of the material to be found in Jung's memoirs that ultimately became the basis of his metapsychology was arrived at through a process that he called "active imagination." This technique, which he developed in order to reach deep into his psyche, was a type of meditation or visualization. After inducing an altered state, Jung would focus on what emerged, concentrating on a single image or event and imagining himself into it. In time the visual images and symbols were used to enter meditative and altered states. Because he allowed these images to develop without exercising conscious control over them, he believed that they unfolded of their own volition and represented the workings of the unconscious. The images and dreams that emerged during the active imagination sessions were then carefully recorded in writing or drawn or painted and a narrative was created around them.

The insights that emerged as he practiced these techniques on himself were then generalized to others. Jung developed "Analytical Psychology," a school of thought that differed from Freudian psychoanalysis in its emphasis on spirituality rather than on sexual or aggressive drives. In his autobiography, Jung (1961/1989) gave details about the rupture in his relationship with Freud; he let his readers know that he found Freud's attitude toward the spirit highly questionable. He noted, "Wherever, in a person or in a work of art, an expression of spirituality . . . came to light, he (Freud) suspected it, and insinuated that it was repressed sexuality" (p. 149). Jung then commented wryly that for Freud sexuality was something to be religiously observed.

His view of the unconscious was also different and more layered than that of Freud. In addition to the personal unconscious—the repository of personal experiences and memories that are outside of awareness—Jung postulated a second layer of unconsciousness, the *collective unconscious* consisting of universal predispositions inherited from common ancestors. In his view, the fact that myths— regardless of geographical origin or chronological time period—share similar themes constitutes evidence of the existence of a universal, inherited level of the psyche.

The collective unconscious was conceptualized as the depository of the archetypes—primordial experiences common to the human race and recurring over the course of generations. The archetypes were organizing principles or predispositions without a form of their own, finding expression in myths, in dreams, and in art forms. Jung's considerable knowledge of mythology, religion, and culture informed his visions and his metapsychology. In his active imagination sessions, Jung experienced these archetypal images as personified entities like the *wise old man* and various mythological creatures with energy and mystical power representing longed-for, idealized objects, as well as feared objects with daemonic power.

These living entities were felt to be separate personalities residing inside the self. Jung identified certain archetypes important in people's lives as representing different parts of personality, such as the *persona* archetype, which is the self that we show the world, and the *shadow* archetype, the darker part of the self, which we view as frightening or evil and that we hide from others and sometimes from ourselves as well. These archetypes are reminiscent of Personalities No. 1 and No. 2 encountered earlier in Jung's self-analysis.

According to Jung, one of the most important archetypes is the *Self*, which is synonymous with the total personality and includes body, ego, spirit, and soul (Samuels, 2000). The Self is composed of both consciousness (ego) and the unconscious. Jung posited that each human being originally has a feeling of wholeness but as a result of differentiation of the psyche that occurs in childhood, wholeness must be regained later in development through a process that Jung called *Individuation*. Individuation or self-realization is the goal of life. Jung was the first to put forth the idea that there is a fundamental striving toward realizing one's potentialities and an innate capacity for integration. Human beings are meant to progress rather than merely to adapt.

Jung's contributions continue to influence psychoanalysis, as well as disciplines outside of psychoanalysis and the culture at large. Terms he used 60 years ago, like *extroversion* and *introversion*, or archetypes like the *shadow* have been incorporated into our vocabulary. Artists of all types and those who are interested in creativity are drawn to Jung; it was a subject that he himself was profoundly interested in. He postulated two different types of creativity, each deriving from a separate unconscious: the *psychological*, which relied on the personal unconscious and was motivated by personal issues, and the *visionary*, which relied on the collective unconscious and operated with archetypes. In the case of the second, the artist is able to transcend the limitations of his personal history and creates a product that has universal significance. Presumably, Jung would consider his own creations to be visionary and locate their source in his collective unconscious.

Jung proposed that art can be used to alleviate or contain feelings of anxiety and fear and can repair, restore, and heal from trauma for the artist as well as for the artist's audience. Through his own personal explorations and his work with patients, he concluded that artistic expression as well as dream interpretation can help restore emotional health and aid recovery from trauma (Malchiodi, 2006).

201

During one of the most difficult times in his adult life, when Jung felt himself in a state of chaos, he discovered the symbol of the mandala. The mandala is a geometrical form in the shape of a circle or square with intricate designs that can be found in ancient and diverse cultures. The mandala supported Jung's understanding of the collective unconscious and its archetypes and came to represent the path to the center, the path to individuation. Almost daily he found himself sketching and painting this image, which seemed to develop out of itself, often without conscious intention. This activity brought him great relief. Eventually he came to understand that it represented his self in transformation. He wrote, "My mandalas were cryptograms concerning the state of the self which were presented to me anew each day. In them I saw the self—that is, my whole being—actively at work" (1961/1989, p. 196).

The symbol of the mandala appears in the work of many contemporary artists, as well as painters inspired by Jung. In the 1930s and 1940s the psychoanalytic ideas of Freud and Jung were popular in artistic and intellectual circles. The sentiment expressed by Picasso, "My work is like a diary, to understand it you have to see how it mirrors my life" (in Richardson, 2009), was not unique. European Surrealism, an artistic and philosophical movement, was especially influenced by Jung's understanding of the relationship between art and the unconscious. Surrealists used a technique called "automatism"—a random, improvisational technique of allowing the hand to wander over the canvas or paper surface without conscious control. Much like automatic writing it was believed to be a true expression of the real functioning of the mind, a way to liberate unconscious imagery. For the Surrealists, automatism provided a visual equivalent to dream imagery or to free association. Similar to the technique of active imagination, it was based on the premise that in a relaxed, trance-like state, the mind was more susceptible to permitting repressed wishes and ideas to flow unrestrained. Even the conscious refinements of these images were assumed to be triggered by unconscious associations.

In America, artists who called themselves Abstract Expressionists were widely influenced in their use of content by Jung's philosophical system, as evidenced in their use of mythological symbols. "Hence, because of its purported universality and timelessness, ostensibly revealing psychological truths common to humanity as a whole, myth became one of the quintessential Abstract Expressionist subjects of the 1940s" (Cernuschi, 1992, p. 7).

Jackson Pollock, an American artist who was influenced by the European Surrealists and by other modern artists like Picasso, was drawn to psychoanalysis as a means to enhance his creativity as well as a way to heal. He suffered from severe bouts of emotional disturbance and alcoholism, and in the late 1930s, after a hospital stay, he sought out a Jungian analyst who had been analyzed by Jung. During his analysis, Pollock produced over 83 drawings varying in style from representational to abstract and in degree of spontaneity from premeditated and carefully detailed to more improvisational. According to the analyst, Pollock had difficulty communicating verbally and the decision to bring the drawings into sessions was meant to encourage discussion and facilitate therapy; the art was a bridge to communication. These "psychoanalytic" drawings seem typical of the work that Pollock was doing at the time—quickly executed, improvised, with variations in themes and styles, many featuring myth-related subjects. The interest of both the analyst and Pollock seemed to be primarily in the archetypal symbolism in the drawings. Pollock is quoted as saying, "the source of my painting is the unconscious" (Cernuschi, 1992, p. 1).

Jung's influence has been far reaching beyond the confines of psychoanalysis. For many years his contributions to psychoanalysis were not truly recognized. His penchant for mystical ideas was off-putting for those who like Freud were intent on legitimizing psychoanalysis as a science based on reason and rational thinking. Yet, Jung's theories had an influence in certain analytic circles outside of the classical community. Some of his ideas were assimilated into Humanistic Psychology and the Human Potential Movement of the 1960s, particularly the emphasis on the release of man's innate capacity for creativity through self-realization. His technique of active imagination can be recognized in various experiential approaches, among them Gestalt therapy, a psychological movement founded by Fritz Perls (1973) and popular in the 1950s through the 1970s. Perls and his followers used phenomenological techniques emphasizing subjective experience over interpretation and analysis. Their focus was on somatic awareness, on mindful meditation, and on dreams. In dreamwork, enactment and integration of dream elements was encouraged. Perls, like Jung, attributed each element in a dream to a subjective part of the dreamer (Bosnak, 2007). The dreamer was guided to re-experience the dream as if it were happening in the present and to assume the role of various dream elements, entering into a dialogue with them. More recently, Robert Bosnak (2007), a Dutch psychoanalyst who acknowledged Jung's influence as well as that of Perls, developed a method of dreamwork that he called "embodied imagination" in order to access psychic states that are normally not within consciousness.

While Perls and his followers were reluctant to speak about the unconscious, Bosnak respected it. According to him, from the point of view of the dreaming state of mind, dreams are real events in real environments, constituting a nonlinear reality where the patient has been. Bosnak maintained that by voluntarily reentering the dream one can come to know parts of the self that are usually seen as alien. The technique of re-entering the dream is to induce a hypnagogic state through a process of questioning by a trained guide/analyst. By reentering the dream, one can access the self-state of the dreamer while at the same time holding on to the self-state of the waking self. The main task of "imaginal" work, according to Bosnak (2003), is to let the variety of selves be aware of one another by networking them through the craft of imagination (p. 688).

This is the phenomenon referred to as "standing in the spaces" by Bromberg, a great admirer of Bosnak's ideas. According to Bromberg (2003), most individuals have the capacity to reenter their own dream space while simultaneously retaining their waking reality, and thus he believes that embodied imagination is a central aspect of working with the human capacity to feel like one self while being many.

He reported that this powerful technique, which he has occasionally used with his patients, is an effective way of bridging psyche and soma, affect and thought, and self-states that have been isolated self-protectively through dissociation (p. 701). When Bromberg spoke about this aspect of dissociation, he referred to it as *normal dissociation*—an aspect of the natural hypnoid capacity of the mind that works in the service of creative adaptation.

It is striking how many of Jung's ideas are similar or compatible with contemporary relational psychoanalysis, yet many of his contributions tend not to be recognized by most psychoanalysts (Fosshage, 2000). For instance, in postulating the objective existence of autonomous, highly energized entities within the individual, Jung was conceptualizing a version of what we have come to view as different self-states. Jung's model of personality is a dissociative model in which the psyche is viewed as a multiplicity of part-selves (Bromberg, 1998; Davies, 1998). A number of Jung's ideas seem ahead of their time and have anticipated some of our current thinking in psychoanalysis—such as the mutual field created by analyst and analysand and the consequent recognition of mutual influence in psychoanalysis (Jacoby, 2000; Jung, 1929/1966; Kalsched, 2000), the necessity of deep involvement on the analyst's part (Jacoby, 2000; Sedgwick, 2000), and the desirability of transformation for both the analyst and the patient (Young-Eisendrath, 2000)—ideas that today we would call postmodern (Fosshage & Davies, 2000; Young-Eisendrath, 2000). Among some of the ideas that are compatible with our current thinking are the primacy of affect (Kalsched, 2000), the importance of transference and countertransference (Jacoby, 2000; Jung, 1946/1966; Sedgwick, 2000), and the belief that development continues throughout one's life (Samuels, 2000).

Despite his ambivalence about the issue of disclosure, Jung's willingness to self-disclose at a time when most analysts were preoccupied with neutrality and anonymity was not only courageous, but also in keeping with his belief that we learn about psychoanalysis not only from patients but from the observation of our own unconscious as well. The attribution of universality to the themes, with which Jung himself struggled, was an ingenious and effective way of using his personal experiences in the service of growth and healing. It must have been a comfort to feel that his struggles were shared, that he was part of the human race, connected rather than isolated as he had once felt.

Jung's journey into his inner life calls attention to the thin line between creativity and madness. Jung understood madness from the inside out. According to his translator and friend, R.F.C. Hull (in Bair, 2003), the *Red Book* offered the most convincing proof that Jung's whole system was based on psychotic fantasies. At the same time Hull noted that Jung had an astounding capacity to stand off from his experiences, to observe and to understand what was happening to him, and thus was not overwhelmed by the psychotic material that was emerging. For Jung, regression was implicated in psychological growth and maturation. He exemplified the strength of the "wounded healer" (Bair, 2003; Samuels, 2000).

Jung took the core danger in his own life as the template for development. The core danger in Jung's life was the ever-present threat of disintegration of self-representation. His metapsychology reflected this theme of the precarious self threatened with dissolution through contact with omnipotent objects (the archetypes) seen as either poised to rescue or to swallow up and to annihilate. He viewed mental illness or neurosis as self-division and posited that the goal of analytical therapy is the establishment of a cohesive self-representation—ideas further developed by those who followed, like Winnicott and Kohut.

Jung's understanding of regression in the clinical situation was tied to the idea of psychological growth and maturation. He encouraged patients to discover from their own fantasies the symbols and myths by which they lived, and to follow his example in drawing and painting images arrived at by means of the active imagination technique. At the same time, he warned that this method could be dangerous and carry the patient too far away from reality.

10

CONFRONTATION WITH
MORTALITY

When he was in his late 60s, Sigmund Freud thought that he had come to the end of his life. He had just been diagnosed with a recurrence of cancer, and he decided to write his last paper. It was an account of his life, interweaving personal history with the history of psychoanalysis, and he titled it *An Autobiographical Study* (1935/1952). His ambivalence about the self-disclosure involved in writing an autobiography came through. For instance, at the end of the piece he wrote,

> And here I may be allowed to break off these autobiographical notes. The public has no claim to learn any more of my personal affairs—of my struggles, my disappointments, and my successes. I have in any case been more open and frank in some of my writings (such as *The Interpretation of Dreams* and *The Psychopathology of Everyday Life*) than people usually are who describe their lives for their contemporaries or for posterity. I have had small thanks for it, and from my experience I cannot recommend anyone to follow my example. (pp. 83–84)

By the time he wrote this piece in 1924, he had already given an account of the development of psychoanalysis on several occasions, (1910, 1914/1924–1950) but this paper was unique in that the narrative was more personal and combined biographical and historical interests. In view of his ambivalent feelings about personal disclosure, it is significant that he chose to write this autobiographical account, which he described as "the story of my life and the history of psychoanalysis" (1935/1952, p. 81).

His decision to write his story speaks to the importance it had for him in integrating this material and offering it for posterity. He was facing death and he was intent on leaving a meaningful legacy behind, not just his theoretical contributions, but his personal experiences and occasionally his feelings. In addition to stating the facts of his life, he revealed his attitudes and resentments, his disappointments and his triumphs; he wrote about his Jewish identity, anti-Semitism, his competitive feelings with peers, and other personal matters. Apparently, despite his public stance on self-revelation, he wanted to be known by his readers.

As it turned out, in 1923 he had surgery that saved his life and extended it by another 16 years, during which he continued to be productive and to write. But according to this autobiography, a significant change took place in the nature of his interests. He was no longer concerned about developing his theories in the natural sciences, medicine, or psychotherapy, and he did not make any further decisive contributions to psychoanalysis. Instead, his interests turned to culture, a subject that had fascinated him in his youth. He described this new period as a "phase of regressive development" (1935/1952, p. 82). I have seen this kind of return to earlier interests in the lives of others and experienced them in my own life, but rather than seeing them in pathological terms like "regressive development," I have conceptualized them as opportunities to develop areas of interest that had remained unfulfilled.

The notion of a last chance to fulfill what had been set aside before it became too late is a powerful theme for those who are confronting their mortality, either as a result of illness, aging, or both. In my view, the examination of one's life in the shadow of death has a powerful impact. While existential issues are ever-present in one's psyche, in illness or in late adulthood, ultimate concerns such as death, isolation, and meaninglessness (Yalom, 1980) move into the foreground and take center-stage. While mortality is always an issue, an awareness of it cannot be readily avoided when it is facing us up close. Both physical illness, whether chronic or sudden, and the gradual deterioration of the body associated with aging can be seen as potentially traumatic events—with an attendant sense of irreparable loss, helplessness, and disturbance of self-image and identity.

Betrayal of the Body

I will begin this section with a discussion of the psychological effects of physical illness and the way in which art-making can allow for the working through of major losses, restore a sense of control, and re-establish a connection with others. Illustrations from the life and artwork of two individuals faced with life-threatening, sudden physical illness will be used to highlight the issues involved.

Judith Alpert (2012), a psychoanalyst and trauma expert, wrote about what she called the "ultimate trauma," referring to the effects of chronic illness on the individual and those who love him/her. In her paper, Alpert focused on the theme of the sick individual "passing" as healthy as long as possible, a condition that she likens to other situations, such as those involving race and religion, in which one's true identity is hidden in the service of avoiding stigma or harsh consequences. Sometimes, according to Alpert, people who have an invisible illness choose to pass in order to keep the well self alive with others and experience some power in a situation that renders them helpless. However, paradoxically this attempt at coping often results in a feeling of deadness, detachment, and disconnect.

The chronically ill person is dealing with both internal and external demands to control, hide, and courageously overcome the illness. Because others are often threatened by their encounter with vulnerability and the prospect of death, they encourage the sick person to pass as healthy and to be strong in overcoming the illness. The sick individual does not only have to deal with the death anxiety of others, but also his own fragmented sense of self. One's sense of identity can be shattered because of the discontinuity of the self-representation as once intact and now damaged. As in other cases of trauma, there is a "before" me and an "after" me, with the sense of continuity disrupted.

Much of what Alpert writes about can be attributed to all trauma survivors, namely, the experience of life before trauma and life after trauma; the struggle about whether to conceal and how much to reveal; and the tendency to live a double life— the public and private persona divided by an insurmountable schism. Elsewhere I have written about the "hidden self" (Richman, 2004), a construct arising from an inner sense of shame and the need to protect the vulnerable self. The "hidden self" like the "damaged self," which Mitchell (1988) described, is an evocative meta- phor that becomes a way of experiencing oneself and serves as the centerpiece of an elaborate psychodynamic configuration that provides continuity and connectedness with one's internal and interpersonal world. The unfortunate consequence of this way of being in the world is that it results in pervasive feelings of inauthenticity and ultimately perpetuates the shame and the alienation it was meant to protect against.

Alpert ended her paper with the statement that, in psychological treatment, the chronically ill can be helped to access authentic emotion and aliveness. Another way, which I propose here, is through engagement in the creative arts. Art-making, in whatever form, can be a means of self-expression for those who struggle with the assault of illness on the body and the mind. Through this medium, with or without psychotherapy, even in cases where the hidden self is a prominent feature, there is an opportunity to process what has happened and to regain a sense of vital- ity and agency. The emotional truth can be revealed through artistic expression, where it can be disguised in symbols that have personal and often universal mean- ing. The work of Catherine Angel (Nathanson, 1995), a talented photographer/ artist whose story follows, testifies to this process through her mixed-media col- lages, photographs, and poetry.

In 1979, at the age of 21 and newly married, Catherine Angel was diagnosed with ovarian cancer. A hysterectomy followed. At such a young age, she was forced to face her own mortality, as well as her inability to bear the children she had longed to have. During her recovery, she produced work dealing with her feel- ings, but it was only after some time had elapsed, about 10 years later, that she was able to explore her experience in greater depth. By that time, the couple had adopted three daughters, and Angel had a stable university teaching career.

The early photographs, done within the first 10 years after her diagnosis and surgery, focused on the agony of her loss.[1] In her portfolio titled *Early Works,* we note a series of stark black-and-white photographs—some self-portraits, some portraits of her husband—that capture the despair in their faces and bodies. Many of these early photographs feature flowers in various stages of decay and disem- bodied hands—sometimes folded in prayer, and at other times, used to cradle and sooth. The camera captured Angel and her husband in different poses and moods, separately and together, some somber, others sensual, and still others playing with incongruity and conveying a sense of irony. For instance, there is a sensual photograph of her husband in his undershirt and briefs, legs spread apart, holding a pot of flowers over his genitals—a poignant image of frustrated sexuality and fertility. One has the sense that Angel is processing and recording her reaction to the news and reality of infertility, and that she is sharing this with the viewer. Through her art, she creates witnesses to her grief.

About 10 years after the initial diagnosis and surgery, Angel produced an evocative series of photomontages and collages that document aspects of her healing process. The primary themes of her work at this period in her life were the physical fragmentation of the body, the loss of identity this precipitated, and a yearning to heal (Brown, 1995). She created an installation of mixed-media collages constructed from fragments of photographs and torn paper covered over with a black gouache to create texture and patina with sections of gold leaf shining through (Nathanson, 1995). These pieces tended to be somber and melancholy and had the quality of faded memories. The visual symbols of death and vulnerability included gravestone shapes, severed body parts, and flowers dying or isolated within an inner space bathed in light and sometimes highlighted in muted colors.

In the piece wistfully titled *Oh, My Love* (see Figure 10.1), Angel juxtaposed the hard lines and edges of a geometric shape reminiscent of a monument that one might find in a cemetery with a small, window-like image at its center, where the viewer can catch a glimpse of a hand cradling a bouquet of delicate flowers. The inner space is enclosed and differentiated by its form as well as by the presence of color. The center image seems fragile yet alive, perhaps representing Angel's core self.

Oh, My Love is part of the collection entitled *To Embrace*. The collection has been the subject of several exhibitions of the artist's work featuring a series of panels alternating between mixed-media collages and mounted pages of text where Angel recorded the narrative of her trauma. The texts comprised journal entries, excerpts of medical reports, quotes from medical journals, discharge summaries, and dictionary definitions of highly charged words like *sterile* or *barren*. By interweaving the factual with the emotional response, Angel communicated her story most effectively (Morgan, 1995). Like the collage images, the words described a world falling apart and tenuously held together by a narrative. Some of the phrases seem to take the shape and character of a poem, but in a personal communication, Angel told me that this was not her intention. She thought of the following words as part of the text to be shown with the images. The piece, titled *To Embrace*, ends with an affirmation:

I am infertile, but I am not devoid.
I am sterile, but I am not unproductive.
I am barren, but I am not lacking.
I was castrated.
I did change.
I did become different.
I now embrace that difference as my own.

Figure 10.1 Catherine Angel, *Oh, My Love* (1990). Photocollage, 16 × 12 inches. Courtesy of the artist. The original in color can be seen at http://catherineangelphotography. com. Portfolios, *To Embrace* 1988–1998.

This is the voice of a survivor whose artistic activity, whether verbal or non-verbal, is part of the healing process and a way for her to redefine herself in a world where her identity as a woman is culturally defined by her capacity to reproduce. Although she seems to have come to terms with her traumatic losses, the confrontation with her mortality has left her acutely aware of the transient nature of existence. At a later period of her life, she refers to a series of photographs of her three adopted daughters:

> My eyes and camera now hold fast to those nearest and dearest to my heart. I hold onto the moments like a madman, the inevitability of loss and the brevity of life nipping at my heels. I hold still the moment as it slips away, making visible this proof of stopping time on film. (Angel, 2004)

It is notable, that so many of the visual artists I present in this book have chosen to express themselves in mixed-media collage (see Shimon Attie, Hannelore Baron, Marilyn Charles, Susan Erony, and David Newman—soon to be discussed). It was not my intention to limit my examples to artists using this particular art form, but on reflection, I can understand why this artistic technique would be so compelling for those who are dealing with trauma. Collage, photomontage, or mixed-media productions involve the active piecing together of separate entities arranged and rearranged into a whole and, as such, seems particularly well suited to the expression of emotional fragmentation and a wish for wholeness, expressing both the instability of part objects and the hope of their reintegration.

Brown (1995), reviewing Angel's work and writing about collage, wrote,

> The process of embracing difference, in determinability, and paradoxically finding within it a sense of self is effectively conveyed through Angel's uses of collage, a continuous process of relating separate entities as parts of a possible whole. Because these parts can be infinitely rearranged, the collage is never absolutely defined: it is always a becoming, rather than a being. (p. 47)

Consistent with this observation is the fact that Angel used this technique at a particular time in her life when she was struggling to unify the shattered pieces of her recollections and to integrate them into a new and meaningful whole. Work prior and subsequent to this period featured photographs in various compositions, in contrast to the cutting and tearing and pasting together characteristic of collage. In this series, Angel is engaged in a continuous process of relating separate entities, arranging and rearranging them into a meaningful narrative. She says about her collage work, "For me the putting together of parts to reveal the whole makes sense" (in Degennaro, 1993, p. 9).

David Newman, a psychoanalyst in private practice, wrote and published a memoir about a period in his life when he was diagnosed with a rare, large, malignant tumor growing at the base of his skull. In his book, *Talking with Doctors*

(2006), Newman examined his complex emotional reactions, his disconcerting experiences with physicians, and the responses of his own patients as they learned about his condition. His narrative provides us with an intimate look at coping with the trauma of facing impending death and having to make a rapid decision with very limited knowledge in a life-and-death situation. The world of medicine that he is suddenly thrust into is an intimidating one, with a different language and competing ideas and philosophies of treatment. Fate requires him to trust a physician—a stranger—with his life.

When the book ends, there is a resolution; Newman tells the reader in the last chapter that five years have elapsed since the surgery without a recurrence of cancer. But we know that recovery has only just begun; as a trauma survivor he now has a long road ahead. It is my contention that the book itself is evidence of the continuation of the working through of his trauma. Sorting through memories and notes, he revisited the five weeks of frantic search for the right treatment and the right physician. In so doing he faced once again the humiliating and crazy encounters with many insensitive, pompous, narcissistic, and frightened doctors, and through his understated but caustic words took revenge on them. He exposed many of them as pretentious fools, hiding behind their professional facades. In retrospect, he made sense of those strange encounters and took control of a situation in which he had once felt helpless and powerless.

It is with particular interest that I found references to the dissociative process in Newman's account of his ordeal, although these instances were not specifically identified as such. For instance, in a chapter titled "Parallel Parking" he gave an account of his decision to consciously block thoughts about his death and its impact on his loved ones. Having tolerated such thoughts for a little over two weeks, he found them unbearable:

> On Sunday, September 26th, in an uncharacteristic gesture, I decided to avoid them—if possible to stop them when they began, or at least to prevent them from being elaborated in any way . . . the feelings were too acute. That explains to me the necessity of the censoring gesture, my unexpected ability to enact it, and its substantial success. (p. 68)

He is struck with the fact that he remembers the details of where he was at the time of this decision:

> I see the field, the sun and shadows . . . It is intriguing why all this landscape comes back to me. Perhaps it was my sharply heightened sense of vulnerability . . . The feeling that I was in something of a cocoon, cut off from my surroundings, paradoxically intensified the sharpness of the light, the darkness of the shadows, and their visual impact on my memory.

I suspect that the title of the chapter, "Parallel Parking," is also a reference to his double awareness of being in the moment and alongside himself at the same time—a feature of dissociation. Newman described in detail his feelings of numbness, disorientation, and the sense of an insurmountable barrier between himself and everybody else. Writing not only rights the wrongs of his experience, it also allows him to reconnect with others. By allowing us to become witnesses to the indignities and pain he has suffered, he brings us into his world.

One of the most interesting aspects of the memoir for me relates to the way in which Newman's experiences were expressed in his paintings and his mixed-media works. He is first and foremost a visual artist, and he devoted one chapter in the memoir to describing the nature of his artwork. His paintings feature books on which he paints using oils on printed and bound paper, tree bark, and wood panels. While each painting begins with a book, they differ dramatically in terms of placement, configurations, colors, states of fragmentation, and compositions. He lets the reader know that he paints on books because of the intensity and intimacy associated with their appearance, texture, content weight, and structure. They create a structure and a boundary, providing a sense of order.[2]

He reported that three months before the diagnosis he had taken on a new art project in which he destroyed and transformed books so that they appeared as if they had been decomposed and reconstructed. Some of the paintings looked as though a fire had been raging over the materials, others like archaeological sites with fossilized remains. For some time, long before the diagnosis, he had been working on paintings that expressed fury and passion. He wrote,

> It was as though I carved flesh and blood from the books or drew them out of the texts and into organic fragments, like the pieces of bark. The presences that emerged from these procedures felt as though they existed on the edge of discontinuity, dissolution, and death. (2006, p. 147)

It seemed so clear to me, as I read these descriptions of his art work, that on some deep level he must have known what was raging in his own body for a long time prior to the diagnosis. The creator self was driven to express what was within, even as this knowledge was not available to the remainder of his personality. In the year or two following his surgery, he found himself cutting large swatches into and out of books and reconstructing them into heads and skulls, but the meaning of this symbolic expression of his trauma did not become apparent to him until a much later time.[3]

In 2008, nine years after his initial tumor diagnosis and surgery, Newman had a recurrence of this life threatening tumor and once again had to desperately search for a trustworthy physician and a viable treatment. At that point the tumor proved to be inoperable and the only form of treatment deemed possible was chemotherapy, a continuous and unrelenting process that goes on to this day.[4]

Several years after this retraumatization, Newman turned to writing once again. He updated his book *Talking with Doctors* (expanded 2nd edition, 2011) by adding a final chapter—"Keeping Howling Dogs at Bay," an evocative title that captures the terror of knowing that survival is tenuous and requires constant vigilance.

Newman told the reader that he lives in a state of limbo with the knowledge that his next MRI could reveal dangerous tumor progression. How does he cope with this horror? His attitude toward life can be best described as a creative one—he wrote, "I try to cultivate everyday feelings of well-being, of wonder, astonishment, and disbelief about what I see, hear, read, and do" (p. 219). He brought his highly developed self-reflective capacity to this chaotic situation. For instance, he observed himself being alternately compliant and self-assertive or gently confrontational with the doctors he interacted with. He was aware of the multiple states of self he experienced. He was surprised by his own tolerance for uncertainty and dispassionately noted his vacillation. His philosophy of living was eloquently expressed in the last sentence of his book:

> I believe that merely apprehending the shadows signifies a smattering of wisdom. My freedom is curtailed and constrained, but I choose again and again what to do and how to do it, however ineptly and mistakenly. I am entangled in a drama, inside and outside, that is gnarled, twisted, mangled, ravaged, and dark, but I am always seeking more light. (2011, p. 222)

I find that it is in Newman's visual art that this drama is most poignantly processed and expressed.[5] After a hiatus of several years, two months after beginning chemotherapy treatment, Newman resumed painting. He sees that action as a direct response to his precarious health and a sense of "if not now, when?" He continues to use the book format for his work and feels that both the presence and the absence of the book engages "my wanting something to hold onto, something that is structured (or even fragmented), an ordering that is often elusive or transient or disappearing or intermingling with the chaotic." Besides giving shape, form, and order to the chaos within, for Newman books also function as witnesses in the sense that they capture fleeting historical experience of trauma or catastrophe. For instance, he writes, "One of the books that appears and reappears in several of the paintings is a history of the Jewish communities in Poland, one of which is where my mother's family is from." Similar to his desire to experience wonder and astonishment in his daily life, in his work he strives to engender surprise, to create the unexpected. "When this occurs," he writes, "I treasure it, and the painting itself is a witness of my being alive."[6] Engendering surprise can be seen as something akin to a violation of expectations (Lachmann, 2008) as a definition of creativity.

In his play with colors and shapes and compositions that are totally under his control, Newman experiences the pleasure of mastery as he expresses and communicates his felt experience of "trembling and dangling." Through the playful manipulation of shapes, spaces, textures, and colors, he creates a mood that reflects his multiple emotional states. In his artist statement, he writes about the creative process—the paint is poured, dripped, splattered, brushed, blown, or sprayed and sometimes tree bark from different types of trees is inserted and painted over.

His art is rich in texture, vibrant and intense—different from the art he created in more "normal" times. He describes the book fragments and the spaces in which they exist as "fragile and formidable, alive and threatened, shattered, gestating, inherited, and abandoned."[7] What I so appreciate about Newman's self-expression is its authenticity and his apparent unwavering commitment to neither minimize nor dramatize his precarious situation. His courage is expressed in the following words: "I see myself as heedful of the possibility of imminent death, but also refusing to succumb to it" (2011, p. 220).

Before It's Too Late

Angel encountered her mortality early in life, when she was barely in her 20s, and Newman in the prime of his life, but for those who are in late adulthood, the specter of death is ever-present. It's a time of decline and a time of endings. The body shows signs of deterioration, losses accrue, contemporaries die, and memories begin to fade. With retirement there is more time to contemplate one's life and the inevitability of death. In the absence of an external structure provided by work, one is faced with the fact that ultimately we are responsible for creating a situation that is satisfying and meaningful. A heightened awareness of our ultimate aloneness and our dependency on the caretaking of others are consequences of both aging and serious illness. At a time when there is an increase in the need for protection and connection, there often exists the recognition of an unbridgeable gap between self and others. For those who do not have the inner resources or the external supports to cope with the aging process, this period of life can be traumatic.

Dramatic changes in the demographics of age in the past century have brought issues of aging into the forefront. While the average life expectancy in 1900 was 47 years of age, today it's 78—more than 30 years longer. Given that fact, it is surprising how little research there is in our field devoted to the aging process in contrast to the voluminous psychoanalytic literature on early childhood development.

One of the few contemporary psychologists who is currently prolific on the subject of creativity and aging, Dean K. Simonton (1989, 1990), has noted that creativity tends to undergo a resurgence in the later years of life and has called this phenomenon the "swan song" or "last works" effects (1989). He identifies this pattern as related to the contemplation of the prospect of death. He cites the literature on classical composers as evidence of last works effects but feels that it applies to other forms of creativity as well.

The psychoanalytic literature on this subject is quite limited as well. Otto Rank, who was acutely aware of the human need for immortality, brought the subject of creativity in the context of death into the literature (1932/1989). According to him, the task for both the individual and for society is mastery of the fact of mortality: "The human creature tries to invent ways to insure some sort of immortality—to perpetuate the self either through procreation, through identification with an

ideology that will outlast the individual self, or through some creative product"
(Menaker, p. 27).

Rank, however, did not posit a life stage theory as did Jung and Erikson, both
of whom conceptualized life as a series of overlapping stages, each presenting
specific challenges as well as opportunities for growth and renewal. Jung divided
the second half of life into middle age and old age. He viewed midlife as a period
of questioning one's long-held convictions and a time for personal transformation
when values shift from a need to succeed in the world to a desire to make cultural
contributions. What may appear as a midlife crisis is the questioning of one's basic
assumptions and prior decisions that can sometimes lead to dramatic actions. It
was his own midlife crisis (see chapter 9) that was the template for the theories
he developed. Similarly he used his own experience of old age to understand the
issues of this period of life. Old age according to Jung is a time of increased introspection and preoccupation with self-evaluation. Toward the end of his life, he
wrote that, with increasing age, memories, contemplation, reflection, and inner
images play a greater role in one's life. He warned, however, that there is some
danger in becoming overly involved in reconstruction of the past; one can remain
imprisoned in memories, and it is important to be able to translate one's emotions
into images or fantasies in order to gain some insight into one's unconscious and
ultimately move forward. Jung continued to be productive—creating, writing, and
developing aspects of his theory well into his 80s. True to his belief that in the final
stage of life it is essential to pass on the wisdom that one has accrued to future
generations, he left us with his rich legacy.

Nevertheless, it is Erik Erikson (Erikson & Erikson, 1998) whose life stage theory is
most often quoted in reference to the aging process. In his lifespan theory of development, Erikson identified several stages of adulthood, including middle and late adulthood. In Middle Adulthood—from about 40 to 65—the primary developmental task is
what he called *generativity*, a term that denotes a desire to make a contribution to society by nurturing and caring for the next generation or by creating something of value
that will live on. Knowing that one will cease to be stirs a desire to leave a mark on the
world, a sign of one's existence—a theory, a work of art, a piece of literature, a musical composition. This is a way of reaching for immortality. In Late Adulthood, from
66 on, the final developmental task according to Erikson is *retrospection*. Depending
on the answer to the question, "Have I lived a full life?" one experiences either a sense
of integrity or a feeling of despair. For Erikson integrity means self-acceptance, taking
responsibility for one's life, and coming to terms with one's mortality.

One of the problems with these stage theories of development is that they tend
to present the outcome to the struggle as either one of failure or success, when
in fact life is more complicated. Despair and integrity coexist as individuals shift
from one self-state to another at different points in time. Major losses are a hallmark of aging and moments of despair are inevitable; it is how one copes with
such moments that make the difference.

Fred Pine (1989) looked at the different stages of development from the perspective of object loss. He identified multiple universal losses in adulthood that

are inherent to the developmental process. These included the loss of omnipotentiality or an awareness of limitation; physical losses such as loss of strength, health, and appearance; loss of children as they go off on their own; and loss of peers through death and the preparation for the ultimate loss of self. Pine pointed out that within the developmental process these losses can be accompanied by personal growth or by adaptive possibilities that temper their effects. He was not explicit about what these might be.

George Pollock (1989a) also emphasized loss in old age, which he understood to be a potential stimulant to creativity. He wrote that creativity in later life has to do with mourning for one's own losses: "if one cannot successfully mourn past states of the self, then one cannot accept the ongoing aging process as a natural event" (1989a, p. 147). He conceptualized the relationship between mourning and creativity as a form of liberation. The creative product is utilized in the service of mourning, and it is also an outcome of the mourning process (Pollock, 1989b, p. 36). When the aging individual is gifted, a creative product can result in a great work of art, music, literature, poetry, or scientific finding; it can function as a memorial. But even in the less gifted, a creative outcome can reflect a change in attitude, a new relationship, or a sense of accomplishment. At times the creative product is not the end result of the mourning process, but represents an attempt at mourning work through creativity. At times the mourning is pathological with a suicidal outcome, such as in the case of Virginia Woolf, Anne Sexton, and Sylvia Plath, among others, but this does not diminish the aesthetic validity of the work.

In my view of this developmental stage in life, the tasks include life review and retrospective evaluation, the maintenance of a sense of continuity over the lifespan, an acceptance of limitations, and a creative adaptation that holds some possibility of transcendence as well as the potential for fulfillment of interrupted or submerged aspects of self. The need to feel that one's life has been meaningful and that one can leave a legacy and be remembered are important themes at this stage of life and beyond.

A number of these themes characteristic of later stages of development are well illustrated in the case of the contemporary writer Louis Begley, who came onto the literary scene in his later years. For over 40 years, Begley had a lucrative career as an attorney in a prestigious law firm, and at the age of 57, while still practicing law, he published his first novel to great acclaim. This success was followed with eight more novels and a number of nonfiction works within the next few years. For Begley, who had been an English literature major in college, retirement provided an opportunity to develop a writing talent that lay dormant while he had concentrated on developing his career.

Most of Begley's novels contain autobiographical elements, but his first one, *Wartime Lies* (1991), was actually more memoir than novel. It dealt with his boyhood in Poland during the Second World War and described how he survived under a false identity by passing as a Christian. This first book was a huge success, garnishing numerous prestigious awards. I personally find it quite compelling and appreciate his deep understanding of the long-term psychological impact of a childhood in hiding: having to lie in order to survive and living under a false identity during an impressionable time of life. I resonate not only with his story, which is so similar to my own, but also with the parallels in our writing of it. Both of us in midlife felt the need to turn to writing as a way to make sense of and come to terms with childhood trauma. In an interview (Atlas, 2002), Begley described his first novel as an attempt to take care of unfinished business before moving forward into novels that address current life issues that have meaning for him. Three of his novels feature Schmidt, an unlikely hero who is anti-Semitic and difficult for many readers to like. In view of Begley's personal history as a victim of the Holocaust, it is striking that he has given his protagonist, whom he claims to have affection for, a German name and anti-Semitic values. One wonders how much of Schmidt is in Begley and how much he is willing or able to acknowledge about their underlying similarities. The author and his protagonist are the same age, in the same profession, and they are both struggling with the ravages of age. Both have led a life of apparent respectability with the trappings of success, yet suffer from a deep sense of emptiness and loneliness. It is easy to see that Begley's childhood experiences of passing have rendered him particularly sensitive to hypocrisies and dissembling. He chooses to write about a life that looks successful from the outside but that belies the banality, conformity, and emotional barrenness that lies beneath.

Schmidt is a man who is awkward with others; he feels different and can't get close to people; he is a man in pain. Begley, as a Holocaust survivor, knows pain well, and it is likely that he is intimately familiar with a sense of isolation. In an interview (Atlas, 2002), he reveals, "I have always been aware of an uncomfortable distance separating me from other people. Perhaps also a distance separating the real me from the other visible me."

In a recent *New York Times* essay (2012a), Begley reflected on aging—its insults to the body and its potential loneliness. He wrote poignantly and somewhat regretfully about his sad relationship with his mother, who died at the age of 94. He described their early relationship as "symbiotic" because of the fact that survival depended on their being extremely close. His need to separate from her resulted in a lifetime of keeping her at arm's length. He described himself as a dutiful but emotionally distant son. By his own admission, he said, "I could speak movingly of Schmidt's loneliness after the loss of his daughter . . . But it has taken me until now, at age 78, to feel in full measure the bitterness and anguish of my mother's solitude."

One wonders how much awareness Begley has about the "not me" aspects attributed to Schmidt. When asked by an interviewer (Albon, 2011) about his choice of Schmidt as a hero, he replied, "One obeys a strange rule when one writes a novel. There are some things characters do out of their own free will that one cannot prevent." Later in a radio interview (Begley, 2012b), he vehemently denied having other than superficial similarities to his character, saying that besides the fact that they're both males and retired lawyers and that they both have a fondness for martinis, the resemblance stops. His denial seems strained and when the interviewer presses him further he acknowledges that "it is fun to play out one's nightmares." He referred to Schmidt as "my doppelganger" or double. A doppelganger who represents one's nightmares and whose similarities are disowned seems to me, at least in this case, to be a version of a "not me" self-state. My guess is that Schmidt represents unacceptable, shameful, and sometimes dissociated aspects of Begley that the author faces and masters through the creative process, hence his fascination with this character.

Begley has been able to make use of an innate talent to accomplish some of the tasks that this stage of life requires for a sense of fulfillment. For many others, however, this time of life represents loss and greater vulnerability and they lack the internal or environmental resources to enjoy more freedom. Nevertheless, they can benefit from the arts, as has been demonstrated by various programs developed for this age group.

There is considerable research confirming the importance of using creative arts with adults. For instance, one study done in 2001 (Cohen, 2001) measuring the impact of a cultural program on older adults found that community-based art programs run by professional artists involved in visual and literary arts, music, poetry, and drama resulted in better health—emotional and physical—as well as more involvement in activities and an improvement in overall functioning. Additionally, there was a positive impact on maintaining independence. The theoretical assumption behind this study was that a sense of control and mastery, as well as the opportunity to engage in meaningful social interactions, was responsible for these positive effects. Other research on creativity and aging has consistently supported these findings (Cohen, 2006).

The Aging Brain

We are learning from neuroscience that age affects the brain selectively and that the normal aging process leaves many mental functions intact. With new imaging techniques and advances in science, neuroscientists are able to revise some of their theories about the nature of the aging brain. There is evidence of *neuroplasticity*— the capacity of the human brain to keep changing—and the evidence supports the idea that environmental influences are important in shaping brain function and structure as well (Davidson & Mc Ewen, 2012). Apparently even into our 70s, our brains continue producing new neurons, and we no longer believe that a vast number of brain cells are lost as we grow older. Having a lifetime of experience and a greater store of knowledge gives older people an advantage with regard to being able to access and combine diverse information. This is likely related to the common notion of wisdom accruing with age.

One of the observations from various sources is that with age there is less concern about the opinion of others. Delbanco (2011) observed that the change that takes place in creativity as artists get older is that gratification turns inward, so that public recognition of the final product seems to be less significant for the creator than the act of making something. Besides a shift in perspective deriving from a foreshortening of time, there is also neurological evidence (Salat et al., 2004) that certain areas of the prefrontal cortex, which affect the emotions, are thinner in the aging brain, accounting for a diminished need to impress or please others. This is also a characteristic attributed to creative individuals.

A fascinating recent discovery relevant to my thesis is that the aging brain resembles the creative brain in several respects. Both are characterized by a broadening focus of attention, and this state allows the individual to hold disparate bits of information in mind and combine them into creative ideas (Carson, 2009; Kim, Hasher & Zacks, 2008). With aging, there is a process of demyelination, gradually starting at the front of the brain and working to the back of the brain, that diminishes cognitive capacities, particularly as they relate to reasoning and memory, resulting in frontal cortex disengagement, which in turn enhances creativity. As the frontal lobes are losing their power and the brain is winding down, creativity is actually enhanced. This is similar to the hypofrontal state that enhances the inspirational aspect of the creative process. Aging is more conducive to the hypofrontal state, which may account for the popularity of the arts with older people (Jung, 2012). Furthermore, the plasticity of the aging brain is enhanced through creative endeavors. Creativity nourishes the brain by providing a challenging, stimulating, and rich environment (Cohen, 2001).

We are revising one of the popular conceptions about the location of creativity in the brain. The idea that creativity resides in the right hemisphere has been popular since the 19th century. Based on his clinical observations, Hughlings Jackson, a physician, theorized that the left hemisphere is involved in language, logical processes, and rational thinking, while the right hemisphere is involved in musicality and synthesis, which are aspects of creativity (Rose, 2001). This idea is challenged today as we are becoming aware that the entire brain is involved in the creative process. The processing of visual and auditory stimuli, spatial manipulation, and artistic ability are all represented bilaterally, but may show right hemisphere superiority. It is of note that there are many contradictory claims and much ambiguity in the literature. Neuroscience as an identifiable field is young; it began in the 1970s and so we can expect profound changes as new discoveries come to light.

One of the most fascinating discoveries in recent years was made by Bruce Miller, a behavioral neurologist working with neurodegenerative diseases. While analyzing a condition called frontotemporal dementia, Miller and his colleagues (Seeley et al., 2008) discovered that, when the dementia is expressed solely on the left side, patients began to show creativity either for the first time in their life or, if they had been artists prior to the illness, there was an enhancement of their creative output with greater experimentation, particularly with new color and forms. It was hypothesized that this type of damage reduced the left hemisphere's ability to inhibit action in the frontal and temporal lobes of the right hemisphere (Kandel, 2012).

Another interesting current finding is that despite the prominent loss of motor skills in Parkinson's disease, artistic capacities remain preserved. Most recent data suggest that artistic creativity may actually be enhanced in patients with

Parkinson's disease who are treated with anti-Parkinsonian therapy (Inzelberg, 2013). In my clinical practice, I have a patient whose serious hobby is photography, a skill that gives him immense pleasure. A couple of years ago he learned that he has Parkinson's disease and has been greatly concerned that the disease might interfere with his ability to take and develop photographs. Yet to his great relief, his skill continues to develop; the images he creates are increasingly beautiful, haunting, and emotional. Despite the progression of the disease, when he is engaged in photography, the tremors, which are so characteristic of Parkinson's, actually stop and his hands are as steady as they ever were.

Alzheimer's is another progressive disease that selectively affects different parts of the brain, and we now know that those parts involved in creativity can remain relatively intact until a much later time. The amygdala, a part of the limbic system that performs a primary role in the processing and memory of emotional reactions, is the part of the brain that responds to the arts (Ellena & Huebner, 2009).Corroboration also comes from studies of the amygdala linking it with emotionally charged memories. The right amygdala was one of the structures that showed heightened activity during traumatic recall, along with increased activity in the visual cortex and reduced activity in Broca's area—the region for language production. These findings are consistent with the notion that traumatic memories are characterized by vivid visual imagery (Schacter, 1996).

A documentary film entitled *I Remember Better When I Paint* (2009) describes a program that involves the use of the creative arts with older adults who suffer from Alzheimer's. The film, which shows patients engaged in various creative activities with the help of trained staff, also includes interviews with relatives who describe with amazement the changes that they have seen as a result of these programs; people with serious memory and cognitive problems can be brought back into active communication with loved ones. The film also features a number of experts from multiple medical fields discussing the latest brain research that indicates that parts of the brain related to emotions and to creativity are largely spared by the disease. By tapping into non-verbal emotional places in the individual, areas of cognitive limitation are bypassed, allowing those with Alzheimer's disease to relate in terms of the strength that they still have. Thus creative expression for aging adults, even for those who are not especially talented artistically, can be an outlet, a release, a way to process complex life events, and a vehicle of communication for those isolated by their disease. Cognitive losses of this magnitude, however, are not typical. We know that people can be very old and still maintain a high degree of intellectual sharpness, as will be illustrated in the clinical case that follows.

Clinical Vignette

The personalities that I have described and used as illustrations for my ideas in the previous sections—Angel and Begley—are not individuals I have known personally or worked with in therapy; hence my descriptions of their lives and their trauma is based on what I have read, either in the literature or on the internet. I have quoted extensively from their own accounts in the hope of truly representing them. My analysis of their psychodynamics and the motivations that I attribute to them is by the nature of such research inevitably limited. In contrast, the vignette that I am about to discuss is based on my clinical work with a patient over many years.

Sylvia first came to see me when she was 71 years old; she is now 89 and for the last 18 years she has rarely missed a session. She initially came to me to deal with a growing depression—precipitated by numerous losses. We mourned and processed the death of her mother, her brother, her ex-husband, and countless relatives and friends. When the depression lifted she decided that the process of examining her life and her feelings was worthy in itself and that she didn't need to be in pain in order to benefit from ongoing dynamic psychotherapy. "Why not, if I can afford it," she said.

Sylvia has been in treatment for most of her life. Even an early experience with a traditional male analyst—judgmental and clueless, as she remembers it—did not shake her faith in the efficacy of the process. What she values in our work together is the opportunity to express herself without the kind of inhibition she often experiences in relationships outside of the consulting room. My role with her has been primarily one of witnessing as she struggles with problems in living and in helping her make sense of her experiences as she reviews her life.

Over the years, the contents of Sylvia's sessions have ranged from revisiting the trauma of having been sexually abused by her grandfather when she was 5 years old, to an exploration of her difficult and complicated relationship with her mother, to her current relationships with her three children and five grandchildren, and ultimately, as she moved into her 80s, to her increasing concerns about decline and death.

The creation of narrative in analysis involves a kind of life review that is so significant at this stage of retrospection. With her sharp intellect and her notable psychological astuteness, Sylvia revisits the significant moments in her life, bringing an ever-evolving and shifting perspective on them. Sometimes lately, when her memory fails her, I as the keeper of her history can remind her of some of the things we have talked about in the past and help her to integrate the material and make new connections.

Sylvia is most engaged when she is talking about her two favorite subjects—the creative arts and her grandchildren. While the arts bring her back into the past as she listens to her favorite musical compositions or revisits and finds new meaning in the plays of Shakespeare, the grandchildren bring her into the future. When her first grandchild was born, she envisioned a long string passing through her and connecting her with her grandmother, her mother, her daughter, and her daughter's daughter, a most imaginative way of describing continuity and generativity.

With her grandchildren, Sylvia is a great supporter and sometimes co-conspirator. Like her grandmother, who took her side in any conflict with her mother, Sylvia does the same with her children's children. We have noted that she gets vicarious pleasure in their rebellion and self-assertion—something that she was incapable of doing with her own controlling mother. Her bitterness toward her mother has always been in consciousness, but the longing for her love and for her recognition was not within awareness until very recently. Of late, a dramatic change has been taking place in Sylvia's internal relationship with her mother. From time to time she finds herself wanting to phone her mother to share some event in her own life. Her mother, who has been dead for at least 16 years, was during her lifetime never experienced as someone who Sylvia could, or would want to, share good news with. For the first time in her conscious memory, Sylvia wishes to have her mother witness the good things in her life. To her great surprise, her mother has become her imaginary witness. This change has coincided with recognition of her mother as a separate individual with strengths as well as weaknesses.

Sylvia has also come to appreciate the fact that her mother supported creative and intellectual endeavors even when she had to assert her wishes over those of Sylvia's father, who did not feel that a young woman needed such an education. Her mother encouraged Sylvia to go to college and arranged for piano lessons that ultimately brought her to Julliard. Although Sylvia showed great promise, her insecurity and fear of failure held her back, and she did not pursue a career after completing college—something she has always regretted.

Sylva married early and immediately began a family. For the most part, Sylvia did not experience marriage and motherhood as satisfying, and it was music and dance that provided her with the escape and solace she needed to cope with the frustrations of domestic life. She describes how when the children were young, she would spend the nights listening to Beethoven in order to soothe herself and find some strength. In describing her experience listening time and again to the chorale movement of Beethoven's 9th symphony, she says, "It goes into me; it enters my soul."

From her late 30s into her 60s, folk dancing was the driving and healing force in her life. By the time I met her in her early 70s, she had stopped dancing and had shifted from being an active participant in the arts to enjoying them as a viewer and listener. These days, her passion is directed to theater and film. She rarely misses a class devoted to the works of Shakespeare given by an actor at a local senior center. The thrill of rereading Shakespeare and seeing new connections is palpable. About Shakespeare, particularly when reading *Hamlet*, she exclaims, "How does he know me so well?" With me, she loves to discuss films. When Sylvia tells me that she has seen a new movie, I take out a pad and pencil—not to analyze her choices but to heed her recommendations. They are always excellent.

A few years ago, at holiday time, Sylvia brought me a gift of one of her favorite movies—a videotape of *Babette's Feast*, a film that had meant a great deal to her and one that I had not seen. What made her pick this film? I asked. "We usually like the same films," she answered. The film which won the 1987 Academy Award for Best Foreign Language Film, is based on a short story written by Isak Dinesen in 1958, when she was 73, four years before her death. Briefly, the plot line is of two sisters, the devout and beautiful daughters of a stern and puritanical minister living in a small, seacoast village in Denmark who give up their chance for love and career to remain devoted to their father and his church. Years after his death, a stranger appears, a woman named Babette who has lost her husband and her son to the bloodshed of the French civil war and barely escaped with her own life. She takes refuge with the two spinsters in their bleak and harsh environment and offers to be their housekeeper and cook for them in return for room and board. Eventually she wins the lottery and with her winnings decides to create a real French dinner for the sisters and their small congregation—a magnificent feast in celebration of the 100th anniversary of the birth of the church. We do not learn about Babette's great talent in the culinary arts until the very end when she confesses that she was once a great artist and a renowned chef in a famous restaurant in Paris.

This simple story is filled with symbolism that has led to a number of interpretations, some religious, others artistic, but the ones most relevant for understanding Sylvia's fascination with this film are the psychoanalytic interpretations of *Babette's Feast* as a parable of trauma (Waldron, 2010) and as a metaphor of impeded mourning and a means of transcending it through artistic creation (Rashkin, 2008). These interpretations fit well in my work with Sylvia, and I believe that she was drawn to this story because of these themes in her life and their unconscious pull for her. According to Rashkin, *Babette's Feast* is a story about the overcoming of an inability to mourn. The dinner has a psychoanalytic function; it enables loss to be talked about and the process of mourning to begin. The preparation and consumption of food serves as the medium of transcendence that permits loss to be swallowed and the process of digestion to begin. According to Rashkin, the metaphor of food functions "as a vehicle for articulating a fundamental connection between artistic creation and bereavement, between literary inscription and psychic memorialization, and between the production of narrative as an aesthetic enterprise and the creation of art as a life-saving act" (p. 26/27). In the film, the congregation's role is as a kind of Greek chorus that echoes the main theme and bears witness to the traumas revealed and to the transformation of suffering into a work of art (Rashkin, 2008).

It was poignant to learn that the author of *Babette's Feast*, Isak Dinesen was suffering from a long, debilitating illness at the time she wrote this story toward the end of her life, and that ultimately she starved to death. She had severe eating problems for many years, presumably caused by advanced syphilis—a disease contracted from her philandering husband—which had attacked her digestive system and left her in an emaciated physical state. Much like Babette, Dinesen had suffered numerous losses in her lifetime, including the loss of country, husband, and a lover who died in a plane crash. Now she faced her own imminent death because of her inability to eat. In that context, it is easy to see how Dinesen would find food to be an apt metaphor for salvation, particularly when served lovingly by a maternal figure like Babette. The book and the film end with hope; the heroine's state of psychic numbness has been transformed into a sense of excitement and aliveness through her creative and loving act. The feast has facilitated mourning for all of the characters in the story and for the readers, for the audience, and presumably for the writer as well. Rashkin pointed out that since *Babette's Feast* is about the creation of a work of art as the therapeutic medium for talking about loss, it is most likely that Dinesen, too, was able to use this narrative for her own therapeutic needs; born out of her need to grieve, this story can be seen as a tale of Dinesen's recipe for mourning.

Sylvia and I spoke for some time about the film and its significance for her. She related to the losses that were so prominent in the film, particularly those of the two sisters who had given up their own opportunities for love and fulfillment in order to fulfill their duty to their father. Sylvia could identify with the failure to choose the more exciting paths in life and staying close to home and parental expectations. When she was young, Sylvia loved to travel and once had found herself powerfully sexually attracted to a young Latin man, but stopped herself from following her passion. "My parents would sit *Shiva* for me if I married him!" she exclaimed. Eventually, she had married someone who her parents thought suitable and within a short time found herself deeply disappointed in her choice. It took many years before she found the strength to divorce him. Like the sisters in the film who were afraid of their passions, Sylvia chose the loveless, safer path and, like them, she did not choose a career despite her musical talent and intellect. Sylvia could well identify with making choices that led to regret.

As we spoke about the feast, Sylvia reminded me about her love of Chinese cooking. We had once discovered that each of us had taken classes with the same master chef, but while I had dabbled in the technique, she had developed her skill into an art. Now as we spoke about it in the context of the film, I realized that, for Sylvia, sensuality and passion were expressed through cooking. She told me that she had taken great pleasure in organizing Chinese banquets for her friends. She loved the shopping, preparing, cooking, and serving of exotic dishes; she described the rich aromas, the delicate tastes, the varied colors and textures of the ingredients. The erotic and sensual, which were suppressed in her life, were expressed here in abundance. But the greatest thrill for her was her sense of mastery over this challenging art. She proudly told me how in time she was able to create her own recipes. This was one of the few areas where she felt in full control and where she was aware of doing her very best. The importance of giving one's all to the artistic enterprise is expressed in Babette's words: "Through all the world there goes one long cry from the heart of the artist: Give me leave to do my utmost" (Dinesen, 1958, p. 53).

Like Babette, who lived in a sterile, colorless environment following her traumatic losses, Sylvia had felt like a stranger in her own family. The adults around her had failed to protect her when she was sexually abused as a child. Even her beloved grandmother, the matriarch of the family and the wife of the abuser, did not come to her aid. There seemed to be no recognition of the abuse that she had endured, nor was there an opportunity for mourning. Sylvia wondered if anyone knew, or if this was a secret that she had to keep; she lived with a pervasive sense of insecurity and developed a façade of independence, behaving as though she didn't need anyone.

The Chinese banquets seemed out of character for her, yet upon reflection I began to see them as an ingenious way to repair the rupture and betrayal experienced in childhood. In her family of origin, dinners were not occasions for bringing a loving family together, nor did they provide psychological nourishment. As a child Sylvia had faded into the background while her mother took center stage at these events. But as an adult, Sylvia gathered a community of friends who could share a meal that was exciting, exotic, and nourishing and that she herself had organized and created. In these situations, she was in control; she could share herself with others and allow herself to shine and to be admired. Food was more than a means of nourishment; it was a sensory experience that transformed her from the insecure person who gave over her power to others to someone who invested her whole self in this communal act.

The film itself served an interesting function between us as well. It began as a gift from Sylvia to me; it was like a good meal that she provided for us to share, rich in complex ingredients and nourishment, which provided us with much to chew on. It led her to talk about the lost opportunities in her life, the regrets she had, and the creative activities that had facilitated mourning and reparation. Our discussion of the movie and the book allowed Sylvia to express unformulated and distanced aspects of self which she could recognize in the characters. The fictionalized account provided the safety to explore her own losses in greater depth. As Rose (1996) has written: "For the audience of art, participation in the aesthetic experience offers the opportunity for regression and/or progression, 'escape' or expansion in a dynamically changing 'living' balance" (p. 111). The pleasure that Sylvia had in introducing me to this film matched the pleasure that I experienced in our discussion of it.

Working with Sylvia has been most gratifying for me. Her desire to know herself continues unabated in her late 80s, and she brings a great deal of insight and wisdom to our sessions. It is a privilege to watch how she copes with aging and to have a role in facilitating her transition into this challenging developmental phase. We talk a great deal about how to prepare for when she is no longer able to live independently. She faces the uncertainties of the future with courage and with grace. She is painfully aware of the passage of time and her most recent dreams are reflecting a sense of urgency—the legacy of this developmental period. Some months ago, she told me the following dream:

> There was something I had to do and I knew that I would not have enough time—maybe fly to Cara's (her daughter). I had a half hour of extra time and wondered should I do something or just make sure that I make the time.

She added,

> In the dream there was a quandary; I felt an internal pressure. I worried about time wasting. There was a sense of urgency—should I do this, or should I not? How shall I use this time? I realize that it's about my old age and making specific plans for the future and it's hard to do.

226

Coda

I want to end this chapter with some words of wisdom from the 96-year-old mother of a friend. Clarice is a tiny woman with sparkling eyes and a ready smile. She's delighted to be interviewed, anticipating that her words will be memorialized in my book. By now she has outlived most of her contemporaries, including her husband, her younger brother, and all of her cousins—even some members of the next generation, like her son-in-law.

When I ask her a question that she is often asked these days—To what do you attribute your longevity?—her response is a variation on much of the material in this book. She answers:

My curiosity; I have a lot of interests, I'm always learning, solving puzzles. I have an interest in philosophy; I ponder the beginnings of life and the ending of life. When my friends ask me, "What's your secret?" I say, "You have to have at least one passion so that when you wake up in the morning you feel strongly about something."

She laughs: "They call me the passion lady!"

She tells me about her two passions—folk dancing and tending to the garden that she has lovingly created. Soon to be 97, she is still dancing but she says wistfully,

I can no longer fly; I'm rooted to the ground. Now that I can't fly, my first passion is gardening. In my garden I see life—that's what it's all about—life is manifested in nature, the life force represents God; life is starting and ending, blossoming. It's ablaze in color and form. It's almost like an orchestra—there are insects and animals and they all have a place. When I go into the garden I'm overwhelmed with a spiritual feeling—like I'm part of the life energy.

Her creative spirit finds an outlet in this garden. She takes cuttings of plants when she moves or travels and grows them in new soil—"I help to create the plants. I root plants, if I have one plant I can have a hundred . . . I facilitate, I bring things together that normally don't go together and see if it works."

Clarice is radiant as she describes her garden—the brilliant colors and patterns, the scent of basil on a breezy day, a wondrous convocation of black noisy crows gathering by a large tree. As she talks, I'm reminded of Alice Walker's beautiful essay and poem *In Search of Our Mothers' Gardens: The Creativity of Black Women in the South* (1983). Walker writes about oppressed black women, mothers, and grandmothers like her own who managed to keep their creativity alive by creating magnificent gardens. She refers to her mother and the generations of women before her as "Artists" and "Creators" who had a powerful drive to express their spirituality and unused talents in whatever way was open to them in their bleak existence. Lacking in the freedom to paint or sculpt or expand their mind, they found an ingenious way to express their vibrant creative spirit—they planted ambitious gardens for all to see and admire. These were a daily reminder of their generativity and their ability to transcend their impoverished environments. Walker gratefully acknowledges that her own creativity has been inspired by her mother's legacy.

Alice Walker's homage to her mother brings us to the conclusion of this chapter, and to the end of this book as well. In her eloquent essay, Walker alerts us to yet another instance of the theme that we have been addressing throughout this book. Here we note that through the transcendent power of art, generations of descendents of slaves, traumatized by subjugation, found a way to keep their spirit alive and to express what was in their soul.

Notes

1. See http://catherineangelphotography.com.
2. Note that the cover image for *Mended by the Muse* is a painting by David Newman. (2010). *By Fire*, 16 × 20 inches, oil on bound paper, bark and wood panel.
3. D. Newman, personal communication, April 2007.
4. Before the following section was written, several years ago, I lost contact with Newman until recently, when I contacted him to obtain permission to use his material in the book. He then shared what had transpired in the interim.
5. Some of the following observations derive from personal communications with D. Newman in March 2013.
6. D. Newman, personal communication March 24, 2013.
7. Artist statement and paintings can be viewed at http://davidnewmanpaintings.com.

REFERENCES

Abend, S. M. (1982). Serious illness in the analyst: Countertransference considerations. *Journal of the American Psychoanalytic Association, 30,* 365–379.

Aberbach, D. (1989). Creativity and the survivor: The struggle for mastery. *International Review of Psycho-Analysis, 16,* 273–286.

Adorno, T. (1982). Commitment. In A. Arato & E. Gebhardt (eds.), *The essential Frankfurt school reader* (pp. 300–318). New York: Continuum. (Originally published 1962).

Albon, M. (2011, December 1). Book Review: Louis Begley's Schmidt steps back. *The Vienna Review.* Retrieved from www.viennareview.net/book-reviews/reinventing-the-anti-hero-the-man-behind-schmidt

Alexander, F. (1964). Neurosis and creativity. *American Journal of Psychoanalysis, 24,* 116–130.

Alpert, J. (2012). Loss of humanness: The ultimate trauma. *The American Journal of Psychoanalysis, 72,* 118–138.

Andreason, N. (1987). Creativity and mental illness: Prevalence rates in writers and their first-degree relatives. *American Journal of Psychiatry, 144,* 1288–1292.

Angel, C. (2004). Catherine Angel Photography. "My Daughters." Retrieved from http://catherineangelphotography.com/mydaughtersstatement.html

Anthony, E. & Kohler, B. (1987). *The invulnerable child.* New York: Guilford Press.

Appelfeld, A. (1994). *Beyond despair.* New York: Fromm International Publishing Corp.

Arieti, S. (1976). *Creativity: The magic synthesis.* New York: Basic Books.

Aron, L. (1991). The patient's experience of the analyst's subjectivity. *Psychoanalytic Dialogues, 1,* 29–51.

Aron, L. (1996). *A meeting of minds: Mutuality in psychoanalysis.* Hillsdale, NJ: Analytic Press.

Atlas, J. (2002). Louis Begley: The art of fiction CLXXII. *Paris Review, 44* no. 162, 110–143.

Attie, S. (1994). *The writing on the wall: Projection in Berlin's Jewish Quarter. Photographs and installations.* Heidelberg, Germany: Edition Braus.

Auerhahn, N., Laub, D., & Peskin, H. (1993). Psychotherapy with Holocaust survivors. *Psychotherapy, 30,* 434–442.

Badiou, A. (2012). *Plato's Republic,* trans. S. Spitzer. New York: Columbia University Press.

Bair, D. (2003). *Jung: A biography.* New York & Boston: Little, Brown and Company.

Balint, M. (1968). *The basic fault: Therapeutic aspects of regression.* New York: Brunner Mazel.

REFERENCES

Barbanel, L. (1980). The therapist's pregnancy. In B. L. Blum (ed.), *Psychological aspects of pregnancy, birthing, and bonding* (pp. 232–246). New York: Human Sciences Press.

Barron, J. W., ed. (1993). *Self-analysis: Critical inquiries, personal visions.* Hillsdale, NJ: Analytic Press.

Basescu, S. (1990). Show and tell: Reflections on the analyst's self-disclosure. In G. Stricker & M. Fisher (eds.), *Self-disclosure in the therapeutic relationship* (pp. 47–59). New York: Plenum Press.

Basescu, S. (2010). Creativity and the dimensions of consciousness. In G. Goldstein & H. Golden (eds.), *Sabert Basescu: Selected papers on human nature and psychoanalysis* (pp. 99–118). New York: Routledge. (Originally published 1967).

Bassin, D. (2011). Reminiscence, ritual, and beyond working through: Commentary on papers by Joyce Slochower and by Laura Impert and Margaret Rubin. *Psychoanalytic Dialogues, 21,* 707–718.

Beebe, B. & Lachmann, F. (2002). *Infant research and adult treatment: Co-constructing interactions.* Hillsdale, NJ: Analytic Press.

Begley, L. (1991). *Wartime lies.* New York: Ballantine Books.

Begley, L. (2012a, March 19). Bitter gifts of getting old. *The New York Times.*

Begley, L. (2012b, March 22). Louis Begley's Schmidt steps back. *The Leonard Lopate Show.* WNYC.

Benjamin, J. (1988). *The bonds of love.* New York: Pantheon Books.

Benjamin, J. (1990). An outline of intersubjectivity: The development of recognition. *Psychoanalytic Psychology, 7S,* 33–46.

Benjamin, J. (1992). Recognition and destruction: An outline of intersubjectivity. In N. Skolnick & S. Warshaw (eds.), *Relational perspectives in psychoanalysis* (pp. 43–60). Hillsdale, NJ: Analytic Press.

Benjamin, J. (2005). From many into one: Attention, energy, and the containing of multitudes. *Psychoanalytic Dialogues, 15,* 185–201.

Beres, D. (1959). The contribution of psycho-analysis to the biography of the artist—a commentary on methodology. *International Journal of Psycho-Analysis, 40,* 26–32.

Bergstein, M. (2010). *Mirrors and memory: Freud, photography, and the history of art.* Ithaca, NY: Cornell University Press.

Bernstein, J. (2000). Making a memorial place: The photography of Shimon Attie. *Psychoanalytic Dialogues, 10,* 347–370.

Bettelheim, B. (1979). *Surviving and other essays.* New York: Alfred A. Knopf.

Betzer, J. & Christensen, B. (producers); Axel, G. (director). (1987). *Babette's feast.* Danish: Nordisk Film Production Company.

Bloch, O. (2012, March 4). Vivienne's songbook: A film about trans-generational trauma. IARPP conference: *The legacy of Stephen Mitchell: Sustaining creativity in our psychoanalytic work.* New York, NY.

Blythe, W. (1998). *Why I write: Thoughts on the craft of fiction.* Boston, MA: Little, Brown and Company.

Bollas, C. (1987). *The shadow of the object.* New York: Columbia University Press.

Bollas, C. (2011). *The Christopher Bollas reader.* New York: Routledge.

Bornstein, M., ed. (2004). The making of psychoanalysts: Personal journeys. *Psychoanalytic Inquiry, 24,* 487–593.

Bose, J. (2005). Images of trauma: Pain, recognition, and disavowal in the works of Frida Kahlo and Francis Bacon. *Journal of the American Academy of Psychoanalysis, 33,* 51–70.

Bosnak, R. (2003). Embodied imagination. *Contemporary Psychoanalysis, 39,* 683–695.

Bosnak, R. (2007). *Embodiment: Creative imagination in medicine, art and travel.* New York: Routledge.

Boulanger, G. (2007). *Wounded by reality: Understanding and treating adult onset trauma.* Mahwah, NJ: Analytic Press.

Brenson, M. (1989, June 2). Pieced-together history: Hannelore Baron's collages. *New York Times* Art Review.

Bromberg, P. (1979). Interpersonal psychoanalysis and regression. *Contemporary Psychoanalysis, 15,* 647–655.

Bromberg, P. (1998). Shadow and substance: A relational perspective on clinical process. In P. Bromberg, *Standing in the spaces: Essays on clinical process trauma and dissociation* (pp. 165–187). Hillsdale, NJ: Analytic Press. (Originally published 1993).

Bromberg, P. (1998). *Standing in the spaces: Essays on clinical process, trauma and dissociation.* Hillsdale, NJ: Analytic Press.

Bromberg, P. (2003). On being one's dream: Some reflections on Robert Bosnak's "embodied imagination." *Contemporary Psychoanalysis, 39,* 697–710.

Bromberg, P. (2006). *Awakening the dreamer: Clinical journeys.* Mahwah, NJ: Analytic Press.

Brown, G. (1995, April). "Catherine Angel" S.R.O. Gallery review. *New Art Examiner, 22,* 47–48. Retrieved from http://catherineangelphotography.com/toembracereviews.html

Bucci, W. (2001). Pathways of emotional communication. *Psychoanalytic Inquiry, 21,* 40–70.

Bucci, W. (2002). The referential process, consciousness, and the sense of self. *Psychoanalytic Inquiry, 22,* 766–793.

Bucci, W. (2007). Dissociation from the perspective of multiple code theory, part I: Psychological roots and implications for psychoanalytic treatment. *Contemporary Psychoanalysis, 43,* 165–184.

Butler, L. (2006). Normative dissociation. *Psychiatric Clinics of North America, 29,* 45–62.

Cardeña, E. (1994). The domain of dissociation. In S. Lynn & J. Rhue (eds.), *Dissociation* (pp. 1–31). Washington, DC: American Psychological Association Press.

Carson, S. (2009, March 30). Creativity and the aging brain. Life as Art. *Psychology Today.* Retrieved from www.psychologytoday.com/blog/life-art/200903/creativity-and-the-aging-brain

Caruth, C. (1996). *Unclaimed experience: Trauma, narrative and history.* Baltimore & London: Johns Hopkins University Press.

Cernuschi, C. (1992). *Jackson Pollock: "Psychoanalytic" drawings.* Durham, NC: Duke University Press.

Charles, M. (2001). Auto-sensuous shapes: Prototypes for creative forms. *American Journal of Psychoanalysis, 61,* 239–269.

Charles, M. (2002). *Patterns: Building blocks of experience.* Hillsdale, NJ: Analytic Press.

Charles, M. (2011). Remembering, repeating, and working through: Piecing together the fragments of traumatic memory. In L. DellaPietra (ed.), *Perspectives on creativity, Volume II.* Newcastle upon Tyne: Cambridge Scholars Publishing.

Chessick, R. (1999). *Emotional illness and creativity: A psychoanalytic and phenomenological study.* Madison, CT: International Universities Press.

Cohen, F. (2007). *From both sides of the couch.* North Charleston, SC: Booksurge.

Cohen, G. (2001). *The creative age: Awakening human potential in the second half of life.* New York: HarperCollins.

Cohen, G. (2006). Research on creativity and aging: The positive impact of the arts on health and illness. *Generations, 30,* 7–15.

Cook, N. (1998). *Music: A very short introduction.* New York: Oxford University Press.

Corbett, S. (2009, September 20). The holy grail of the unconscious. *New York Times Magazine.* Retrieved from www.nytimes.com/2009/09/20/magazine/20jung

Crastnopol, M. (1997). Incognito or not? The patient's subjective experience of the analyst's private life. Psychoanalytic Dialogues, 7, 257–280.

Csikszentmihalyi, M. (1990). *Flow: The psychology of optimal experience.* New York: Harper & Collins.

Csikszentmihalyi, M. (1996). *Creativity: Flow and the psychology of discovery and invention.* New York: HarperCollins.

Csikszentmihalyi, M. (2004). Ted Talks: Mihaly Csikszentmihalyi: Flow the secret to happiness. Retrieved from www.ted.com/talks/mihaly_csikszentmihalyi_on_flow.html

Davidson, R. & Mc Ewen, B. (2012). Social influences on neuroplasticity: Stress and interventions to promote well-being. *Nature Neuroscience, 15,* 689–695.

Davies, J. M. (1996). Linking the "pre-analytic" with the postclassical: Integration, dissociation and the multiplicity of unconscious process. *Contemporary Psychoanalysis, 32,* 553–576.

Davies, J. (1998). Multiple perspectives on multiplicity. *Psychoanalytic Dialogues, 8,* 195–206.

Davies, J. & Frawley, M. (1994). *Treating the adult survivor of childhood sexual abuse: A psychoanalytic perspective.* New York: Basic Books.

Davoine, F. & Gaudillière, J. (2004). *History beyond trauma: Whereof one cannot speak, thereof one cannot stay silent.* New York: Other Press.

Degennaro, C. (1993, June). Pieces of a dream: The inner landscapes of Catherine Angel. *Art View* (Sacramento, CA). Retrieved from http://catherineangelphotography.com/toembracereviews.html

Delbanco, N. (2011). *Lastingness: The art of old age.* New York: Grand Central Publishing.

Denes, M. (1997). *Castles burning: A child's life in war.* New York: W. W. Norton.

Deri, S. (1990). The homeostatic and the representational function of the symbolic process; with reference to the "rat man's" obsessive ideation. *Psychoanalytic Review, 77,* 525–534.

Dewald, P. A. (1982). Serious illness in the analyst: Transference, countertransference, and reality responses. *Journal of the American Psychoanalytic Association, 30,* 347–363.

Dietrich, A. (2003). Functional neuroanatomy of altered states of consciousness: The transient hypofrontality hypothesis. *Consciousness and Cognition, 12,* 231–256.

Dietrich, A. (2004a). The cognitive neuroscience of creativity. *Psychonomic Bulletin & Review, 11,* 1011–1026.

Dietrich, A. (2004b). Neurocognitive mechanisms underlying the experience of flow. *Consciousness and Cognition, 13,* 746–761.

Dietrich, A. (2007). Who is afraid of a cognitive neuroscience of creativity? *Methods, 41,* 518–524.

Dietrich, A. & Kanso, R. (2010). A review of EEG, ERP and neuroimaging studies of creativity and insight. *Psychological Bulletin, 136,* 822–848.

Dinesen, I. (1958). *Babette's feast.* New York: Penguin Books.

Ehrenberg, D. (1995). Self-disclosure: Therapeutic tool or indulgence? *Contemporary Psychoanalysis, 31,* 213–229.

Ehrenzweig, A. (1967). *The hidden order of art.* Berkeley & Los Angeles: University of California Press.

Eigen, M. (1983). A note on the structure of Freud's theory of creativity. *Psychoanalytic Review, 70,* 41–45.

Ellena, E. & Huebner, B. (2009). *I remember better when I paint* [documentary]. Paris, France: French Connection Films.

Epstein, H. (2009a, November 23). Culture vulture: Reading Jung's *Red Book,* part one. *The Arts Fuse.* Retrieved from http://artsfuse.org/3674/culture-vulture-reading-jungs-red-book-part-one/

Epstein, H. (2009b). Whose story is it? Constructing narrative in analysis and memoir. *Psychoanalytic Perspectives, 6,* 76–89.

Erikson, E. & Erikson, J. (1998). *The life cycle completed; extended version.* New York: W. W. Norton.

Erikson Bloland, S. (2005). *In the shadow of fame.* New York: Viking.

Falzeder, E. (2005/2006). Psychoanalytic filiations. *Cabinet.* Retrieved from http://cabinetmagazine.org/issues/20/falzeder.php

Fenster, S., Phillips, S. & Rapoport, E. (1994). *The therapist's pregnancy: Intrusion in the analytic space.* Hillsdale, NJ: Analytic Press.

Ferenczi, S. (1988). *The clinical diary of Sandor Ferenczi,* ed. J. Dupont, trans. M. Balint & N. Z. Jackson. Cambridge, MA: Harvard University Press. (Original work published 1932).

Forgeard, M. (2013). Perceiving benefits after adversity: The relationship between self-reported posttraumatic growth and creativity. *Psychology of Aesthetics, Creativity and the Arts, 7,* 245–264.

Fosshage, J. (2000). Afterward: A view from the outside. *Psychoanalytic Dialogues, 10,* 509–512.

Fosshage, J. & Davies, J. (2000). Analytical psychology after Jung with clinical case material from Stephen Mitchell's influence and autonomy in psychoanalysis. *Psychoanalytic Dialogues, 10,* 377–388.

Frank, G. (1991). Sublimation: Inquiries into theoretical psychoanalysis. Hans W. Loewald. New Haven, CT: Yale University Press, 1988. *Psychoanalytic Review, 78,* 475–478.

Frank, K. A. (1997). The role of the analyst's inadvertent self-revelations. *Psychoanalytic Dialogues, 7,* 281–314.

Frankel, F. (1994). Dissociation in hysteria and hypnosis: A concept aggrandized. In S. Lynn & J. Rhue (eds.), *Dissociation: Clinical and theoretical perspectives* (pp. 80–93). New York: Guilford Press.

Frankl, V. (1967). *Psychotherapy and existentialism: Selected papers on logotherapy.* New York: Simon & Schuster.

Frankl, V. (1984). *Man's search for meaning.* New York: Washington Square Press. (Originally published 1946).

Frankl, V. (1997). *Viktor Frankl recollections: An autobiography.* New York: Insight Books.

Freud, S. (1910). The origin and development of psychoanalysis. *American Journal of Psychology, 21,* 181–218.

Freud, S. (1912). Recommendations to physicians practicing psychoanalysis. *The standard edition of the complete psychological works of Sigmund Freud,* vol. 12 (pp. 109–120). London: Hogarth Press.

Freud, S. (1924–1950). *On the history of the psycho-analytic movement. Collected Papers,* vol. 1. London: Hogarth and Institute of Psycho-Analysis. (Originally published 1914).

Freud, S. (1952). *An autobiographical study.* New York: W.W. Norton & Company. (Originally published 1935).

Freud, S. (1953). The Moses of Michelangelo. In J. Strachey (ed. & trans.), *The standard edition of the complete works of Sigmund Freud,* vol. 13 (pp. 209–238). London, England: Hogarth Press. (Original work published 1914).

Freud, S. (1958). The relation of the poet to day dreaming. In S. Freud *On creativity and the unconscious: Papers on the psychology of art, literature, love, religion* (pp. 44–54). New York: Harper & Brothers. (Originally published 1908).

Freud, S. (1961). Dostoyevsky and parricide. In J. Strachey (ed. & trans.), *Standard edition,* vol. 21 (pp. 177–194). London: Hogarth Press. (Originally published 1929).

Freud, S. (1999). *Leonardo Da Vinci: A memory of his childhood.* New York: Routledge. (Originally published 1910).

Gabbard, G. O. & Lester, E. P. (1995). *Boundaries and boundary violations in psychoanalysis.* Washington, DC: American Psychiatric Publishing.

Gaddis, J. (2002). *The landscape of history: How historians map the past.* New York: Oxford University Press.

Gaines, R. (1997). Detachment and continuity. *Contemporary Psychoanalysis, 33,* 549–571.

Gambetta, D. (June 1, 1999). Primo Levi's last moments. *Boston Review.* Retrieved from www.bostonreview.net/diego-gambetta-primo-levi-last-moments

Gandy, S. (2009). "I remember better when I paint": Treating Alzheimer's through the creative arts. Retrieved from www.irememberbetterwhenipaint.com

Gedo, J. (1989). *Portraits of the artist.* Hillsdale, NJ: Analytic Press.

Gerson, B. (1994). An analyst's pregnancy loss and its effects on treatment: Disruption and growth. *Psychoanalytic Dialogues, 4,* 1–17.

Gerson, B., ed. (2001). *The therapist as a person: Life crises, life choices, life experiences, and their effects on treatment.* Hillsdale, NJ: Analytic Press.

Gerson, S. (2009). When the third is dead: Memory, mourning and witnessing in the aftermath of the Holocaust. *The International Journal of Psychoanalysis, 90,* 1341–1357.

Ghent, E. (1992). Paradox and process. *Psychoanalytic Dialogues, 2,* 135–159.

Ghent, E. (1999). Masochism, submission, surrender: Masochism as a perversion of surrender. In S. A. Mitchell & L. Aron (eds.), *Relational psychoanalysis: The emergence of a tradition* (pp. 211–242). Hillsdale, NJ: Analytic Press. (Originally published 1990).

Gilbert, E. (2009). Ted Talks: Elizabeth Gilbert: Your elusive creative genius. Retrieved from www.ted.com/talks/elizabeth_gilbert_on_genius.html

Glennon, S. (2003). The facilitation of mourning through artistic expression. *Psychologist-Psychoanalyst, 23,* 47.

Glover, E. (1943). The concept of dissociation. *International Journal of Psycho-Analysis, 24,* 7–13.

Goodman, N. & Meyers, M., eds. (2012). *The power of witnessing: Reflections, reverberations, and traces of the Holocaust.* New York: Routledge.

Graf, M. (1942). Reminiscences of professor Sigmund Freud. *Psychoanalytic Quarterly, 11,* 465–476.

Grand, S. (2010). *The hero in the mirror: From fear to fortitude.* New York: Routledge.

Greenacre, P. (1957). The childhood of the artist—libidinal phase development and giftedness. *The Psychoanalytic Study of the Child, 12,* 47–72.

Greenacre, P. (1958). The family romance of the artist. *Psychoanalytic Study of the Child, 13*, 37–43.

Greenacre, P. (1959). Play in relation to creative imagination. *The Psychoanalytic Study of the Child, 14*, 61–80.

Greenberg, J. & Mitchell, S. (1983). *Object relations in psychoanalytic theory.* Cambridge, MA: Harvard University Press.

Greenberg, J. R. (1995). Psychoanalytic technique and the interactive matrix. *The Psychoanalytic Quarterly, 64*, 1–22.

Greenberg, M. & van der Kolk, B. (1987). Retrieval and integration of traumatic memories with the painting cure. In B. van der Kolk (ed.), *Psychological trauma* (pp.191–215). Washington, DC: American Psychiatric Press.

Greene, G. (1980). *Ways of escape.* New York: Simon & Schuster.

Grimbert, P. (2004). *Memory.* New York: Simon & Schuster.

Grinberg, L. & Grinberg, R. (1989). *Psychoanalytic perspectives on migration and exile.* New Haven, CT: Yale University Press.

Guntrip, H. (1975). My experiences of analysis with Fairbairn and Winnicott. In K. Frank (ed.), *The human dimension in psychoanalytic practice* (pp. 49–68). New York: Grune & Straton.

Hagman, G. (1995). Mourning: A review and reconsideration. *International Journal of Psychoanalysis, 76*, 909–925.

Hagman, G. (2005). The musician and the creative process. *The Journal of the American Academy of Psychoanalysis and Dynamic Psychiatry, 33*, 97–118.

Hagman, G. (2010). *The artist's mind: A psychoanalytic perspective on creativity, modern art and modern artists.* New York: Routledge.

Hanly, C. (1986). Psychoanalytic aesthetics: a defense and an elaboration. *Psychoanalytic Quarterly, 55*, 1–22.

Harris, A. (2004). *Gender as soft assembly.* New York: Routledge.

Hartmann, H. (1955). Notes on the theory of sublimation. *Psychoanalytic Study of the Child, 10*, 9–29.

Haynal, A. (2003). Childhood lost and recovered. *International Forum of Psychoanalysis, 12*, 30–37.

Herman, J. (1992). *Trauma and recovery.* New York: Basic Books.

Hilgard, J. (1970). *Personality and hypnosis: A study of imaginative involvement.* Chicago: University of Chicago Press.

Hilgard, E. (1977). *Divided consciousness: Multiple controls in human thought and action.* New York: John Wiley & Sons.

Hirsch, M. (1996). Past lives: Postmemories in exile. *Poetics Today, 17*, 659–686.

Hoff, E. (2004). A friend living inside me: Forms and functions of imaginary companions. *Integration, Cognition and Personality, 24*, 151–189.

Hoff, E. (2005). Imaginary companions, creativity and self-image in middle childhood. *Creativity Research Journal, 17*, 167–181.

Hoffman, I. (1998). *Ritual and spontaneity in the psychoanalytic process.* Hillsdale, NJ: Analytic Press.

Holst-Warhaft, G. (1992). *Dangerous voices: Women's laments and Greek literature.* London: Routledge.

Holst-Warhaft, G. (2014). *Theodorakis: Myth and politics in modern Greek music.* Athens, Greece: Metronome. (Original work published 1980).

Holst-Warhaft, G. & Orfanos, S. D. (2013, December 14). Greek hero Theodorakis is inducted into Athens Academy. *The National Herald*, p. 5.

Howell, E. (2005). *The dissociative mind.* Hillsdale, NJ: Analytic Press.

Howell, E. (2007). Inside and outside: "Trauma/dissociation/relationality" as a framework for understanding psychic structure and problems in living. *Psychoanalytic Perspectives, 5*A, 47–67.

Inzelberg, R. (2013). The awakening of artistic creativity and Parkinson's disease. *Behavioral Neuroscience, 127,* 256–261.

Jacobson, E. (1949). Observations on the psychological effect of imprisonment on female political prisoners. In K. R. Eissler (ed.), *Searchlights on delinquency* (pp. 341–368). London: Imago.

Jacoby, M. (2000). The growing convergence of contemporary psychoanalysis and Jungian analysis. *Psychoanalytic Dialogues, 10,* 489–503.

Jameson, F. (2009). *Valences of the dialectic.* London Verso.

Jamison, K. (1989, May). Mood disorders and patterns of creativity in British writers and artists. *Psychiatry, 52,* 125–134.

Jamison, K. (1995). *An unquiet mind: A memoir of moods and madness.* New York: Vintage Books.

Jung, C. (1966). Problems of modern psychotherapy. In *Collected Works,* vol. 16. Princeton, NJ: Princeton University Press. (Originally published 1929).

Jung, C. (1966). The psychology of the transference. In *Collected Works,* vol. 16. Princeton, NJ: Princeton University Press. (Originally published 1946).

Jung, C. (1989). *Memories, dreams, reflections.* New York: Random House. (Originally published 1961).

Jung, C. (2009). *The red book,* edited by S. Shamdadani. New York: W. W. Norton & Company.

Jung, R. (2012, March 22). Creativity and the everyday brain. Retrieved from www.onbeing.org/program/creativity-and-everyday-brain/1879/history

Kalsched, D. (2000). Jung's contribution to psychoanalytic thought. *Psychoanalytic Dialogues, 10,* 473–488.

Kandel, E. (2012). *The age of insight.* New York: Random House.

Kestenberg, J. & Brenner, I. (1996). *The last witness: The child survivor of the Holocaust.* Washington, DC: American Psychiatric Press.

Khan, M. (1978). Secret as potential space. In S. Grolnick, L. Barkin, & W. Muensterberger (eds.), *Between reality and fantasy.* New York: Aronson.

Kidd E., Rogers, P., & Rogers, C. (2010). The personality correlates of adults who had imaginary companions in childhood. *Psychological Reports, 107,* 163–172.

Kim, S., Hasher, L., & Zacks, R. T. (2008). Aging and a benefit of distractibility. *Psychonomic Bulletin & Review, 14,* 301–305.

Klein, G. (1976). *Psychoanalytic theory: An exploration of essentials.* New York: International Universities Press.

Kligerman, C. (1980). Art and the self of the artist. In Goldberg, A. (ed.), *Advances in self psychology* (pp. 383–396. Madison, CT: International Universities Press.

Knafo, D. (1991a). Egon Schiele's self-portraits: A psychoanalytic study in the creation of self. *Annual of Psychoanalysis, 19,* 59–90.

Knafo, D. (1991b). Egon Schiele and Frida Kahlo: The self-portrait as mirror. *Journal of the American Academy of Psychoanalysis, 19,* 630–647.

Knafo, D. (1993). The mirror, the mask, and the masquerade in the art and life of Frida Kahlo. *Annual of Psychoanalysis, 21,* 277–299.

Knafo, D. (2003). Creative transformations of trauma. *Israel Journal of Psychoanalysis, 1,* 537–564.

Knafo, D. (2008). The senses grow skilled in their craving: Thoughts on creativity and substance abuse. *Psychoanalytic Review, 95,* 571–595.

Knafo, D. (2009). *In her own image: Women's self-representation in twentieth-century art.* Cranbury, NJ: Associated Universities Press.

Knafo, D. (2012). *Dancing with the unconscious:* New York: Routledge.

Kogan, I. (2012). *Canvas of change: Analysis through the prism of creativity.* London: Karnac Books.

Kohut, H. (1957). Observations on the psychological functions of music. *Journal of the American Psychoanalytic Association, 5,* 389–407.

Kohut, H. (1966). Forms and transformations of narcissism. *Journal of the American Psychoanalytic Association, 14,* 243–272.

Kohut, H. (1971). *The analysis of the self.* New York: International Universities Press.

Kohut, H. (1979). The two analyses of Mr. Z. *International Journal of Psycho-Analysis, 60,* 3–28.

Kołodziej, M. (2009). *The Labirinths. Passing 2.* Gdansk, Poland: The Baltic Sea Cultural Center.

Krim, M. (1999). A review of Otto Rank: A psychology of difference. The American Lectures. *Contemporary Psychoanalysis, 35,* 166–170.

Krippner, S. (1999). Altered and transitional states. In M. Runco & S. Pritzker (eds.), *Encyclopedia of creativity,* vol. 1. London: Academic Press.

Kris, E. (1952). *Psychoanalytic explorations in art.* New York: International Universities Press.

Kris, E. (1953). Schizophrenic art: Its meaning in psychotherapy. Book review. *Psychoanalytic Quarterly, 22,* 98–101.

Krystal, H. (1988). *Integration and self-healing: Affect, trauma, alexithymia.* Hillsdale, NJ: Analytic Press.

Kubie, L. (1958). *Neurotic distortion of the creative process.* New York: Farrar Straus & Giroux.

Kuchuck, S. (2014). *Clinical implications of the psychoanalyst's life experience.* New York: Routledge.

Kuriloff, E. (2010). The Holocaust and psychoanalytic theory and praxis. *Contemporary Psychoanalysis, 46,* 395–422.

Lachmann, F. (2001). Words and music. In A. Goldberg (ed.), *The narcissistic patient revisited. Progress in self psychology,* vol. 17 (pp. 167–178). Hillsdale, NJ: Analytic Press.

Lachmann, F. (2008). *Transforming narcissism: Reflections on empathy, humor, and expectations.* New York: The Analytic Press.

Lachmann, F. (2012, April). *Goosebumps.* Paper presented at the Thirty-fourth Annual Spring Meeting of the Division of Psychoanalysis of the American Psychological Association, Santa Fe, NM.

Lachmann, F. & Lachmann, A. (1996). Ibsen: Criticism, creativity, and self-state transformations. *The Annual of Psychoanalysis, 24,* 187–204.

Laub, D. (1992). An event without a witness: Truth, testimony, and survival. In S. Felman & D. Laub (eds.), *Testimony: Crises of witnessing in literature, psychoanalysis, and history* (pp. 75–92). New York: Routledge.

237

Laub, D. (2005). Traumatic shutdown of narrative and symbolization: A death instinct derivative? *Contemporary Psychoanalysis, 41,* 307–326.

Laub, D. & Auerhahn, N. (1989). Failed empathy—a central theme in the survivor's Holocaust experience. *Psychoanalytic Psychology, 6,* 377–400.

Laub, D. & Auerhahn, N. (1993). Knowing and not knowing massive psychic trauma: Forms of traumatic memory. *International Journal of Psychoanalysis, 74,* 287–302.

Laub, D. & Lee, S. (2003). Thanatos and massive psychic trauma: The impact of the death instinct on knowing, remembering and forgetting. *Journal of the American Psychoanalytic Association, 51,* 433–464.

Laub, D. & Podell, D. (1995). Art and trauma. *International Journal of Psychoanalysis, 76,* 991–1005.

Lepore, S. J. & Smyth, J. M., eds. (2002). *The writing cure: How expressive writing promotes health and emotional well-being.* Washington, DC: American Psychological Association.

Levenson, E. (2005). The Fallacy of understanding & the ambiguity of change. New York: Routledge.

Levenson, E. (2012). Psychoanalysis and the rite of refusal. Psychoanalytic Dialogues, 22, 2–6.

Levi, P. (1987). *Moments of reprieve.* New York: Simon & Schuster.

Levi, P. (1996). *Survival in Auschwitz.* New York: Simon & Schuster. (Originally published in Italian in 1947).

Leys, R. (2000). *Trauma: A genealogy.* Chicago: University of Chicago Press.

Loewald, H. (1980a). Book review essay on the Freud/Jung letters. In H. Loewald, *Papers on psychoanalysis* (pp. 405–418). New Haven, CT: Yale University Press. (Originally published 1977).

Loewald, H. (1980b). Some considerations on repetition and repetition compulsion. In H. Loewald, *Papers on psychoanalysis* (pp. 87–101). New Haven, CT: Yale University Press. (Originally published 1973).

Loewald (1980c). Primary process, secondary process, and language. In H. Loewald, *Papers on psychoanalysis* (pp. 178–206). New Haven, CT: Yale University Press. (Originally published 1978).

Loewald, H. (1988). *Sublimation: Inquiries into theoretical psychoanalysis.* New Haven, CT: Yale University Press.

Loewy, J., Steward, K., Dassler, A., Telsey, A., & Homel, P. (2013). The effects of music therapy on vital signs, feeding, and sleep of premature infants. *Pediatrics, 131,* 5, 902–918.

Lowenfeld, H. (1941). Psychic trauma and productive experience in the artist. *Psychoanalytic Quarterly, 10,* 116–130.

Ludwig, A. (1995). *The price of greatness: Resolving the creativity and madness controversy.* New York: Guilford Press.

Maher, A. (1993). Creativity: A work in progress. *Psychoanalytic Quarterly, 62,* 239–262.

Mahler, M. (1988). *The memoirs of Margaret S. Mahler,* ed. P. Stepansky. New York: Free Press.

Malchiodi, C. (2005). *Art therapy in expressive therapies.* New York: Guilford Press.

Malchiodi, C. (2006). *Art therapy sourcebook.* New York: McGraw Hill Professional.

Martindale, C. (1999). Biological bases of creativity. In R. Sternberg (ed.), *Handbook of creativity* (pp. 137–151). Cambridge: Cambridge University Press.

Maslow, A. (1962). *Towards a psychology of being.* Princeton, NJ: D. Van Nostrand Co.

May, R. (1994). *The courage to create*. New York: W.W. Norton & Company. (Originally published 1975).

McCue, J. & Cohen, L. (1999). Freud's physician-assisted death. *Archives of Internal Medicine, 159*, 1521–1525.

McDougall J. (1995). The artist and the outer world. *Contemporary Psychoanalysis, 31*, 247–262.

Meissner, W. W. (2002). The problem of self-disclosure in psychoanalysis. *Journal of the American Psychoanalytic Association, 50*, 827–867.

Menaker, E. (1982). *Otto Rank: A rediscovered legacy*. New York: Columbia University Press.

Menaker, E. (1989). *Appointment in Vienna: An American psychoanalyst recalls her student days in pre-war Austria*. New York: St. Martin's Press.

Menaker, E. (1990). Transference, countertransference, and therapeutic efficacy in relation to self-disclosure by the analyst. In G. Stricker & M. Fisher (eds.), *Self-disclosure in the therapeutic relationship* (pp. 103–115). New York: Plenum Press.

Menaker, E. (1996). *Separation, will, and creativity*. Northvale, NJ: Jason Aronson University Press.

Meyer, L. B. (1956). *Emotion and meaning in music*. Chicago: Chicago University Press.

Micheels, L. (1989). *Doctor 117641: A Holocaust memoir*. New Haven, CT: Yale University Press.

Miller, A. (1988). *Banished knowledge: Facing childhood injuries*. New York: Random House.

Milner, M. (1950). *On not being able to paint*. Madison, CT: International Universities Press.

Milner, M. (1987). The framed gap. In M. Milner, *The suppressed madness of sane men: Forty four years of exploring psychoanalysis* (pp. 79–82). London & New York: Tavistock Publications. (Originally published 1952).

Milner, M. (1987). Psychoanalysis and art. In M. Milner, *The suppressed madness of sane men: Forty four years of exploring psychoanalysis* (pp. 192–215). London & New York: Tavistock Publications. (Originally published 1956).

Milner, M. (1987). The ordering of chaos. In M. Milner, *The suppressed madness of sane men: Forty four years of exploring psychoanalysis* (pp. 216–233). London & New York: Tavistock Publications. (Originally published 1957).

Milner, M. (1987). The hidden order of art. In M. Milner, *The suppressed madness of sane men: Forty four years of exploring psychoanalysis* (pp. 241–245). London & New York: Tavistock Publications. (Originally published 1967).

Milner, M. (1988). *An experiment in leisure*. London: Virago. (Originally published 1937).

Milner, M. (2011). *A life of one's own*. New York: Routledge. (Originally published 1934).

Milner, M. (2011). *Eternity's sunrise*. London: Routledge. (Originally published 1987).

Mitchell, S. (1988). *Relational concepts in psychoanalysis: An integration*. Cambridge, MA: Harvard University Press.

Mitchell, S. (1993). Foreword. In J. W. Barron (ed.), *Self-analysis: Critical inquiries, personal visions*. Hillsdale, NJ: Analytic Press.

Mitchell, S. (1997). Commentaries on Kenneth A. Frank's the role of the analyst's inadvertent self-revelations. *Psychoanalytic Dialogues, 7*, 319–322.

Mitchell, S. & Aron, L. (1999). *Relational psychoanalysis: The emergence of a tradition*. Hillside, NJ: Analytic Press.

Molnar, M., ed. (1992). *The diary of Sigmund Freud 1929–1939: A record of the final decade.* London: Hogarth Press.

Morgan, A. (1995, February). Review of the art work of Catherine Angel in the *Art of Healing* (catalogue). Valencia College, Orlando, FL. Retrieved from http://catherine angelphotography.com/toembracereviews.html

Morrison, A. L. (1997). Ten years of doing psychotherapy while living with a life-threatening illness: Self-disclosure and other ramifications. *Psychoanalytic Dialogues, 7,* 225–241.

Myers, W. (1979). Imaginary companions in childhood and adult creativity. *Psychoanalytic Quarterly, 48,* 292–307.

Nachmani, G. (2005). Proof of life: A discussion of Dori Laub's "traumatic shutdown of narrative and symbolization." *Contemporary Psychoanalysis, 41,* 327–340.

Nagel, J. J. (2013). *Melodies of the mind: Connections between psychoanalysis and music.* New York: Routledge.

Nass, M. (1989). From transformed scream, through mourning, to the building of psychic structure: A critical review of the literature on music and psychoanalysis. *The Annual of Psychoanalysis, 17,* 159–181.

Nathanson, C. (1995). *Women's rites of passage: Telling the story.* Dayton, OH: Wright State University Art Galleries.

Naumburg, M. (1950). *Schizophrenic art: Its meaning in psychotherapy.* New York: Grune & Stratton, Inc.

Neruda, P. (1983). Heroes, trans. M. Sayers Peden. In M. Neruda & M. O. Silva (eds.), *Passions and impressions* (p. 11). New York: Farrar Straus Giroux.

Newman, D. (2006). *Talking with doctors.* Hillside, NJ: Analytic Press.

Newman, D. (2011). *Talking with doctors. Expanded 2nd edition.* Montclair, NJ: Keynote Books.

Niederland, W. (1968). Clinical observations on the "Survivor Syndrome." *International Journal of Psycho-Analysis, 49,* 313–315.

Niederland, W. (1976). Psychoanalytic approaches to artistic creativity. *Psychoanalytic Quarterly, 4,* 185–212.

Niederland, W. (1981). The Survivor Syndrome: Further observations and dimensions. *Journal of the American Psychoanalytic Association, 29,* 413–425.

Nowosielski, K. (2009). *Marian Kołodziej—the Labirinths.* Gdansk, Poland: The Baltic Sea Cultural Centre.

Noy, P. (1968). The development of musical ability. *The Psychoanalytic Study of the Child, 23,* 332–347.

Noy, P. (1972). About art and artistic talent. *International Journal of Psycho-Analysis, 53,* 243–249.

Noy, P. (1979). Form creation in art: An ego-psychological approach to creativity. *Psycho-analytic Quarterly, 48,* 229–256.

Ogden T. (2000a). Borges and the art of mourning. *Psychoanalytic Dialogues, 10,* 65–88.

Ogden, T. (2000b). A picture of mourning: Commentary on paper by Jeanne Wolff Bern-stein. *Psychoanalytic Dialogues, 10,* 371–375.

Oltarsh-McCarthy, V. (2007). Vivienne's songbook. *Psychoanalytic Perspectives, 5,* 141–147.

Oppenheim, L. (2013). *Imagination: From fantasy to delusion.* New York: Routledge.

Oremland, J. (1998). Play, dreams, and creativity. *The Psychoanalytic Study of the Child, 53,* 84–93.

Orfanos, S. D. (1997). Mikis Theodorakis: Music, culture, and the creative process. *Journal of Modern Hellenism, 14*, 17–37.

Orfanos, S. D. (1999). The creative boldness of Mikis Theodorakis. *Journal of Modern Hellenism, 16*, 27–39.

Orfanos, S. D. (2006, April 22). *The sound and passion of mourning.* Paper presented at the annual meeting of the Division of Psychoanalysis (39) of the American Psychological Association. Philadelphia.

Orfanos, S. D. (2010). "Song of Songs": Music and a relational aesthetic. *Psychoanalytic Perspectives, 7*, 318–339.

Orfanos, S. D. (2012). Foreword: Voyaging the relational Sea Change. In L. Aron & A. Harris (eds.), *Relational Psychoanalysis: Evolution of Process*, (pp. xix–xxx). New York, London: Routledge.

Orfanos, S. D. (2013). A hero's aesthetics [Review of the book *Becoming Achilles: Child-sacrifice, war, and misrule in the Iliad and beyond*]. *PsycCRITIQUES, 58*(6). Retrieved from www.psycinfo.com/psyccritiques

Orne, M. (1959). The nature of hypnosis: Artifact and essence. *Journal of Abnormal and Social Psychology, 58*, 277–299.

Ornstein, A. (1985). Survival and recovery. *Psychoanalytic Inquiry, 5*, 99–130.

Ornstein, A. (2004). *My mother's eyes.* Cincinnati, OH: Emmis Books.

Ornstein, A. (2006a). Artistic creativity and the healing process. *Psychoanalytic Inquiry, 26*, 386–406.

Ornstein, A. (2006b). Memory, history, autobiography: Psychoanalytic and literary perspectives Discussion of papers by Sophia Richman, Ph.D. and Elaine Freedgood, Ph.D. *Contemporary Perspectives, 42*, 657–669.

Ornstein, A. (2010). The missing tombstone: Reflections on mourning and creativity. *Journal of the American Psychoanalytic Association, 58*, 631–648.

Ornstein, A. (2013, January 20). The function of "memorial spaces": Further comments on mourning following multiple, traumatic losses. Panel presentation at the American Psychoanalytic Association, New York City.

Orwell, G. (1949). *1984.* New York: Signet Classic.

Oswald, P. (1997). The healing power of music: Some observations on the semiotic function of the transitional objects in musical communication. In M. A. Runko & R. Richards (eds.), *Eminent creativity, everyday creativity and health* (pp. 213–239). Greenwich, CT: Ablex Publishing.

Parens, H. (2004). *Renewal of life: Healing from the Holocaust.* Rockville, MD: Schreiber Publishing.

Pérez-Fabello, M. & Campos, A. (2011). Dissociative experiences, creative imagination and artistic production in students of fine arts. *Thinking Skills and Creativity, 6*, 44–48.

Perls, F. (1973). *The gestalt approach & eyewitness to therapy.* Palo Alto, CA: Science and Behavior Books.

Phillips, A. (1988). *Winnicott.* Cambridge, MA: Harvard University Press.

Pine, F. (1989). The place of object loss in normal development. In D Dietrich & P. Shabad (eds.), *The problem of loss and mourning: Psychoanalytic perspectives* (pp. 159–173). Madison, CT: International Universities Press.

Pizer, B. (1997). When the analyst is ill: Dimensions of self-disclosure. *The Psychoanalytic Quarterly, 67*, 450–469.

Pizer, S. (1998). *Building bridges: The negotiation of paradox in psychoanalysis.* Hillsdale, NJ: Analytic Press.

Poland, W. (2000). The analyst's witnessing and otherness. *Journal of the American Psychoanalytic Association, 48*, 17–34.

Pollock, G. (1978). On siblings, childhood sibling loss, and creativity. *Annual of Psychoanalysis, 6*, 443–481.

Pollock, G. (1989a). *The mourning-liberation process,* vol. 1 and 2. Madison, CT: International University Press.

Pollock, G. (1989b). The mourning process, the creative process, and the creation. In D. Dietrich & P. Shabad (eds.), *The problem of loss and mourning: Psychoanalytic perspectives* (pp. 27–59). Madison, CT: International Universities Press.

Proust, M. (1908–1912). A la recherche du temps perdu. In H. Segal, *Dream, Phantasy and Art* New York: Routledge.

Rado, S. (1977). *Codename Dora: the memoirs of a Russian spy Sandor Rado.* London: Abelard.

Rank, O. (1958). *Beyond psychology.* New York: Dover Publications. (Originally published 1941).

Rank, O. (1989). *Art and artist: Creative urge and personality development.* New York: W.W. Norton & Company. (Originally published 1932).

Rashkin, E. (2008). Devouring loss: A recipe for mourning in *Babette's Feast.* In: *Unspeakable secrets and the psychoanalysis of culture* (pp. 25–46). New York: Suny Press.

Raymond, L. W. & Rosbrow-Reich, S., eds. (1997). *The inward eye: Psychoanalysts reflect on their life and work.* Hillsdale, NJ: Analytic Press.

RAZOR & TIE in co-production with THIRTEEN in association with WNET.ORG (Producer), & Wharton, M. (Director). (2009). *Joan Baez—How sweet the sound* [Documentary]. Available from www.cmajor-entertainment.com/catalogue/show/id/2534

Reik, T. (1949). *Fragment of a great confession: A psychoanalytic autobiography.* New York: Farrar & Strauss.

Reik, T. (1953). *The haunting melody: Psychoanalytic experiences in life and music.* New York: Farrar, Straus and Young.

Reis, B. (2009). Performative and enactive features of psychoanalytic witnessing. *The International Journal of Psycho-Analysis, 90*, 1359–1372.

Renik, O. (1999). Playing one's cards face up in analysis: An approach to the problem of self-disclosure. *The Psychoanalytic Quarterly, 68*, 521–539.

Richards, R., ed. (2007). *Everyday creativity.* Washington, DC: American Psychological Association.

Richardson, J. (2009). *A life of Picasso—the prodigy 1881–1906.* New York: Alfred A. Knopf.

Richman, L. (1975). *WHY? Extermination camp Lwów (Lemberg) 134 Janowska street Poland.* New York: Vantage Press.

Richman, S. (2002). *A wolf in the attic: The legacy of a hidden child of the Holocaust.* New York: Routledge.

Richman, S. (2004). From hiding to healing: A psychoanalyst's narrative of personal trauma. *NYSPA Notebook, 16*, 2–7.

Richman, S. (2006a). When the analyst writes a memoir: Clinical implications of biographic disclosure. *Contemporary Psychoanalysis, 42*, 367–392.

Richman, S. (2006b). Finding one's voice: Transforming trauma into autobiographical narrative. *Contemporary Psychoanalysis, 42*, 639–650.

Richman, S. (2006c). Remembering to forget to remember: Response to Ornstein. *Contemporary Psychoanalysis, 42*, 673–680.

Richman, S. (2007). Roundtable discussion: Last Witnesses: Child survivors of the Holocaust. *Psychoanalytic Perspectives, 4*, 1–50.

Richman, S. (2009). Secrets and mystifications: Finding meaning through memoir. *Psychoanalytic Perspectives, 6*, 67–75.

Richman, S. (2012). "Too young to remember": Recovering and integrating the unacknowledged known. In N. Goodman & M. Myers (eds.), *The power of witnessing: Reflections, reverberations, and traces of the Holocaust* (pp. 105–118). New York: Routledge.

Richman, S. (2013). Out of darkness: Reverberations of trauma and its creative transformations. *Psychoanalytic Dialogues, 23*, 362–376.

Rose, F. C., ed. (2001). *Twentieth century neurology: The British contribution.* London: Imperial College Press.

Rose, G. (1987). *Trauma and mastery in life and art.* Madison, CT: International Universities Press.

Rose, G. (1996). *Necessary illusion: Art as witness.* Madison, CT: International Universities Press.

Rose, G. J. (2004). *Between couch and piano: Psychoanalysis, music, art and neuroscience.* New York: Brunner-Routledge.

Rotenberg, C. (1988). Selfobject theory and the artistic process. In A. Goldberg (ed.), *Learning from Kohut: Progress in self psychology*, vol. 4 (pp. 193–213). Hillsdale, NJ: Analytic Press.

Roth, P. (1986). A conversation with Primo Levi. In P. Levi, *Survival in Auschwitz* (pp. 175–187). New York: Simon & Schuster.

Rothenberg, A. (1990). *Creativity and madness.* Baltimore, MD: Johns Hopkins University Press.

Rudnytsky, P. L. (2000). *Psychoanalytic conversations: Interviews with clinicians, commentators, and critics.* Hillsdale, NJ: Analytic Press.

Salat, D. et al. (2004). Thinning of the cerebral cortex in aging. *Cerebral Cortex, 14*, 721–730.

Samuels, A. (2000). Post-Jungian dialogues. *Psychoanalytic Dialogues, 10*, 403–426.

Sapp, M. & Hitchock, K. (2003). Creative imagination, absorption, and dissociation with African American college students. *Sleep and Hypnosis, 5*, 95–104.

Sawicki, P. (2009, June). I was rescuing my own humanity: Interview with Kołodziej. *Oś Oświęcim—People—History—Culture Magazine*, no. 6. Retrieved from www.facebook.com/note.php?note_id=156449270447

Schachtel, E. (1984). *Metamorphosis: On the development of affect, perception, attention and memory.* New York: Da Capo Press. (Originally published 1959).

Schacter, D. (1996). *Searching for memory.* New York: Basic Books.

Schaffner, I. (2001). *Hannelore Baron: Works from 1969 to 1987.* Washington, DC: Smithsonian Institution.

Schmidt, R. S.J. (producer) & Schmidt, J. (director). (2010). *The labyrinth: The testimony of Marian Kołodziej* [documentary]. Hollywood, CA: December 2nd Productions. Retrieved from www.thelabyrinthdocumentary.com

Schur, M. (1972). *Freud: Living and dying.* New York: International Universities Press.

Schwarz, D. (1997). *Listening subjects: Music, psychoanalysis, culture.* Durham, NC: Duke University Press.

Sedgwick, D. (2000). Answers to nine questions about Jungian psychology. *Psychoanalytic Dialogues, 10*, 457–472.

Seeley, W. et al. (2008). Unravelling Bolero: Progressive aphasia, transmodal creativity and the right posterior neocortex. *Brain, 131*, 39–49.

Segal, H. (1964). *Introduction to the work of Melanie Klein*. New York: Basic Books.

Segal, H. (1991). *Dream, phantasy and art*. New York: Routledge.

Seiden H. (1996). The healing presence: Part I: The witness as self-object function. *Psychoanalytic Review, 83*, 685–693.

Shabad, P. (2001). *Despair and the return of hope: Echoes of mourning in psychotherapy.* Northvale, NJ. Aronson.

Sharrock, D. (2008, June 17). Out of the war, into a book and in a rage. *The Australian Times.* Retrieved from: www.theaustralian.com.au/arts/

Simonton, D. K. (1989). The swan-song phenomenon: Last-works effects for 172 classical composers. *Psychology and Aging, 4*, 42–47.

Simonton, D. K. (1990). Creativity in later years: Optimistic prospects for achievement. *Gerontologist, 30*, 626–631.

Simonton, D. K. (1999). *Origins of genius: Darwinian perspectives on creativity.* New York: Oxford University Press.

Singer, E. (1971). The patient aids the analyst: Some clinical and theoretical observations. In D. B. Stern, C. H. Mann, S. Kantor, & G. Schlesinger (eds.), *Pioneers of interpersonal psychoanalysis* (pp. 155–168). Hillsdale, NJ: Analytic Press.

Singer, E. (1977). The fiction of analytic anonymity. In K. A. Frank (ed.), *The human dimension in psychoanalytic practice* (pp. 181–192). New York: Grune & Stratton.

Skolnick, N. & Davies, J. (1992). Secrets in clinical work: A relational point of view. In N. Skolnick & S. Warshaw (eds.), *Relational perspectives in psychoanalysis* (pp. 217–238). Hillsdale, NJ: Analytic Press.

Slavin, J. (2002, November). Sexuality—yours, mine and ours: Relational forays into under explored dimensions of sexual experience and sexual identity. Invited discussion. The International Association for Relational Psychoanalysis and Psychotherapy, New York.

Slavin, M. (2012). Original loss: Psychoanalysis, human evolution, and the existential origins of our need for art and music. Unpublished paper.

Slochower, J. (1993). Mourning and the holding function of Shiva. *Contemporary Psychoanalysis, 29*, 352–367.

Slochower, J. (2004). *Holding and psychoanalysis: A relational approach.* Hillsdale, NJ: Analytic Press.

Slochower, J. (2011). Out of the analytic shadow: On the dynamics of commemorative ritual. *Psychoanalytic Dialogues, 21*, 676–690.

Sobel, E. (2003, Fall/Winter). Art healing and hell: Marian Kołodziej Auschwitz prisoner #432. *Wild Heart Journal: Art, creativity and spiritual life, 6*(2). Retrieved from www.eliezersobel.com/wildheartjournal/hell.pdf

Spiegel, H. (1974). *Manual for the hypnotic induction profile* (rev. ed.). New York: Soni Medica.

Spiegel, D. & Cardeña, E. (1990). New uses of hypnosis in the treatment of posttraumatic stress disorder. *Journal of Clinical Psychiatry, 51*, 39–43.

Spiegel, D. & Cardeña, E. (1991). Disintegrated experience: The dissociative disorders revisited *Journal of Abnormal Psychology, 100*, 366–378.

Spiegel, H. & Spiegel, D. (2004). *Trance and treatment: Clinical uses of hypnosis* (2nd ed.). Arlington, VA: American Psychiatric Publishing.

Spivey, N. (2005). *Songs on bronze: Greek myths retold.* New York: Farrar, Straus and Giroux.

Stein, A. (2004a). Music and trauma in Polanski's *The Pianist* (2002). *International Journal of Psycho-analysis, 85,* 755–765.

Stein, A. (2004b). Music, mourning, and consolation. *Journal of the American Psychoanalytic Association, 52,* 783–811.

Stein, A. (2012). Psychoanalysis and music. In G. O. Gabbard, B. E. Litowitz, & P. Williams (eds). *Textbook on psychoanalysis* (2nd ed., pp. 551–565). Washington, DC: American Psychiatric Publishing.

Sterba, R. F. (1965). Psychoanalysis and music. *American Imago, 22,* 96–111.

Sterba, R. (1982). *Memoirs of a Viennese psychoanalyst.* Detroit, MI: Wayne State University Press.

Stern, D. B. (1997). *Unformulated experience: From dissociation to imagination in psychoanalysis.* Hillsdale, NJ: Analytic Press.

Stern, D. B. (1999). Unformulated experience: From familiar chaos to creative disorder. In S. A. Mitchell & L. Aron (eds.). *Relational psychoanalysis: The Emergence of a tradition* (pp. 77–107). Hillsdale, NJ: The Analytic Press. (Originally published 1983).

Stern, D. B. (2010a). *Partners in thought: Working with unformulated experience, dissociation and enactment.* New York: Routledge.

Stern, D. B. (2010b). Human nature and psychotherapy. In G. Goldstein & H. Golden (eds.), *Sabert Basescu: Selected papers on human nature and psychoanalysis* (pp. 119–138). New York: Routledge.

Stern, D. B. (2012). Witnessing across time; accessing the present from the past and the past from the present. *Psychoanalytic Quarterly, 81,* 53–81.

Stern, D. N. (2010). *Forms of vitality: Exploring dynamic experience in psychology, the arts, psychotherapy, and development.* Cary, NC: Oxford University Press.

Stolorow, R. (1999). The phenomenology of trauma and absolutisms of everyday life. *Psychoanalytic Psychology, 16,* 464–468.

Stolorow, R. & Atwood, G. (1979). *Faces in a cloud: Subjectivity in personality theory.* New York: Jason Aronson.

Storr, A. (1985, Winter). The sanity of true genius. *Virginia Quarterly Review,* 1–19.

Storr, A. (1988). *Solitude: A return to the self.* New York: Ballantine Books.

Storr, A. (1993). The dynamics of creation. New York: Ballantine Books.

Strozier, C. B. (2001). Heinz Kohut: The making of a psychoanalyst. New York: Farrar, Strauss & Giroux.

Tec, N. (1982). *Dry tears: The story of a lost childhood.* New York: Oxford University Press.

Tedeschi, R. & Calhoun, L. (2004). Posttraumatic growth: Conceptual foundations and empirical evidence. *Psychological Inquiry, 15,* 1–18.

Tedeschi, R., Park, C., & Calhoun, L., eds. (1998). *Posttraumatic growth: Positive changes in the aftermath of crisis.* Mahwah, NJ: Lawrence Erlbaum Associates.

Thomas, K. & Siller, J. (1999). Object loss, mourning, and adjustment to disability. *Psychoanalytic Psychology, 16,* 179–197.

Thomson, I. (2005). The genesis of "if this is a man". In S. Pugliese (ed.), *The legacy of Primo Levi* (pp. 41–58). New York: St. Martin's Press.

Thomson, I. (2012, June 29). Talked into life: How "if this is a man" came to be. *Times Literary Supplement* (*TLS*).

Toll, N. (1993). *Behind the secret window: A memoir of a hidden childhood during World War Two*. New York: Dial Books.

Toll, N. (1998). *When memory speaks: The Holocaust in art*. Westport, CT: Praeger.

Trilling, L. (2000). Artists and neurosis. In L. Wieseltier (ed.), *The moral obligation to be intelligent: Selected essays* (pp. 87–104). New York: Farrar, Straus and Giroux.

Ullman, C. (2006). Bearing witness. Across the barriers in society and in the clinic. *Psychoanalytic Dialogues, 16,* 181–198.

Valent, P. (1998). Resilience in child survivors of the holocaust: Toward the concept of resilience. *The Psychoanalytic Review, 85,* 517–535.

Van der Hart, O. & Horst, R. (1989). The dissociation theory of Pierre Janet. *Journal of Traumatic Stress, 2,* 1–21.

van der Kolk, B. (1987). *Psychological trauma*. Washington, DC: American Psychiatric Press.

Wadlington, W. (2001). Otto Rank's art. *The Humanist Psychologist, 29,* 280–311.

Waldron, S. (2010). An interpretation of *Babette's Feast* as a parable of trauma. *Journal of Analytical Psychology, 55,* 556–573.

Walker, A. (1983). *In search of our mothers' gardens: The creativity of black women in the south: Womanist prose*. San Diego, CA: Harcourt Brace.

Weissman, P. (1967). Theoretical considerations of ego regression and ego functions in creativity. *Psychoanalytic Quarterly, 36,* 37–50.

Weissman, P. (1968). Psychological concomitants of ego functioning in creativity. *International Journal of Psycho-Analysis, 49,* 464–469.

Wheelis, A. (1999). *The listener: A psychoanalyst examines his life*. New York: W. W. Norton.

Whiteman, D. (1993). Holocaust survivors and escapees—their strengths. *Psychotherapy, 30,* 443–451.

Wilson, E. (1932). *The wound and the bow: Seven studies in literature*. New York: Houghton Mifflin Company.

Winnicott, D. W. (1953). Transitional objects and transitional phenomena. *International Journal of Psycho-Analysis, 34,* 89–97.

Winnicott, D. W. (1958). The capacity to be alone. *International Journal of Psycho-Analysis, 39,* 416–420.

Winnicott, D. W. (1965). Communicating and not communicating leading to a study of certain opposites. In *The Maturational Processes and the Facilitating Environment* (pp. 179–192). New York: International Universities Press. (Original work published in 1963).

Winnicott, D. W. (1964). Memories, dreams, reflections. *International Journal of Psycho-Analysis, 45,* 450–455.

Winnicott, D. (1965). *The maturational processes and the facilitating environment: Studies in the theory of emotional development*. New York: International Universities Press.

Winnicott, D. (1967). The location of cultural experience. *International Journal of Psycho-Analysis, 48,* 368–372.

Winnicott, D. (1990). *Playing and reality*. New York: Routledge. (Originally published 1971).

REFERENCES

Wittgenstein, L. (1999). *Tractatus logico-philosophicus*. London and New York: Dover. (Originally published 1918).

Wolfenstein, M. (1966). Goya's dining room. *Psychoanalytic Quarterly, 35,* 47–83.

Wortis, J. (1954). *Fragments of an analysis with Freud.* New York: Simon and Schuster.

Yalom, I. (1980). *Existential psychotherapy.* New York: Basic Books.

Young-Eisendrath, P. (2000). Self and transcendence: a postmodern approach to analytical psychology in practice. *Psychoanalytic Dialogues, 10,* 427–440.

Zemeckis, R. (2000). *Cast away.* USA: Twentieth Century Fox & Dreamworks Pictures.

INDEX

Please note: page numbers in *italics* indicate figures.

Abstract Expressionism 8, 202
Adorno, Theodor 102, 164
adversity, relationship to creativity 91
affective attunement 159–60
affective illness and creativity 58
aging 215–19; Clarice interview 227–8;
    Sylvia, clinical vignette 221–26;
    see also neuroscience
Alexander, Franz 56–7
Allende, Salvador 148
allow, use of term (Stern) 81
Alpert, Judith 207
altered states 58–9, 75–7; Jung and 200;
    trance logic 59–60
Alzheimer's disease 221
amnesia, historical 167
Analytical Psychology, development of
    (Jung) 200
analytic space, intrusion into 185–8
Angel, Catherine 208–11, 215; *Early
    Works* 208; *To Embrace* 209, 210;
    Oh, My Love 209, *210*
anti-Semitism 168
Appelfeld, Aharon 122
archaic residue, use of term 31
archetypes 201
area of creation 39–40, 80
Arieti, Silvano 39, 46, 58
Aristotle 54
Aron, L. 184–5, 192
art, therapeutic actions in creation of 13,
    93–7
artist, use of term 42
artists and substance abuse 58–9
art of trauma 6, 9, 123
Attie, Shimon 90

Atwood, G. 42, 79, 196
Auerhahn, N. 103–4
Auschwitz: concentration camp 163–4;
    poetry writing and 102; self-expression
    in 104; *see also* Holocaust, survivors
autobiographical narratives 174–9,
    209–14; *Autobiographical Study, An*
    (Freud) 32, 206–7; Jung's memoirs
    194–200

Babette's Feast (film) 223–6
Bacon, Francis 92–3
Baez, Joan 126
Balint, Michael: on area of creation 39–40,
    80; on benign and malignant regression
    71; on creativity 46
Baron, Hannelore 118–23; *Untitled 119*
Baron, Mark 129n6
Basescu, Sabert 53, 60, 191
Bassin, D. 27
Beebe, B. 161
Beethoven, Ludwig van 158
Begley, Louis 217–19
Benigni, Roberto 155n2
Benjamin, Jessica 63
Beres, D. 35
Berlin, historical photographs of 90
Bernstein, Jeanne Wolff 90–1
Bernstein, Leonard 159
biographic self-disclosure 7, 179–83
Black Books (Jung) 197
Black Milk (film) 135–6
"blank screen," psychoanalyst as 174
Bloch, Ofra 131–6, 154; Binyamin (uncle)
    132–3, 136; *Black Milk* (film) 135–6;
    David (husband) 133–5; interview

249

Made in the USA
Lexington, KY
13 August 2018